EXPLORING SPORT AND FITNESS

Exploring Sport and Fitness is a comprehensive guide to the development of essential professional and interpersonal skills in the sport, leisure and fitness sector. Designed to bridge the gap between the classroom and the workplace, this book introduces the fundamental principles of reflective practice in sport and fitness, and explains how students and professionals can develop their personal effectiveness and workplace performance.

The book draws together important material from a wide range of academic and professional sources, including articles from leading experts in sport management, psychology and coaching, and explores key topics such as:

- Reflective practice
- The importance of effective communication
- Motivation
- Leadership
- Working in teams
- Working with customers
- Learning and instructional frameworks for coaches/instructors
- Organisational cultures in sport and fitness.

Exploring Sport and Fitness is essential reading for all students of sport, leisure and fitness management, sports coaching or sports development, and for all sport and fitness professionals looking to improve their performance and practice.

Caroline Heaney is an academic on the Award in Sport and Fitness in the Faculty of Education and Language Studies at The Open University. She has previously worked in sports science support, fitness instruction, and personal training roles.

Ben Oakley is Head of Award in Sport and Fitness in the Faculty of Education and Language Studies at The Open University. His specialist area is UK sports policy and national elite sport systems and more recently he has investigated oral assessment procedures.

Simon Rea is an academic on the Award in Sport and Fitness in the Faculty of Education and Language Studies at The Open University. He combines extensive experience within the fitness industry with consulting, course design and external verification for higher and further education.

EXPLORING SPORT AND FITNESS

WORK-BASED PRACTICE

This Reader forms part of the Open University course *Working and learning in sport and fitness*. This is a 60-point course and is part of the Foundation Degree in Sport and Fitness.

Details of this and other Open University courses can be obtained from the Student Registration and Enquiry Service, The Open University, PO Box 197, Milton Keynes MK7 6BJ, United Kingdom: tel. +44 (0)845 300 6090, e-mail general-enquiries@open.ac.uk

Alternatively, you may visit the Open University website at http://www.open.ac.uk where you can learn more about the wide range of courses and packs offered at all levels by The Open University.

EXPLORING SPORT AND FITNESS

WORK-BASED PRACTICE

**EDITED BY
CAROLINE HEANEY, BEN OAKLEY AND
SIMON REA**

Routledge
Taylor & Francis Group

LONDON AND NEW YORK

The Open University

First published 2009
by Routledge
2 Park Square, Milton Park, Abingdon, Oxon, OX14 4RN

Simultaneously published in the USA and Canada
by Routledge
270 Madison Avenue, New York, NY 10016

Routledge is an imprint of the Taylor & Francis Group, an informa business

Published in association with The Open University, Walton Hall, Milton Keynes MK7 6AA

© 2009 Compilation, original, and editorial material, The Open University

Typeset in Zapf Humanist and Eras by Keyword Group Ltd.

Printed and bound in Great Britain by
CPI Antony Rowe, Chippenham, Wiltshire

British Library Cataloguing in Publication Data
A catalogue record for this book is available from the British Library

Library of Congress Cataloging in Publication Data
Exploring sport and fitness : work-based practice / edited by Caroline Heaney,
Ben Oakley, and Simon Rea.
        p. cm.
1. Physical education and training. 2. Physical education and training–Administration.
I. Heaney, Caroline. II. Oakley, Ben. III. Rea, Simon.
GV341.E93 2009
613.7–dc22   2009008434

ISBN13: 978-0-415-49155-6 (hbk)
ISBN13: 978-0-415-49156-3 (pbk)

ISBN10: 0-415-49155-X (hbk)
ISBN10: 0-415-49156-8 (pbk)

CONTENTS

V

ACKNOWLEDGMENTS

Routledge would like to thank the following publishers for permission to use their material in this book:

CHAPTER 1

Edited from *Reflection: Principles and Practices*, *FHS*, 2001 with kind permission of The National Coaching Foundation (brand name sports coach UK). All rights reserved. Sports coach UK subscription and membership services provide a range of benefits to coaches, including insurance and information services. For further details, please ring 0113-274 4802 or visit www.sportscoachuk.org

CHAPTER 3

Figure 3.2 from Ghaye, Tony and Lillyman, Sue, *Learning Journals and Critical Incidents: Reflective Practice for Health Care Professionals*, Quay Books, 1997, and Figure 3.3 from Ghaye, Tony and Lillyman, Sue, *Reflection: Principles and Practice for Healthcare Professionals*, Quay Books, 2000, both reprinted with the kind permission of Quay Books

CHAPTER 6

Palgrave MacMillan for permission to reprint the chapter *Reflective Practice* from N. Thompson, *People Skills,* 2nd edition, Palgrave, 2002

CHAPTER 9

Reproduced by permission of SAGE Publications, London, Los Angeles, New Delhi and Singapore from K.B. Everard, Geoff Morris and Ian Wilson, *Effective School Management*, Copyright © Sage, 2004

CHAPTER 10

Table 10.2 reproduced with permission of SAGE Publications, London, Los Angeles, New Delhi and Singapore from Shaw, G. and Williams A.M, *Choices for Self-Managing Schools*, Sage, 2004, Copyright © Sage, 2004

CHAPTER 11

Wiley for permission to reproduce part of S. Bull, *The Game Plan: Your Guide to Mental Toughness at Work* (2006), Capstone, Copyright © 2006 Steve Bull

CHAPTER 14

The McGraw Hill Companies for permission to reproduce part of J.M. Williams, *Applied Sport Psychology*, McGraw-Hill, London, © 2006 McGraw Hill

CHAPTER 15

Palgrave MacMillan for permission to reprint the chapter *Valuing Diversity* from N. Thompson, *People Skills,* 2nd edition, Palgrave, 2002

CHAPTER 16

The YMCA George Williams College for permission to reprint part of Doyle, M.E. and Smith, M.J. (1999) *Born and Bred: Leadership, Heart and Informal Education*, London: YMCA George Williams College/The Rank Foundation, © 1999 YMCA George Williams College

CHAPTER 17

Table 17.1 reproduced with permission of SAGE Publications, London, Los Angeles, New Delhi and Singapore from Fidler, B., Russell, S. and Simkins, T. (1997) Choices for Self-Managing Schools, Paul Chapman Publishing (now Sage), Liverpool. Copyright © Sage, 1997

CHAPTER 19

This article was published in Hoye, R., Westerbeek, H., Stewart, B., and Nicholson, M., *Sport Management: Principles and Applications*, Butterworth-Heinemann, as a chapter titled *Organizational Cultures*, pp. 145–161, Copyright © Elsevier, 2006

CHAPTER 20

Figure 20.3 reprinted with permission of Pearson Education Limited from C. Carnall, *Managing Change in Organizations 5e*, Pearson Education, 2007. Copyright © C. Carnall, 2007

CHAPTER 22

Figure 22.1 provided by the courtesy of Nobelprize.org. Link to the original image: www.nobelprize.org/educational_games/medicine/pavlov/ Copyright © Nobel Web AB 2008

CHAPTER 24

Adapted content reproduced with permission of John Wiley & Sons Ltd. from McMorris, T., and Hale, T., *Coaching Science*, 2006. Copyright © 2006 John Wiley & Sons, Ltd

CHAPTER 26

Figure 26.1 reproduced with permission of Pearson Education Limited from Doyle, P., *Marketing Management Strategy, 2e*, Hemel Hempstead, Prentice Hall Europe, 1998. Copyright © Doyle, P., 1998

Figure 26.2 Reprinted from Business Horizons, May-June, 1985, Berry, L.L., Zeithmal, V.A. and Parasuraman, A., *The Roots of Customer Satisfaction*, p. 47. Copyright 1985, with permission from Elsevier

Figure 26.3 Reprinted from MIT Sloan Management Review, Spring, 1991, Parasuraman, A., Zeithmal, V.A. and Berry, L.L., *The Zone of Tolerance*, p. 42. Copyright 1991, with permission from Tribune Media Services

CHAPTER 29

Pearson Education Limited for use of material from J. Beech and S. Chadwick, *The Marketing of Sport* (2007) Financial Times, Prentice Hall. Copyright © J. Beech and S. Chadwick, 2007

INTRODUCTION

This book is the second text developed by the Open University in the subject area of sport and fitness. It has been stimulated by the continued development of the sector and of undergraduate courses in the subject, including vocationally focused work-based learning and Foundation Degrees. The book is being used as a 'Reader' on the Open University module E113 *Working and Learning in Sport and Fitness*, which is part of a Foundation Degree in Sport and Fitness. Therefore, this text is rather different compared with other academic work in the field in that its remit is to support the learning that takes place in the workplace which often happens informally. A great deal is learnt outside the classroom and books by trial and error, learning by doing and general 'experience'. This learning is often captured by the use of reflective practice techniques, which are an important theme throughout the book and are addressed in the first section of the text. The book also differs in that it is partly designed for a distance-learning audience which means that clarity is particularly important.

The terms 'sport and fitness' have been used together in this book to capture the range of settings and motivations that may be involved in such activities and to explicitly include sports coaches, health and fitness instructors and those managing sports facilities. The focus on coaching and instruction, which can also be described as a 'leadership' activity, is another theme of this book.

WORK-BASED LEARNING

The book has been written in a period when the shape of Higher Education is changing with a growth in participation in general and increasing take-up of part-time study options. There is also a continuing interest in the relationship between universities and the work place, leading to calls for more active engagement of employers (Leitch, 2006), more 'skills' development and a greater emphasis on work or practice-based learning.

The Open University's Practice Based Professional Learning Centre defines work or practice-based learning as:

> learning which arises out of, or is focused on, working practice in a chosen job, voluntary work, career or profession.

and works from the basis that:

> Practice-based learning raises student employability and promotes learning outcomes that are hard to develop through conventional courses.
>
> (Yorke, 2006: p. 1)

The sometimes elusive relationship between learning and action, theory and practice, academic and vocational approaches is tackled in many Higher Education Institutions (HEIs) by work placements or sandwich years in which students undertake a prolonged period of work. Many aspects of this book will support learning in such placements.

The relationship between academic and work-place learning remains one of intense discussion and is linked to debates on the nature of professional and practitioner knowledge and expertise. For example, Eraut (1994) argues that practitioners act on the basis of personal knowledge, and this is acquired both through workplace experience and through learning academic knowledge. Like many others, Eraut notes the importance of integrating academic knowledge with work-based understanding and experience through a process of reflection. Other commentators have explored the distinction between learning as the acquisition of knowledge and learning as participation (Sfard, 1998), the latter often represented as learning through communities of practice (Lave and Wenger, 1991; Wenger, 1998).

The idea that theory is relevant and useful to practice is encouraged by HEI work placements. Students on such work placements are often asked to reflect and write about how the knowledge from their studies applies to the work place. The use of *reflective practice* techniques underpins such an approach and until now it has not featured widely in sport and fitness texts. A series of new and existing readings on reflective practice have therefore been developed to support work-based learning, which feature as the first section and topic of this book.

For those undertaking work placements a 'learning contract' is often established between the student, employer and HEI in which the student can shape the topics they focus and reflect on to adapt to their own circumstances and interests. This element of student choice is considered by many to be an important feature. With this in mind the decision of what other topics should be included in this book (see below) is not meant to limit such choice of what might be possible to study at work. As much as possible we have chosen areas of knowledge that apply to a number of different sport and fitness settings.

CHOICE OF TOPICS

This book takes a multidisciplinary approach towards sport and fitness, using definitions, concepts, theories and methods from a range of disciplines, including management, psychology, linguistics and education.

In keeping with the vocational focus of this book, we concentrate on some of the most important generic topics for employers and their staff, and address these with a range of readings that can connect with practice. In order to ensure relevance, we have consulted with leading employers, a government training council called SkillsActive which develops 'national occupational standards' and employee surveys. This consultation suggested that the topics of *interpersonal communication* and *customer focus* were very highly valued by employers and as a result these feature as sections of the book. Furthermore, since this book has an instructional, coaching and leadership bias we also carefully considered what work-based knowledge would support those progressing their career in these roles. As a result we have also developed sections on the topics of *motivation, leadership* and *instruction*. These five topics, together with the recurring theme of reflective practice, make up the six main sections of the book.

STRUCTURE OF THE BOOK

The book is structured in six main sections, each considered to be important to a range of roles within the sport and fitness sector. Within each section, different contributors provide expert knowledge in their particular field of expertise. The six main sections are:

1 Reflective practice
   This section looks at the role reflective practice can play in helping the individual to develop their skills and knowledge in their chosen field of practice.
2 Motivation
   This section examines the development of a motivational climate to ensure that individuals are able to produce the best possible results, whether this is on the sports field, in the gym or in the workplace.
3 Communicating effectively
   Effective communication is central to working in sport and fitness. This section considers the components of effective communication and addresses the important areas of ethics and diversity.
4 Leadership
   Leadership in its broadest sense is addressed in this section. The readings consider what makes an effective and ethical leader in a range of different contexts (individual, group, organisational and strategic).
5 Learning and instructing
   This section looks at how learning physical skills and learning how to be a coach/instructor can be better understood by considering an overview of the most important research findings. The focus moves from learning to instruction with simple frameworks that can be applied to better understand practice.
6 You and your customers
   This section addresses the value of understanding customers and their needs, both in terms of how schedules are adjusted to provide what they want and in developing effective ways of communicating with them.

The sequencing of chapters has been carefully chosen so that each section starts with chapters which introduce the area under consideration. These ideas are then extended in later chapters in each section. At the start of each section there is an editorial introduction that explains the outline content of each chapter. There is also a little background information about the author(s) that will help readers to understand the particular perspective that they are writing from.

A particular strength of the book is the broad mix of authorial voices behind the different chapters. These range from established academics from leading sports universities, commercial managers, hands-on facility managers and those with broad coaching experience.

REFERENCES

Eraut, M. (1994) *Developing Professional Knowledge: A Review of Progress and Practice*. London: Falmer.

Lave, J. and Wenger, E. (1991) *Situated Learning: Legitimate Peripheral Participation*. Cambridge: Cambridge University Press.

Leitch, S. (2006) *Review of Skills: Prosperity For All in the Global Economy – World Class Skills*. London: HMSO.

Sfard, A. (1998) On two metaphors of learning and the dangers of choosing just one. *Educational Researcher*, 27(2): 4–13.

Wenger, E. (1998) Communities of practice. Learning as a social system. *Systems Thinker*. Available online: www.co-i-l.com/coil/knowledge-garden/cop/lss.shtml (accessed August 2008).

Yorke, M. (2006) *Good Practice; Better Practice: A Review of Practice-Based Professional Learning in Four Central Academic Units in the Open University*. The Open University.

ABOUT THE EDITORS

Caroline Heaney is an academic on the Foundation Degree in Sport and Fitness at The Open University. She has been lecturing in sport and fitness for several years and has a strong vocational background in the field. Caroline is a British Association of Sport and Exercise Sciences (BASES) Accredited Sport Psychologist, and has provided sport psychology support to a wide range of teams and individuals, including several world class performers. Her research interests lie in the areas of applied sport psychology and the psychological aspects of sports injury.

Ben Oakley is the Head of Award for the Open University's Foundation Degree in Sport and Fitness. His sporting interest has taken a prominent role in past jobs, having been full-time Olympic coach for the Games held in Seoul (1988) and Barcelona (1992) in the sport of windsurfing. He has lectured in sports policy at UK and European Universities, and was a member of Sport England's Regional Board, which made decisions about the distribution of National Lottery funds to local projects. He is the academic consultant on the BBC Olympic Dreams series.

Simon Rea is an academic on the Foundation Degree in Sport and Fitness at The Open University. He combines extensive experience within the sport and fitness industry with fourteen years lecturing experience in higher and further education. He is an external verifier for a major examining board and has co-authored five course text books. He has run his own personal training company as well as working in the private and public sectors. In addition he worked as a performance coach in first class cricket, advising players on nutrition, psychology and physical conditioning.

SECTION 1

REFLECTION IN WORK-BASED PRACTICE

INTRODUCTION

Reflective learning and reflective practice are gaining increasing prominence in the training of sport and fitness professionals. The development of reflective techniques is central to many undergraduate programmes and in the professional development of sports coaches, fitness professionals and sports managers. Reflection seeks to make the most of an individual's knowledge and the workplace experiences they have so they can maximise their learning. By reflecting on knowledge and experiences a practitioner can understand their practice and the effectiveness of the actions they take. They can also start to develop new ways of acting and dealing with work role situations.

The section starts with two accessible readings that will assist newcomers to this field. Chapters 3–5 use a slightly more academic approach to the topic whilst the final two chapters explain distinct aspects of the field.

Chapter 1 is by Tony Ghaye, Director of Reflective Learning UK (RL-UK) which is a not-for-profit social enterprise. He is the founder and editor of the international journal 'Reflective Practice'. Tony has written extensively about reflective learning and its role in continuing professional development. This chapter represents an introduction to the area of reflective practice and how such an approach can improve coaching or instruction. It addresses the importance of asking 'reflective questions' to trigger the reflective process and provides four principles to guide reflective practice.

Chapter 2 is written by Simon Rea and Ben Oakley of the Open University. It provides an accessible starting point for those interested in using reflection in learning and in practice. It summarises what is meant by the term 'reflective practice', the value of implementing reflective techniques, and how reflective can be done in a deliberate way.

Chapter 3 is authored by Zoe Knowles and Hamish Telfer. Zoe Knowles is a senior lecturer in sport psychology and coaching science at Liverpool John Moores University. She is a BASES accredited sport psychologist whose clients include professional football clubs and Olympic/World championship athletes and staff. Hamish Telfer is a senior lecturer in coaching practice and sports studies at the University of Cumbria. He has been a Great Britain team coach in three sports and has coached his own squad of athletes. He also contributes to coach education as a Senior Tutor with Sports Coach UK and Running Sports. Both authors have written extensively on the subject of reflective practice. The authors trace the development of reflective practice in other professions and show its relevance to sport and fitness environments and how it can be applied by sport and fitness practitioners. This is followed by an outline of models which can be used to direct an individual's reflection.

Chapter 4 is written by the same authors as the previous chapter, Hamish Telfer and Zoe Knowles. They explain how reflective practice helps us to focus on and learn from our experiences and how different types of knowledge contribute to the knowledge of our 'craft'. The process of 'getting started' with reflection and the use of reflective questioning are explored.

Chapter 5 is written by Lindsey Dugdill, Reader in Exercise and Health and Associate Dean (Research) for the Faculty of Health and Social Care at the University of Salford. Dugdill's chapter uses a case study-based approach to show how reflective practice can contribute towards the development of 'professionalism' and, in particular, when working with people from different professions. She shows the role of reflective as being central to the process of evaluation.

Chapter 6 is written by Neil Thompson who is a director of Avenue Consulting. Thompson introduces what he understands by the term 'reflective practice' and then looks at the process of applying theory to practice and establishes why it is important that practice as based on theory focuses on the importance of relating theory to practice, the role reflection plays in developing an understanding of theory, and understanding the application of theory to our practice.

Chapter 7 is written by Jennifer A. Moon of the educational department at the University of Exeter. She is an experienced teacher and course leader in education and professional training. She is also a leading expert on reflective learning strategies. Dr Moon's chapter examines how to write in a reflective manner. An incident that the author has witnessed is presented in four reports; each report becomes more reflective than the previous report. It shows the difference between reporting facts and developing a reflective approach to an event one has been involved in.

CHAPTER 1

REFLECTION[1]
Principles and practices

Tony Ghaye

REFLECTIVE PRACTICE

In this chapter the author discusses reflective practice within the field of sports coaching. However, all that is noted within the coaching context here could equally apply to those in leadership positions or those working in health and fitness. Rather than change the text to be more generic, the sports coaching references have been maintained with this introduction acting as a reminder that what follows can also be applied to a range of sports and fitness settings.

REFLECTION: PRINCIPLES AND PRACTICES FOR BETTER COACHING ... BETTER SPORT

'Everyday' reflective practice

There are many views about what reflection is, how it's done and what people get out of it. It is commonly referred to as 'what we do anyway, quite naturally' and as 'thinking again about what we do'. It can be done well or badly, successfully or unsuccessfully. Many people see the purpose of reflection as focusing on what went wrong and then trying to put it right. Understanding

---

[1] Edited from Ghaye, T. (2001) *Faster Higher Stronger*, pp. 9–11, The National Coaching Foundation.

reflection as an aid to learning about practice is often expressed in a number of different ways:

- Navel gazing
- Learning from what we've just done
- Going over and over things, round and round
- Being honest with yourself
- Questioning what you do
- Thinking about things more deeply
- Looking back over your shoulder
- Justifying what you do
- Getting better at things
- Doing what I know and knowing why I do it

These everyday expressions say something, but by no means everything, about reflection.

Reflection is a complex process and makes an important contribution to better coaching

I am going to put it to you that reflection is much more than thinking again about what we do. Additionally, being reflective does not always come natural to us but it can be developed and done so in different ways. There are many types of reflection. For example, there is the common type called descriptive reflection (a re-telling and re-living of past experiences usually done soon after an event and often told to another person). Very different kinds are creative and critical reflection. Here reflection is used to try to move our thinking about what we do and our actions (e.g. coaching elite performers) forward in some way. Creative reflection means learning from past experiences and then trying out something new, or doing something we've always done, in a new and novel way. It is both backward and forward looking. Critical reflection includes questioning routines, habitual practices, challenging the 'conventional wisdom' on the matter and being able to ask others and ourselves 'why-type' questions (e.g. why do I/we coach in this way?).

Reflection is not just something that we always do alone and privately. It can be done with others, with reflections being publicly shared and constructively critiqued. This is particularly relevant if the activity in question involves team-work. It is wrong to characterise reflection as simply soft, warm, 'touchy-feely'

6

stuff, that's bland, pappy and very subjective. Reflection of one kind or another can also have a tough, militant and political face, especially if the purpose of reflection is to try to improve our practice (not just understand it better) and improve the context in which our practice takes place. For example, being skilful at critical-creative forms of reflection is important if better coaching and better sport depends upon improving the whole way the sport is coordinated, managed and funded (i.e. developing youth policies, nurturing talent, engaging with local communities, the role of sports academies and centres of excellence, securing new sources of funding, developing new and better network, using 'e' technologies, developing more holistic, interdisciplinary approaches to practice, etc.). So let's be clear. There is reflection:

- For self-development, personal renewal and growth (self-knowledge, self-awareness, self-esteem, self-confidence, self-efficacy, etc.).
- For improving our understanding about our work as a practitioner (sense making that contributes to safe and accountable practice, self-regulation and so on).
- For improving our practice (actually improving what we do, with and for others).

There is also another type of reflection called reflection-*on*-action, completed after an event. In contrast, there is also something called reflection-*in*-action. This is about the ways we 'think on our feet', make split-second decisions, involve gut feelings, intuition and the way we adapt our practice in the light of the ongoing actions in front of us. Reflection, therefore, should be central to a practitioner's ability to understand their practice. In the case of coaching, reflection of this kind is central to the art and science of coaching because it is about the way coaches handle and resolve difficulties and challenges while actually in the act of coaching. It is thinking about doing something while actually doing it. We need to know much more about reflection-in-action irrespective of the leadership role we undertake.

Reflecting on Schön: Joining up what we say with what we do

Donald Schön is one person who has made an enormous contribution to our understanding of reflective practice (Schön, 1983, 1987, 1991). One of his ideas, further developed in his work with Chris Argyris (Argyris and Schön, 1992) is particularly relevant when using reflection to try to improve coaching. It centres on the idea of a theory-of-action. This comes in two parts. One is called our espoused theories, the other our theories-in-use. The former is about what we say or *claim we do*, or want to do, in our coaching sessions. The latter is about *what actually happens* in practice. Reflecting on the congruence between what we say and what we do is a critical component in the improvement process. Sometimes we say one thing and do something quite different. We should get into the habit of reflecting on the reasons for this. Focusing on congruence and contradiction in coaching work is an important step in the direction of improving practice.

What can usefully trigger reflection?

The reflective process is usefully triggered by an ability to ask questions about your practice. For example, reflection-for-improvement is about being able to ask confrontational questions, where you confront your own practice. Naturally this can be disturbing and threatening. But responses to the following questions can help to develop a creative response to improving aspects of what you do. You might ask yourself:

- What is my practice like?
- Why is it like this way?
- How has it come to be this way?
- What aspects of it would I like to improve? (be realistic!)
- Whose interests are being served (or denied) by my practice?
- What nourishes and/or constrains what I do?
- What pressures prevent/limit me from practice in alternative ways?
- What alternatives are available to me right now?

Asking a good reflective question, in the right way and at the right moment, is a skilful business.

Four of the guiding principles of reflective practice

There is a growing body of research which suggests that reflective practice has the potential to transform both who we are and what we do. Reflection is much more than a collection of methods, or a set of tools. Rather, it needs to be seen as a whole way of being, a disposition towards practice, a whole approach to the job (Dewey, 1933). Would you say that you were a 'reflective coach'? Would you know one if you were working with one? What would be their qualities, disposition and skills?

8

Four of the guiding principles of reflective practice for all practitioners are:

1   Reflective practice is about you, your role and your work (coaching, managing, leading).
    The focus is on you and those you coach, manage or lead. It starts and ends with your practice. It is reflection on what you did, or thought you did, as well as on what you might, should or could have done. The 'context' in which your coaching takes place is a big influence on this.
2   Reflective practice is about learning from your experience of coaching and leading.
    Reflection on experience should be a conscious and intentional activity. There is no virtue in simply claiming that we have lots of leadership experience, whether coaching or managing others. The key attribute of excellent leaders is what they actually do with their experience! If we fail to learn from our experience we are likely to commit the mistakes of yesterday. Top coaches have an ability to turn experience into learning (through reflection).
3   Reflective practice is about valuing what you do and why you do it.
    Better coaching is linked to improving our knowledge about coaching. So what and whose knowledge is worth knowing? Generally it is wise to view all knowledge as 'uncertain', rather than fixed and unable to be reviewed.
4   The reflective conversation is at the heart of the process of reflecting-on-practice.
    This is not a standard debrief, not just a drink and a chat after an event. It is a hugely skilful and complex process. Good leaders need to be taught how best to facilitate this, amongst themselves and with those who they coach or manage. Its defining characteristic is its focus on values. Our values make us the kind of coach (and sports person) that we are. Our values give us reasons for doing things. Coaches, I suggest, need to know them, justify and try to live them out.

Developing a culture of reflection within your own practice

The new United Kingdom Coaching Certificate (UKCC), licensing and developing standards in sport relating to equity, disability and safeguarding, now place a greater responsibility on sports practitioners to audit their own practice. In common with other service industries, good sports practitioners should be aiming to offer the best level of service practice they can, whether they are coaches, managers or fitness leaders. The aspiration of elevating the sports industry to a profession can only be achieved if practitioners take responsibility for their own practice and are accountable. Much can be learned from the experiences of other emerging professions and the process of gaining an understanding of your own practice and being able to develop it is both exciting and challenging. Being the best we can should be the vision we all share and should guide our own professional development. We know that 'without a vision for tomorrow, hope is impossible' (Freire, 1998: p. 45). It is hoped that through reading this brief introductory chapter that you will come to understand the pivotal role of reflection in making your practice more robust through your own vision of what your practice should aspire to. It is my belief that reflective practices and reflective practitioners will be potent parts of a joined up or 'connected profession', with the clarity of thinking and sensitivities to work towards a sporting future that is inclusive of all.

REFERENCES

Argyris, C. and Schön, D. (1992) *Theory in Practice: Increasing Professional Effectiveness*. San Francisco: Jossey Bass.
Dewey, J. (1933) *How We Think: A Restatement of the Relation of Reflective Thinking to the Educative Process*. Chicago: Henry Regnery Publishers.
Freire, P. (1998) *Pedagogy of the Heart*. New York: Continuum Press.
Schön, D. (1983) *The Reflective Practitioner*. New York: Basic Books.
Schön, D. (1987) *Educating the Reflective Practitioner*. San Francisco: Jossey Bass.
Schön, D. (1991) *The Reflective Turn: Case Studies in and on Educational Practice*. New York: Teacher's College Press.

CHAPTER 2

USING REFLECTIVE PRACTICE – AN OPEN UNIVERSITY PERSPECTIVE

Simon Rea and Ben Oakley

This chapter provides an accessible starting point for those considering using reflective practice. It assumes little prior knowledge of the concept and systematically explains what it is about, the likely focus of reflection, and frameworks for how it might be approached. It uses the authors' experience of embedding these ideas into an Open University course in which students from many different 'work roles' (including voluntary coaching) study at a distance.

INTRODUCTION

Reflective practice is a way of learning that is used to improve performance. It is about learning from the experiences we have had by thinking about them in a deliberate or structured way, undertaking 'cycles of enquiry'. The term 'cycle' is used to capture the way a reflective learner moves between reflection and future action; there is a sense in which taking action will result in our doing things differently and we can then reflect on what happened next (Ramsey, 2006). Another key word here is 'deliberate'. At some time or other we have all thought about what we have just done and wondered how else we could have acted. It is a somewhat different process, however, to set about improving our work performance on purpose by actively considering how we should behave, then designing and carrying out a new action before stepping back to consider whether the new action has made a difference.

Reflective practice is used in sport and fitness by those who want to understand their effectiveness whether they are sports coaches, fitness instructors or those in leadership positions. As these types of work role move towards professional status with training, set standards and self-regulation, reflection has an important role to play in encouraging self-improvement, flexibility and awareness.

LINKING KNOWLEDGE AND PRACTICE

In educational environments reflective practice is recognised as the link between knowledge and practice. Research into the effectiveness of coach education courses found that, while coaches on these courses increased their knowledge, it rarely improved the effectiveness of their coaching in practice (Douge *et al.*, 1994; cited in Knowles and Borrie, 2001). Therefore, many degree courses will include an element of work experience so that students can take the theory and concepts that have been learnt in study and try them out in the workplace. This suggests that you need to deliberately reflect on new knowledge you gain to consider how you will use it in practice. Thus, reflection is the link between theory and practice and provides a new kind of knowledge that cannot be gained from watching other people or reading about it (Jasper, 2003: p. 1).

PROBLEM-SOLVING

Your workplace is a rich source for learning because you are presented with new experiences or situations on a daily basis. If things go wrong at work you may discuss these with a colleague to help make sense of the situation or you will mull it over yourself until you understand it better – if you don't seek to understand the situation you will keep making the same mistakes.

Reflection is done for many reasons; the most basic is to develop strategies to enable us to be more effective at work and in life. Ramsey (2006) considers that:

> Too often managers in organisations when faced with difficult problems resort to 'just trying harder'. A crucial part of learning is doing things differently and being able to evaluate the success of these new practices
>
> (p. 7)

In your workplace you may find that certain issues do not have straightforward answers, such as how to deal with particularly difficult people or groups. The answer is often to try out new approaches and learn from them. This links well to the idea of 'professional practice', which is a central subject of the influential writer on reflective practice, Schön (1983, 1987). He examined how professionals, such as architects, psychotherapists and managers practice their professions on a daily basis, and this has significance for people in sport and fitness. Edwards (1999), writing about Schön's work, explains that 'professionals do not receive ready-made problems' (Edwards, 1999: p. 72) so a set solution cannot be applied. Edwards (1999) goes on:

> Schön argues that each professional builds up a set of experiences and draws on these to help in the task of problem solving.
>
> (Edwards, 1999: p. 72)

Both writers identified the importance of 'practical professional knowledge' which is used to solve problems. However, problem-solving can only be done after a period of reflection to identify the problem; or, 'problem setting'. Problem setting is often ignored in the workplace and you can probably identify situations when a solution was hurriedly applied to a problem before the complexities of the actual problem had been fully identified. As a result the problem would remain.

WHAT TO REFLECT ON

You may feel that we are suggesting you reflect about everything you do. This really is not the case; it is likely that most of what you do at work is perfectly successful and achieves what you intended. However, sometimes you will achieve something which is exceptionally good, such as the way you managed a difficult session. Alternatively, sometimes you may have an exceptionally bad experience, such as a participant making a complaint about the way they were treated. Both of these should be seen as potentially rich learning experiences and could form a focus for reflection.

As a starting point, the focus of your reflection could be any of the following:

- A significant event.
- Applying new knowledge you have gained.
- A specific ongoing issue in your practice.

Let's briefly consider each of these in turn. Significant events describe the positive and negative experiences described above and can provide valuable learning. In instructional or leadership contexts such events happen quite often and as a result this will be referred to again later in the chapter.

13

Applying new knowledge you have gained refers to the value of using reflection to make sense and apply new information, for example, undertaking a training course or reading a book such as this. Earlier in this chapter there was discussion under the heading of 'linking knowledge and practice' which considered the importance of this type of reflection.

The final aspect to reflect on we termed 'a specific ongoing issue in your practice'. By this we mean that there may be aspects of your current practice that you would like to improve or understand more about. For example, you may feel that there are certain participant groups you don't seem to be able to communicate effectively with or you may feel that you are struggling to motivate children in your sessions.

In general, all these situations would benefit from some deliberate thought and discussion and you will notice as you read further that much reflection is triggered by asking appropriate questions. Questioning is a central feature of the reflective frameworks explained later in the chapter.

Looking overall at what to reflect on, Ghaye and Lillyman (2006) suggested five core competencies of good practice that could be investigated using reflection (see Table 2.1). They suggested a selective approach in which you consider which is most important and appropriate to your own situation. This table therefore provides a useful prompting list of what can be the focus of reflection.

Having looked at the role of reflection and what you may reflect on we will now explain how you can use frameworks of reflection to give it a systematic structure.

FRAMEWORKS FOR REFLECTION

Frameworks can be very helpful in pointing us to what issues we should consider and can also help us to be thorough in our reflection. A framework is a way of breaking that 'thinking about' into distinct activities that follow logically on from each other.

The frameworks we introduce below should be used as guides only and can be adapted to suit your purposes.

If you research reflective practice further you will discover that there are many frameworks for reflective practice. We have carefully chosen two frameworks that we feel work best for sport and fitness learning in a variety of work and

14

Table 2.1 Core competencies of good practice

Competency	Explanation	Specific aspects
Communication	Look at the communication between you and your colleagues and you and your customers/participants	Verbal and non-verbal aspects Your questioning skills Your listening skills Your responses
Decision-making	You will constantly be making decisions, most of them quickly, and the outcomes you get are the result of these decisions	Speed Timing Effectiveness Consequences Options taken or not taken
Teamwork	If appropriate, look at how well and willing people are to work together to achieve aims and objectives	Quality of interaction Leadership: who leads and how? Your own leadership skills Cohesion within the team Individual contributions to the team
Observation	Your own observation skills are important in judging how other people react, feel and are acting	Who or what are you observing: People, their relationships or their environment? Consequences of what you observed
Judgement	You will act all the time on your judgement of situations and people. How accurate are your judgements?	Colleagues, staff and customers Information for the basis of your judgement Accuracy Consequences

Source: Adapted from Ghaye and Lillyman (2006)

study situations. They are the Reflective Practice (RP) and the Significant Event (SE) frameworks.

The Reflective Practice (RP) framework

This framework focuses reflection on:

- A specific ongoing issue in your practice.
- Applying new knowledge you have gained.

The RP framework that we are proposing has been adapted from a similar approach used on an Open University course, 'Working with Young People'

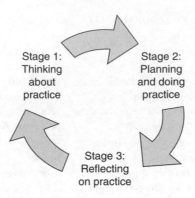

Figure 2.1 The reflective practice learning process

Source: Open University (2006), p. 3

(Open University, 2006), which is adapted from Kolb (1984); it moves learners through three main stages in which you are thinking about, planning and reflecting on practice. These stages are represented in Figure 2.1.

Table 2.2 Some key questions at each stage of the reflective practice process

Stage 1 Thinking about practice (or specific aspects of your role)	What do I know about my current practice? What do I know and believe about this area of practice? What new ideas do I want to explore or try out?
Stage 2 Planning and doing practice	How am I going to explore these new ideas? Who am I going to work with? How will I get feedback on this work?
Stage 3 Reflecting on practice	What have I learnt about my practice and values? How will my learning change my practice now and in the future? What other aspects of my practice do I need to develop?

Source: Adapted from Open University (2006)

GUIDANCE ON USING THE RP FRAMEWORK

Each stage can be broken down into a group of related prompting questions and Table 2.2 sets out the different questions which may be addressed at each stage of the process. Prompting questions are merely there to trigger thinking and reflection and can be adapted to the topic or circumstances. Indeed you should adjust such questions in conjunction with a mentor or colleagues so that they are appropriate to your own situation.

This RP framework works best when used to examine specific aspects of your practice or perhaps when you have recently learnt new knowledge through a training course or readings such as those in this book. If the framework and associated questions are used it prompts you to think about how you can use the new ideas you may have learnt.

The above framework is a very logical model of how we learn. However, it is not always as simple as that since thoughts and behaviour aren't always rational. A key part of reflective practice is to help us become more thoughtful and less impulsive in our actions, but we do need to include our feelings and their effect on our actions in our reflection. The second framework we want to introduce to you is helpful in this respect, especially in how you react to specific events or incidents.

The Significant Event (SE) framework

This second framework is more precise than the previous one in that it focuses on significant events. When we use the term 'significant event' we mean something, positive or negative, that has stuck in your mind which you would like to explore further. The SE framework is based on a model of reflection developed by Gibbs (1988). This 'reflective cycle' consists of six stages that guide you through an event by asking simple prompting questions. The reflective cycle is shown in Figure 2.2 and starts with a description of what happened. Box 2.1 that follows gives guidance about how to use the SE framework.

Different uses of the two frameworks

It is perhaps useful to compare how these two frameworks have been used in Open University learning to illustrate the differences. The RP framework is used for considering how the new knowledge and insights presented in a course of study will be applied and evaluated in people's work roles. In contrast, the SE framework focuses on specific events that happen. The word 'events' is significant here; only you can decide which events are significant enough to learn from.

17

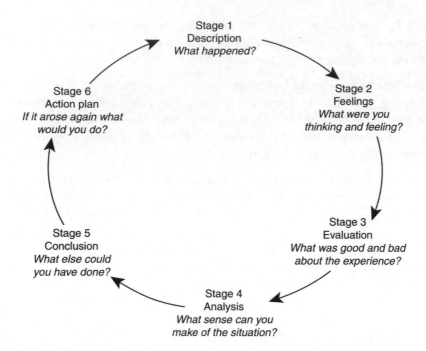

Figure 2.2 Significant Event framework

Source: Adapted from Gibbs (1998)

BOX 2.1: GUIDANCE ON EACH STAGE OF THE SE FRAMEWORK

Stage 1: Description of the event

The starting point is to write down a description of the event; you need to recall as much as you can of the event. You may include where you were, the sequence of events, the other people involved and what they were doing.

Stage 2: Feelings

Now recall how you were feeling when the event started, how your feelings changed through the course of the event and why they may have changed.

Stage 3: Evaluation

As you evaluate something, you are comparing the experience against your expectations and trying to understand what happened. You may ask questions such as: what was good and what was bad about the experience?

Stage 4: Analysis

When we analyse something we break it down into smaller parts or look at the detail. You need to question in a deeper way:

What went well?
What did I do well?
What could be improved?

This is a good point at which to analyse some of the core competencies from Table 2.1: communication, decision-making, teamwork, judgement and observation.

Stage 5: Conclusion

Once you have produced some results from the evaluation and analysis stages you perhaps have sufficient information to make a judgement. You should have developed some insight into your own and other people's behaviour and how they contributed to the outcome. You may not be entirely satisfied with your contribution but it may give you a chance to learn about yourself and develop new ways of working.

Stage 6: Action plan

Once you have come to a conclusion about how you acted during the event you need to draw up a list of actions which will help you become more effective in the future. You may consider that you need more knowledge and more skills, and you could identify who might assist in this. The SE cycle ends here; the next time an event occurs it will become the focus of another reflective cycle.

19

INCLUDING OTHERS

Now that you have an idea about how to structure reflection using the frameworks, you might consider trying it out on your own first. However, for a more thorough analysis of your practice you should also consider the benefit of including other people in your reflection. For example, if you were struggling to motivate a group of children, you may not understand why you are finding it difficult or be sure about the solution. At this point it would greatly help to discuss the issue with someone else to gain a new perspective on it. We would suggest that you identify someone you trust with whom you can talk openly and in confidence. These people are often called mentors, or critical friends, and in some cases may be trusted supervisors. They should be able to ask you questions or discuss new strategies, help illuminate what the problem may be and develop possible solutions. Or, if appropriate, you may ask the children in a group for feedback as part of a debriefing, as their perspective may differ from yours. In summary, the more viewpoints you have then the more information will be available to establish the likely reality of a situation.

RECORDING YOUR REFLECTION

Ghaye also stresses the importance of creating a record of your reflective work:

> If you don't create a written account you don't know where you have come from. It is difficult to know what progress you have made because you can't see a trail. There are no footprints there. It is really important to make some kind of record of your learning.
>
> (Open University, 2009)

It is useful to store your reflective work, perhaps in a reflective journal. This can be hand written or word processed. Some people also like to use visual methods, such as pictures or story boards. Recording reflection is good practice, as it is increasingly used in professional accreditations to demonstrate 'professional development' and a commitment to ongoing learning.

CONCLUSION

You may have found much of the information presented in this chapter familiar because most people reflect in some way. The difference here is that the reflection is deliberate and structured and also recorded in some way. You have been presented with many new ideas and you may find it difficult to put them all into practice straight away. Learning new skills takes time so give yourself the time and space to improve your reflective skills. Keep trying out new ideas and find out what works for you. As you get more comfortable with the process you should notice the benefits of reflective practice.

REFERENCES

Edwards, A. (1999) Reflective practice in sport management. *Sport Management Review*, 2: 67–81.

Ghaye, T. and Lillyman, S. (2006) *Reflection and Writing a Reflective Account. United Kingdom.* Maisemore: The Institute of Reflective Practice–UK.

Gibbs, G. (1988) *Learning By Doing: A Guide to Teaching and Learning Methods.* Oxford Brookes University, Oxford: Further Education Unit.

Jasper, M. (2003) *Beginning Reflective Practice.* Cheltenham: Nelson Thornes.

Knowles, K. and Borrie, A. (2001) Reflection works. *Faster, Higher, Stronger*, 10: 9–11.

Kolb, D.A. (1984) *Experiential Learning: Experience as the Source of Learning and Development.* New Jersey: Prentice Hall.

Ramsey, C. (2006). *Introducing Reflective Learning.* Milton Keynes: The Open University.

Schön, D.A. (1983) *The Reflective Practitioner: How Professionals Think in Action.* New York: Basic Books.

Schön, D.A. (1987) *Educating the Reflective Practitioner: Toward a New Design For Teaching and Learning in the Professions.* San Francisco: Jossey-Bass.

The Open University (2006) *Working with Young People (E118) Study Guide.* Milton Keynes: Open University.

The Open University (2009) *Working and Learning in Sport and Fitness (E113) Course DVD: Film 1 Reflective Practice in Action.* Milton Keynes: Open University.

CHAPTER 3

THE WHERE, WHAT AND WHY OF REFLECTIVE PRACTICE[1]

Zoe Knowles and Hamish Telfer

INTRODUCTION

This chapter aims to plot the origins and development of reflective practice in sport and fitness. Concepts, techniques and practices of reflection have been 'borrowed' from other allied health/education-based professions, and researchers are now working with these principles in the sport domain. Definitions of reflective practice and models which show the process of reflective practice are presented. Finally the authors propose a rationale as to why practitioners in sport professions should engage in reflective practice.

SECTION 1: WHERE HAS REFLECTIVE PRACTICE DEVELOPED FROM IN SPORT?

Researchers and educators in sport have drawn on the more developed expertise of allied health/education professions who have used reflective practice as a learning tool. For example, examples can be seen in nursing (e.g. Ekeburgh, 2007); teacher education (e.g. Lee, 2007); health promotion (e.g. Fleming, 2007); social work (Ruch, 2007) and physiotherapy (Donaghy and Marss, 2007). Typically, in principles of reflection, models demonstrating the process of reflection and developed techniques have been 'borrowed' from these disciplines. This range of professions all have a common theme which involve dealing with people (interpersonal relationships), a dynamic and changing practice environment; the ability to make decisions in practice

---

[1] 'The multiprofessional international journal established in 2001 'Reflective Practice' bears testimony to the range of professional fields using reflective practice as a learning strategy, see www.tandf.co.uk/journals.'

and the need to learn from experience. For example, a fitness instructor works with clients, other fitness professionals, medical staff or physiotherapists, within the course of their duties. The fitness suite is a constantly changing environment and no two client training plans are the same. Decisions on exercise and training are often made quickly in response to client condition and for both trainee instructors *and* experienced trainers the fitness suite is their primary learning environment. A sports coach may work with athletes, assistant coaches, medical staff, agents and sports scientists. The training and competitive arena is a constantly changing environment (e.g. involving tactical play). Decisions by the coach are sometimes made quickly (substitutions, tactical play, training loads in practice sessions) and again, as with fitness professionals, for coaches the training and performance environments are their primary sources of learning.

However, it is important to take account of roles, working environments, support and opportunities for learning and how practitioners are made accountable for their practice within sport and fitness which may differ considerably. It is with this focus in mind that the reader is asked to follow the current and subsequent chapter and make their own links between the ideas and theories proposed with their own practical and learning environments.

Coaching is seen as an episodic process which integrates performance characteristics with the development of skills and knowledge. This process is best conceptualised as a spiral process constantly moving coaching practice forward. This allows practitioners to identify different aspects of coaching roles and management of a range of demands influencing not only performers themselves but also within the performance environment. These demands range from actual coaching practices to dealing with support staff and/or sports coaching teams and funding agencies, to facilitating athletes' social and psychological development. Despite this range of challenges, education and evaluation of sports coaching is almost exclusively focused on competitive performance outcomes. One consequence of this is that sports coaches are rarely judged on the quality of their *own* practice, such that the understanding and improvement of this element of practice is often ignored (Knowles *et al.*, 2005). In a similar sense the success of fitness instructors/personal trainers is usually measured through retention rates, which in turn are influenced by the outcomes the clients have achieved and whether they have achieved their goals.

Studies exploring the practice of expert coaches and expert-novice differences coaching practice have shown that coaching expertise is linked to cognitive skills, decision-making and the personal practice-based knowledge created through experience. In other words, expert coaches learn from 'doing the job' through experience and this is something which cannot be created within a typical and often formally taught education structure (e.g. lectures, demonstrations, etc.). In response to this literature, the focus for coach educators is a shift away from developing *what* coaches do (roles such as trainer, tactician, etc.) to how coaches *think* (i.e. how they learn). The question still remains for all educators across the sport and fitness professions as to how practitioners, whether novice or expert, learn from *their* practice. In order for practitioners to generate 'practice-based knowledge' reflective practice has been suggested as a strategy in sport and exercise science which could help practitioners explore decisions and experiences and so increase their understanding and management of themselves and their practice (Anderson *et al.*, 2004).

WHAT IS REFLECTIVE PRACTICE?

To us, reflective practice can be viewed in many ways. It is more than simply thinking over and over what has happened. Reflective practice is a cognitive (thinking) process which brings together deliberate exploration of thoughts, feelings and evaluations focused on practitioner skills and outcomes. The outcome of reflection is not always preparation for change, or action based, but perhaps confirmation/rejection of a theory or practice skill option. For example, it may be that an outcome of reflection is seen through understanding how certain training techniques actually work in practice (e.g. you may discover that you can be successful by adapting communication skills in certain ways for a target audience but not others). Reflective practice is a process by which we can generate self-awareness, focus on our practice and others that we may work with and formulate new knowledge and ways of working.

Within the literature definitions of reflection incorporate these ideas:

> ... a generic term for the intellectual and affective activities in which individuals examine their experiences in order to develop new understanding and intrapersonal appreciation ...
> (Knowles *et al.*, 2006: p. 165)

Here Knowles *et al.*, refer to reflection as being both a thought (intellectual) and action-based (affective) process, suggesting there are activities or 'ways' in which we can examine our practice. Understanding is proposed here as one outcome of reflection. Chapter 4 discusses further this notion, amongst others, as the product of reflection.

> … Reflective practice can refer to the ability to analyse one's own practice, the incorporation of problem solving into learning by doing or application of critical theory to the examination of professional practice …'
>
> (Edwards, 1999: p. 67)

In Edward's definition, critical theory includes questioning routines or habitual practices and challenging the 'norm'. We should ask of ourselves and others 'why'-type questions. For example, why do I coach in this style? Why does our pre-match warm-up work in the same way each week? Why do we do different exercises in each training session? Examples of these types of questions are seen in the reflective models presented later in the chapter.

> … Reflection could provide a bridge linking knowledge gained from professional experience, observations, coaching theory and education …'
>
> (Nelson and Cushion, 2006: p. 175, citing Buysse et al., 2003)

Nelson and Cushion highlight how reflection can be used to transfer knowledge into our own 'local' practice (i.e. our own working environment) which may be through observation or discussion of others' experiences, formal taught education through courses or our own practice knowledge. We can actually reflect on how this information would be applicable to ourselves. For example, we may consider:

> … that wouldn't work for my players, they are not skilled enough …
> … that wouldn't work in my fitness suite as we don't have the space …
> … I couldn't work that fitness test as I don't have the knowledge to understand the administration or analysis of data …

Reflection can be an individual or shared activity and it is important to understand how we can learn from reflecting with others as well as on our own. We suggest as reflective practitioners that both are important to reflective learning. Observation of others in practice or discussing practice/events after they have occurred creates opportunities for us to question practice too, albeit not derived from our own experience. Further examples of both individual and shared activities are presented in the following chapter. An interesting point to note here is whilst working with reflection knowledge can be generated that you are unlikely to see in academic textbooks. However, good examples can be found in the UK within FA Insight magazine; BGA Coaching Craft; SCUK Faster Higher Stronger; and Coaching Edge. Thus:

> … Reflective practice is an approach to practice that involves creating opportunities to access, make sense of and learn from tacit knowledge in action we use in our daily work … this knowledge in action incorporates values, prejudices, experience, knowledge and social norms.
>
> (Knowles *et al.*, 2007)

In this final definition the authors note 'tacit knowledge' (often used inter-changeably within the literature with 'craft knowledge'), that is that knowledge which we cannot perhaps trace back to any formal, educationally derived material but that which is associated with the 'craft' of the coaching role. Have you ever watched a coach or instructor and thought that they have a wealth of ideas and approaches to practice or dealing with issues that perhaps you can't trace back to education from an education course? These individuals, if asked about their practices, would probably tell you their ideas emerged from experience, watching others and trial and error rather than within the specifics of a course. Craft knowledge is linked to experience but having a lot of experience doesn't automatically mean a substantial craft knowledge base. Reflective practice provides a means through which craft knowledge can be identified and documented.

Through the process of reflection we may challenge our values and prejudices and indeed that of 'what we say we do and what we actually do'. We could therefore see reflective practice as a means to validate ethical practice. For example, if asked to note down some of your values about your work you might start your sentence with 'I believe that …' A football academy coach may state that:

> I … believe all of my players have the right to equal amounts of my time and direction when in a session …

This may be challenged however if the coach then knows that the players are due for release or not to be selected for the upcoming match and therefore he may want to focus more time on those who are eligible.

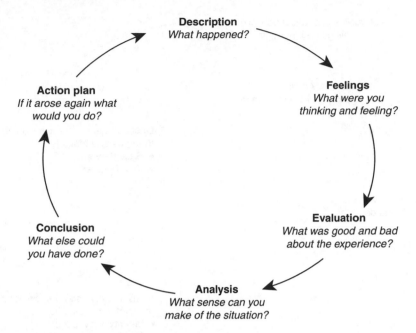

Figure 3.1 Gibbs' (1988) six-staged model of reflection

So far we have established that the practicalities of engaging in reflective practice allow you to focus on you and your work practices as well as perhaps uncover your values and beliefs. The process of reflection itself can be spontaneous or planned, undertaken as an individual or as a shared activity. The outcome of reflection can be preparation for change (action) or understanding/generation of knowledge.

To engage in any form of technique, a reflection guide or model might be used to facilitate the process of reflection. For example, Gibbs' (1988) six-staged cyclical model (Figure 3.1) poses questions designed to increase the practitioner's movement from a start point of description through awareness of feelings, evaluation/analysis, conclusion and formulation of action plan.

Gibbs' cycle should also be considered alongside that of Atkins and Murphy (1994) since the process of reflection can be both continuous (Gibbs) as well as disjointed (Atkins and Murphy), allowing stages in the process to build and resurface at varying points.

This is developed in the following chapter, which deals with the practicalities of how individuals engage in practice. Atkins and Murphy's (1994) model depicts the start point for reflection as being that of a negative one (see Figure 3.2).

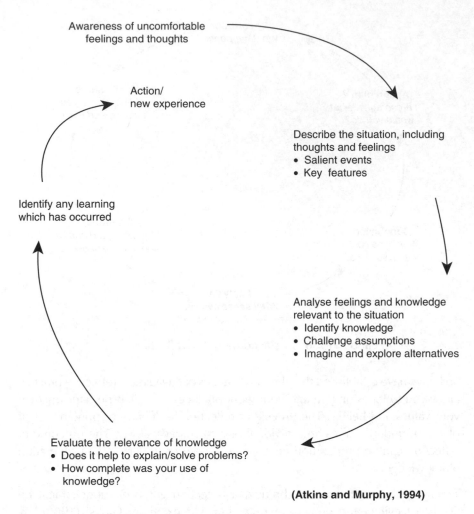

Awareness of uncomfortable
feelings and thoughts

Action/
new experience

Describe the situation, including
thoughts and feelings
• Salient events
• Key features

Identify any learning
which has occurred

Analyse feelings and knowledge
relevant to the situation
• Identify knowledge
• Challenge assumptions
• Imagine and explore alternatives

Evaluate the relevance of knowledge
• Does it help to explain/solve problems?
• How complete was your use of
  knowledge?

(Atkins and Murphy, 1994)

Figure 3.2 Model of reflective practice. From: Atkins, S. and Murphy, K. (1994) in Ghaye, T. and Lillyman, S. (1997)

We would argue as authors that reflection should be about focusing on the positive aspects of 'what went well?' in practice. When people evaluate they often focus only on negatives, which does not always give a true picture of reality if this becomes a habit. Continuously focusing on what went wrong is a demotivating process, albeit one which is perhaps natural to us as practitioners working in sport and fitness where our attention is directed mainly towards a specific outcome as well as the welfare and performance of our clients/athletes. Without a balance of focus on aspects of good practice as practitioners and ourselves as well as our clients, we perhaps leave the likelihood of good practice happening again to chance and missing opportunities to see how well we are doing and giving ourselves a pat on the back! Atkins and Murphy's model however perhaps provides further questions under each stage of the cycle, which may help the novice reflective practitioner. Cyclical models of reflection represent an experiential learning cycle and highlight the dynamic and ongoing nature of learning as an iterative process. Often reflection guides are used when writing a reflective diary or sharing practice with others as a form of 'agenda' to shape the discussion.

Johns (1994) argues that it is necessary to have a detailed model that guides and supports practitioners in their attempts. Indeed, Gibbs' or Atkins and Murphy's model may be useful to practitioners who wish to start developing reflective writing skills or used as a framework to shape shared reflection activities. Johns developed a more complex structured reflection procedure that incorporates a series of 21 questions designed in a linear model to guide the practitioner into his or her experience and facilitate reflection. Specifically, the questions are arranged sequentially (with a start and end point clearly defined) to examine actions, thoughts and feelings in an attempt to develop a deeper understanding of their practice. The model also encourages practitioners to consider the *consequences* of their actions and whether alternative action may have been more appropriate. As an example of the 'borrowing' of practice from other professions and contextually adapting this to sport-based reflective practice referred to in Section 1, Anderson (1999), a trainee practitioner in sport science, used John's model for six months and recommended several changes to the structured procedure. These changes included re-writing some questions to clarify their meaning and increase their relevance for sport science and reorganisation of the structure of the questions to avoid repetition of reflection. Table 3.1 illustrates the revised reflection questions.

Table 3.1 Johns' (1994) structured reflection procedures (as revised by Anderson, 1999)

Core question – What information do I need access to in order to learn through this consulting experience?

Cue questions

1.0 Description of the consulting experience

1.1 Phenomenon:	Describe the 'here and now' of the experience (*where, when, what*)
1.2 Causal:	What essential factors contributed to this experience (*why?*)

(continued)

Table 3.1 (continued)

1.3 Context:	Who are the significant background actors[2] in this experience?
1.4 Clarifying:	Put it back together and establish what the key issues are in this experience that I need to pay attention to.

2.0 Reflection

2.1	What was I trying to achieve?
2.2	Why did I intervene as I did?
2.3	What internal factors influenced my actions? *(Thoughts, feelings, previous experience)*
2.4	What external factors influenced my actions? *(Other people, organisational factors, time)*
2.5	What sources of knowledge did/should have influenced my decision-making?

3.0 Consequences of actions

3.1	What were the consequences of my actions for *(what did I learn/realise – cognitive component):*
	Myself?
	The athlete[3]?
	The people I work with?
3.2	How did I feel about this experience *when it was happening (affective)?*
3.3	How did the athlete[3] feel?
3.4	How did I know what the athlete felt like?

4.0 Alternative tactics

4.1	Could I have dealt with the situation better?
4.2	What other choices did I have?
4.3	What would be the consequences of these choices?

5.0 Learning

5.1	How do I now feel about this experience?
5.2	How have I made sense of this experience in light of past experiences and future practice?
5.3	Action: Write down the key lessons in your notebook.

[2] Readers may wish to consider the term 'others' here.
[3] The term 'athlete' may be substituted for 'client'.

WHY REFLECT?

Unlike many professions from where sport has 'borrowed' principles and techniques for reflective practice, sports coaching does not have a professional body responsible for governing practice. The British Government created the Sports Strategy Coaching Task Force (CTF) (2002) as part of an overall strategy for British sport to support initiatives to improve the standards of coaching, including the development and implementation of the UK Coaching Certificate (CTF, 2002). Sports coaching is now responding to various CTF initiatives, some of which are strongly focused on the improvement of coaching skills. Reflective practice is recognised as a key tool with which coaches should engage in order to improve practice (Knowles *et al.*, 2001, 2005, 2006).

With the welcome introduction of a nationally led coach education programme and more paid coaching roles comes the increasing influence of being account-able for this financial support together with assessment of impact. In the sport and fitness industries, performance outcomes are usually based on the achievements of performers or clients. In high-performance sport, lottery funding is dependent on demonstrating medal-winning potential and thus achieving it at major championships. It is no surprise therefore that as practitioners we simply direct our attention to ensuring performers' or clients' goals are met, rather than focus on our own accountability. Without any formal Governance for the professions (i.e. the stick and carrot approach) it is often left for locally based initiatives (staff appraisals) or even individuals to take responsibility for accountability processes and engagement.

It is the author's belief that if we can focus on improving the self in our respective roles, indirectly we will make a positive impact on performance/experience of others. Reflective practice can be used to increase a practitioner's accountability (Ghaye and Lillyman, 1997). Within sport science for example, Anderson *et al.* (2002) suggested that reflective practice could be used to self-evaluate practice and increase the sport psychologist's accountability to their client, themselves and their profession. Their advice across all three areas is applicable to all sport and fitness professionals. First, practitioners can use reflective practice to be accountable to the client (or performer) by examining and justifying their practice to increase confidence that they are providing the best service possible. Second, by engaging in reflective practice the practitioner takes personal responsibility for monitoring their practice and striving to increase their professional effectiveness (Johns, 1995). For example, Anderson (1999) highlighted how this process increased her accountability to herself when she noted, 'in short, reflective practice enabled me to justify my practice to myself' (p. 328). Third, reflective practice can be used to increase the practitioners' accountability to their profession. Many professional training programmes in coaching and fitness education incorporate a model of supervision. Reflective practice may be used to facilitate this by providing a method of monitoring and documenting the novice practitioner's development whilst learning in practice.

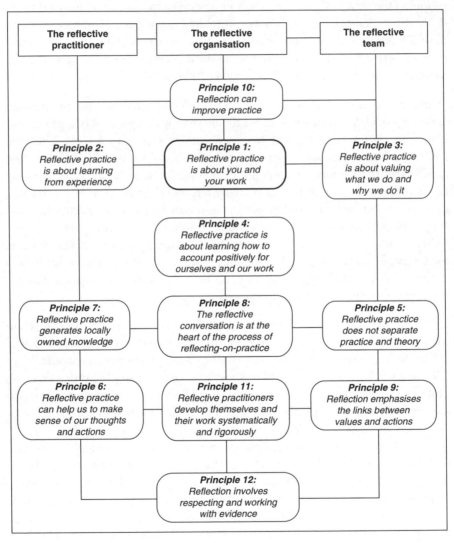

Figure 3.3 From: Ghaye, T. and Lillyman, S. (2000)

zoe knowles and hamish telfer

Professional groups such as the British Association of Sport and Exercise Sciences (BASES) have recently modified the requirements for completion of their Supervised Experience programme, which leads to Accreditation as a Sport and Exercise Psychologist, to include evidence of reflective practice (BASES, 2004). Reflective practice, it seems, is emerging as a technique for learning, encompassed by professional bodies in sport with a keen interest to develop practitioners in practice.

CONCLUSION

To conclude, reflection is a process which involves the whole person, including their thoughts and emotions. A simple definition of reflective practice is therefore difficult and Ghaye and Lillyman (2000) proposed that it is beneficial to see the principles of reflection represented as a 'landscape map' as shown in Figure 3.3. The focus on self and workplace, generating practice specific (craft) knowledge; exploring thought and feelings; evidencing reflection and the role of accountability have all been highlighted in this chapter. The map highlights not only the reflective individual but how they also feature within a reflective team (e.g. a coaching team, management team) and the reflective organisation (e.g. sports centre or national governing of sport). It is beyond the scope of this chapter to focus on these aspects and the interested reader is directed to Ghaye and Lillyman (2000) for further information.

REFERENCES

Anderson, A.G. (1999) Reflections of a budding sport psychologist: First meetings. In H. Steinberg and I. Cockerill (eds), *Sport Psychology in Practice: The Early Stages* (pp. 30–37). Leicester: British Psychological Society.

Anderson, A., Knowles, Z. and Gilbourne, D. (2004) Reflective practice for applied sport psychologists: A review of concepts, models, practical implications and thoughts on dissemination. *The Sport Psychologist*, 18: 188–201.

Anderson, A.G., Miles, A., Mahoney, C. and Robinson, P. (2002) Evaluating the effectiveness of applied sport psychology practice: Making the case for a case study approach. *The Sport Psychologist,* 16: 433–454.

Atkins, S. and Murphy, K. (1994) Reflective practice. *Nursing Standard*, 8(39): 49–56.

BASES (2004) *BASES Psychology Section: Guidelines to the Supervised Experience Framework*. Leeds: BASES.

CTF (2002) *The Coaching Task Force – Final Report*. London: Department for Culture, Media and Sport.

Donaghy, M. and Marss, K. (2007) Evaluation of frameworks for facilitating and assessing physiotherapy students' reflection on practice. *Physiotherapy Theory and Practice*, 23: 83–94.

Edwards, A. (1999). Reflective practice in sport management. *Sport Management Review*, 2: 67–81.

Ekeburgh, M. (2007) Lifeworld based reflection and learning: A contribution to the reflective practice in nursing and nursing education. *Reflective Practice*, 8: 331–343.

Fleming, K. (2007) Reflection: a neglected art in health promotion. *Health Education Research*, 22: 658–664.

Ghaye, T. and Lillyman, S. (1997) *Learning Journals and Critical Incidents: Reflective Practice for Health Care Professionals*. Salisbury: Mark Allen Publishing.

Ghaye, T. and Lillyman, S. (2000) *Reflection: Principles and Practice for Healthcare Professionals*. Salisbury: Quay Books.

Gibbs, G. (1988) *Learning by Doing: A Guide to Teaching and Learning Methods*. Oxford Brookes University, Oxford: Further Education Unit.

Johns, C. (1994) Guided reflection. In A. Palmer, S. Burns and C. Bulman (eds), *Reflective Practice in Nursing* (pp. 110–130). Oxford: Blackwell Science.

Johns, C. (1995) The value of reflective practice for nursing. *Journal of Clinical Nursing*, 4: 23–30.

Knowles, Z., Borrie, A. and Telfer, H. (2005) Towards the reflective sports coach: issues of context, education and application. *Ergonomics*, 48: 1711–1720.

Knowles, Z., Gilbourne, D., Borrie, A. and Nevill, A. (2001) Developing the reflective sports coach: a study exploring the processes of reflective practice within a higher education coaching programme. *Reflective Practice*, 2: 185–207.

Knowles, Z., Tomlinson, V., Anderson, A. and Gilbourne, D. (2007) Reflections of the application of reflective practice for supervision in applied sport psychology. *The Sport Psychologist*, 21: 109–122.

Knowles, Z., Tyler, G., Gilbourne, D. and Eubank, M. (2006) Reflecting on reflection: Exploring the practice of sports coaching graduates. *Reflective Practice*, 7: 163–179.

Lee, I. (2007) Preparing pre service English teachers for reflective practice. *ELT Journal*, 61: 321–329.

34

Nelson, L.J. and Cushion, C.J. (2006) Reflection in coach education: The case of the NGB coaching certificate. *The Sport Psychologist*, 20(2): 174–183.

Ruch, G. (2007) Reflective practice in contemporary childcare social work: The role of containment. *British Journal of Social Work*, 37: 659–680.

CHAPTER 4

THE 'HOW TO' OF REFLECTION

Hamish Telfer and Zoe Knowles

SETTING THE SCENE

This chapter will focus on using reflective practice as a way of thinking critically about practice and also as a means of validating practice. Reflective practice helps practitioners develop as critical thinkers in gathering evidence for understanding more about our skills as a practitioner. Of equal importance, reflective practices enhance and augment awareness about our learning as well as serving to support and develop our practitioner skills and competencies in general.

One of the key purposes of reflective practice is to be able to learn from our experiences in a way that structures our thoughts, our decisions and actions when engaged in coaching, managing or instructing. Often we allow key moments to pass without being able to use the circumstances in a way that will enhance the structure of our future practice. Jasper (2003) talks about this by encouraging us to think about our experiences in a *purposeful* way. The process of reflection involves conscious thinking about what we do and why we do it with a view to developing active strategies that direct our practice in potentially different ways. Consequently, this enhances the development of the practitioner and increases their range of potential skills. Reflection is therefore about engagement in an active learning process.

Johns (2004), Ghaye *et al*. (1996) and Jasper (2003) all comment on the need to authenticate or validate our practice through evidence-based practice. They also encourage us as practitioners to consider being able to use reflective techniques across a wide range of practice situations, positive as well as not so positive. Since sport is usually associated with outcomes (and usually the outcomes of others, i.e. performers or clients), there is sometimes the tendency for sport and fitness practitioners to focus on what went wrong rather than what went well in achieving desired outcomes. A balanced approach is essential when reflecting upon practice. All experiences provide the practitioner with information for learning about themselves. As practitioners we also need to be receptive to the environments in which we work, and this chapter outlines some basic approaches to being able to interrogate your practice with a view to being able to take these experiences and, through reflection, understand them better to action plan for future situations. Learning from experience is a key principle that good sports practitioners embrace although actually 'getting at' a meaningful understanding of these experiences is sometimes problematic.

One of the central strategies we therefore suggest in engaging with reflective practice is to think about coaching, managing or instructing as having a range of underpinning skills or behaviours. These skills or behaviours can be technical skills (e.g. how to kick, jump or throw); methodological skills (e.g. breaking down skills into meaningful parts and building them); skills of communication (e.g. how and when we communicate, when we give feedback and the nature and use of language); and the way in which we make decisions as practitioners. Chapter 3 encouraged you to think of your practice as a *whole* since this is what is known within sports coaching as 'craft' knowledge (Knowles *et al.*, 2005). It is also useful to use reflection in a focused way in order to make sense of specific

Table 4.1 Key knowledge bases for reflection

Subject matter knowledge – knowledge about things	What is delivered: the key skills and techniques; the key components and the types and nature of knowledge that underpin the skills, techniques or concepts.
Pedagogical knowledge – 'knowing how to' – 'delivery'	How things are taught: e.g. methods and processes; how things were broken down and how they were structured; the situational or contextual issues.
Decision-making – 'developing expertise'	How did I make this or that decision? What was the recommended way of acting ('script') and what components did I base the decision upon? How did I narrow choices? Did I follow a 'procedure' or did I speed things up by applying concepts? Were these concepts transferred from other situations?

Source: Developed from Lyle (2002), pp. 139–140, 202–204

parts of our practice. Table 4.1 (Lyle, 2002) gives an idea of how this might work for the sport and fitness practitioner. Some key elements of practice that might be identified by the reflective practitioner are as outlined.

Reflective practice allows us to connect 'knowing about things' to 'knowing how to', thus connecting theory to practice and vice versa. We are often able to communicate something about what we know, but being able to state how we do things is often more problematic. However, this task is of critical importance to the practitioner as without being able to understand why we do what we do, our practice often develops unevenly or, not at all. Practice should also be informed by experience and each and every engagement by the practitioner adds to the sum of knowledge and contributes to their learning. Given that many situations in sport and fitness practice are situationally specific, being able to identify potential common characteristics will enable our practice to become more informed, individualised, robust and responsive.

GETTING STARTED

One of the first steps to using reflective practices is being able to understand how you make sense of things when you think experiences through. This becomes more important to understand when we move from reflection-on-action, which is the usual start point for initial reflective learning (which as it suggests is reflection after the event) to reflection-in-action, which is often seen as the key reflective skill of the more experienced practitioner as it involves decision-making moments in real time. Lyle (1999) alludes to these decision-making moments in sports coaches as a 'stream-of-consciousness flow' and makes the point that a coach's abilities in decision-making (referred to by Lyle as 'naturalistic decision-making') are often the key marker between the skilled practitioner and the simply 'competent' practitioner (Cross and Lyle, 1999: p. 212).

Being able to identify the stage you are at as a reflector can help you understand how you make sense of your practice. King and Kitchner (1994) used the work of Perry (1970) in their study of thinking and specifically in the development of reflective thinking. King and Kitchner (1994) developed a structure allowing us to locate and recognise where our start point may be in beginning to develop as reflective practitioners. Table 4.2 below gives an idea of where one may be, what it means and gives a simple example.

Our ability to be reflective varies not only individually, but also from situation to situation. It is important for us therefore to recognise that reflective skills may need to be 'learned'. Table 4.2 summarises the nature of these varied individual abilities. Within the process of reflective learning we often start as

38

Table 4.2 Reflective thinking – position 'Labels'

'Label'	Meaning	Example
The Dualist	Tend to think of solutions as right or wrong/black or white/yes or no.	Think of how you claim to decide how many repetitions are required for a performer in a training session – it is usually clearly defined with little or no room for negotiation.
The Multiplist	Begins to accept no one right answer; shades of grey – 'it depends' on surfaces.	We usually operate at this level in situations which demand more long-term strategies especially where the environmental aspects of the activity dictate, thus requiring 'flexibility'.
The Critical Reflector	Able to fully differentiate between situations and is able to separate out components of practice. Answers are dependent on situations.	This level of operation is often evident in situations where there is equity in leader/performer relationships (i.e. the power relationship is different) and/or where there may be a requirement for multi-layered decision-making in performance.

Source: Adapted from King and Kitchner (1994)

a dualist or multiplist but through practice develop towards a critical reflector. Being able to recognise our start points is an important first step. Whether we adopt a 'dualist' or a 'multiplist' position takes us down the road in being able to understand how we think about our practice. Since reflection is about being able to interrogate our practice, it is vital that we have some insight into how we think about what we do. Being the 'Critical Reflector' can come easier to some than others. However, whatever the stage, the practitioner must start with some understanding of how they make sense of their practice, thus being able to ascribe a label to it gives the practitioner a start point to develop their learning through reflection.

COMPONENTS OF PRACTICE

Getting started in reflection also entails that we understand what the components of our practice are, as well as how we think about them. Thus we need to put

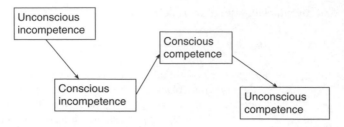

Figure 4.1 Stages of competence awareness

Source: Adapted from Fleishman and Howell (1982)

together what we understand by practice alongside how we think about it. Our views about our competencies therefore gain a degree of clarity in terms of where we might be as practitioners in terms of how competent we think we may be. Figure 4.1 characterises how we might think of this.

If we think that we often start not really knowing what our competence in practice is like and, more to the point, often unable to know where to seek information, we run the risk of being stuck in the area of 'not knowing what we are not good at' (unconscious incompetence). Reflection can help unlock this dilemma. For most practitioners being able to at least get to the point where we can spot less competent practice is a significant first step to being able to improve our practice (so-called 'conscious incompetence'). Moving this to the next stage starts to mark out the more competent and skilful practitioner, who by definition may now be very aware of the areas of strength and weakness in their practice ('conscious competence'), while the more sophisticated practitioners seemingly undertake practice in a fluid and 'natural' way. They do of course think about their practice, but just at higher levels. This is sometimes referred to as achieving practitioner 'expertise' (Côté *et al.*, 1995; Saury and Durand, 1998).

MOVING FORWARD

Being able to put both our reflective position and our practitioner competence together allows us now to be able to apply reflective skills in a way that helps us interrogate our practice. Essentially, what is required for our practice to become more competent and skilful is that we become more honestly self-aware in order to gain greater knowledge about ourselves and our practice through this process of stimulated recall. The reflective practitioner must be an independent thinker as well as responding to the views of others. Being able to assimilate information about our practice is the first step to being able to self-reference the evidence about our practice. This is what Ghaye *et al.* (1996) call 'validating our practice'. Being able therefore to think critically about our practice and to seek the evidence for the outcomes, is one of the key points of reflective practice.

At this point it might be useful to think of an aspect of your practice from a recent event. You might identify not only how you thought about what happened but also where that particular example places you in relation to Table 4.2 in thinking about what you discovered about your own practice. For example, in communicating a required action, clients/performers might have completely misunderstood you, leading to a complete breakdown of the activity or task. While you thought you were clear, what was it about what you said, the way you said it and how it was said that led to this breakdown? Could you have simplified the task? Was enough information given or did you take the level of understanding for granted?

QUESTIONING PRACTICE IN A STRUCTURED WAY

In using reflection to build 'capacity' for our practice to develop, it is important to develop a range of reflective skills and familiarity with reflective techniques that meet the variety of situations and experiences that are inherent within sports practice. This develops awareness of our practice. Asking 'what did I do?', 'why did I do that?' and 'what happened as a consequence?' are good starting points. Being able to follow these questions with further more searching questions such as 'what would others have done?', 'how did I know that this was the thing to do?' and 'what did I learn from this?' are natural extensions of the initial questions.

It is helpful if these questions are used in the context of a structured process that allows us to make sense of the answers. Gibbs' cycle, described in Chapter 3, is one model which sits comfortably with sport and fitness practice. A reflective cycle such as Gibbs often relies on the practitioner being able to select a particular experience as a *significant event* (sometimes referred to as a *critical* or *significant incident*). This means something that is of significance to the practitioner. Such an event may either be an event that is positive or negative about practice and it is worth emphasising that practitioners should guard against being overly negative in their selection of these critical moments. Putting the events or incidents into a series of stages allows the practitioner to work through reflection in a manner that makes sense.

Observations of, and descriptions about, our practice therefore naturally come from things that are considered at the poles of our practice. In essence, situations that went really well, as well as things that went wrong; things that made us feel comfortable or pleased, as well as more uncomfortable situations especially when dealing with individuals. Also of importance are the observations others make about us and, of course, the interpersonal elements that are at the core of a practitioner's work.

Jasper (2003) talks of the four key descriptive words to ask in 'trigger' questions (who, what, where and when) as well as following these up with the more analytical, interpretive and deeper questions of 'why' and 'how' in relation to situating the nature of questioning within a reflective cycle. Being able to 'frame' our actions in order to confirm or seek alternatives is important in reflective learning. Framing is also a consequence of interrogating our practice and is at the heart of reflective practice.

CHOOSING WHAT TO FOCUS ON

This leaves us to consider how and what you reflect upon. Reflecting on actions and ideas is a good start point. Being able to engage with how we felt as we went about our practice is also useful (e.g. was I nervous and if so, why?). Bolton (2005) encourages us to think of our practice as fluid and therefore a degree of certain uncertainty is always present. This is certainly true of sport and fitness practice environments where often no two situations (or clients/performers) are exactly alike. Sometimes this can be daunting for practitioners, who like more certainty within their role or practice and who may also be apprehensive of what they might discover about themselves. Bolton (2005) talks of 'going through the looking glass' and getting underneath our practice. She goes on to comment that 'self-protectiveness against exploring the unknown of oneself arises from a fear of uncovering unpalatable things' (Bolton, 2005: p. 35). It is useful, therefore, to think of reflective practices as a series of dialogues one has with oneself as long as the prerequisite present is being honest in your appraisals.

Capturing reflective moments are essential; therefore thinking of when it might take place (giving time for reflection) and where and how it might happen are going to be important. Think of using statements written cryptically or even single words. Some reflective learners think better in colours rather than words and so use colour-coded approaches (red for something not very good, amber for something uncertain and green for what went well). Others use mind maps as thinking in more pictorial ways allows them to make sense of what happened.

Whatever the medium, it is usual that reflective learners start with committing their reflections in writing in some form. Being able to locate what you are reflecting about can then be put into an action cycle that allows for action points to be created.

CAPTURING REFLECTION

The key to getting started with reflective practice is to do it 'simple and quick' about something that has impacted in particular. It is often best not to bother about whether what is committed to paper is 'messy' or structured; its what you do with it that then allows you to untangle the thoughts in a way that makes sense to you. What is vital is that you capture the moment in a simple format. Table 4.3 gives some examples.

Reflective journals are popular since they are convenient and simple. They can include colours, mind maps and can be 'big picture' concepts or small building blocks. They should also include what actually happened alongside what and when you were thinking, thus linking action in practice to outcome of practice. Sometimes the answers are not easily or instantly accessed and revisiting the journal allows you thinking time. Discussion forums or reflective conversations open the practitioner to outside 'gaze' and can sometimes feel threatening especially in the early stages of practice. However these moments are usually rich in evidence and information about practice. Self-talk (i.e. recording thoughts as they come into our minds) is a complex activity and is usually seen as a more advanced reflective skill used by practitioners who may be used to fast, in-the-moment, decision-making.

What is essential is that you find your own simple method, are constructively critical and try to relate it to the key knowledge areas in order to build your practice through cycles which result in action (action cycles).

GETTING MORE SOPHISTICATED

One of the markers of your progression as a reflective practitioner will be your ability to move your reflection from 'on action' to 'in action'. Furthermore, you will find that your journey develops your thoughts in such a way that what was once 'black and white' becomes more malleable and you are now able to function as a critical reflector. As you develop your practice it is also important to develop your range of reflective skills.

Table 4.3 Methods and approaches to capturing reflection

Format	Benefits	How to go about it
Journals	Written evidence; able to come back to it; can jog memory; useful immediately post-event. Allows critical/significant incidents to be recorded and then interrogated.	Bullet points, brief statements, full sentences, mind maps, colour coded. What you did/what you thought 'about'. Write as yourself/another person/as the 'other'/storytell or write as if you are sending yourself a memo.
Discussion forums in groups	Allows thinking time; allows alternatives to surface, therefore contextualising. Often balances situational and practitioner elements. Develops 'craft' reflection. Can throw up the unexpected.	Establish learning set group; agree boundaries and limitations; set agendas; limit time; ensure everyone speaks; record.
Reflective conversations with 'critical friend'	Usually focused and structured; gets at the 'why' and 'how' questions. Challenges self-perceptions.	Choose critical friend relative to the issue or situation; record; track 'what' happened to 'why' and then 'how' and follow on to action planning for future. You can set up 'hypothetical' conversations.
Taped narrative ('in action')	Gets at reflection-in-action; allows for in-the-moment questions and observations and what the practitioner is thinking.	Need digital voice recorder; ability to self-talk while thinking (making decisions).

Being able to engage with others and enter into what we know as reflective conversations is one sign of growing reflective self-confidence. Using others is also a means of opening a window on our practice and allows for transparency in practice, a key ethical principle. It also stops the process of reflection becoming an isolated activity. Sharing practice dilemmas with peers, supervisors and others (e.g. critical friends) develops self-awareness. Being able to use self-critical prompt words also indicates a growing ability to understand more of where answers might lie (e.g. 'were my methods correct?', 'how did I come over?' and 'did I time that well?'). However, it is also important to understand and accept the importance of being able to reflect in safety knowing that others respect the confidentiality of the process. Capturing reflection in writing is also solely for the purpose of developing self-awareness and practice competencies and the reflective practitioner must be able to undertake reflective learning in safety and without fear of judgement by others.

Being able to capture your impressions of how others see you is also a sign of growing reflective maturity. Getting hold of the lived experience of the sports practitioner is a challenge and might demand a deeper understanding of more developed skills, as well as understanding that while reflective practice is a window on your own practice for you, it also entails that you develop an understanding of your own dispositional traits. For example, working 'on action' often leads the practitioner with hindsight to view the incidents as how they *think* they read them as opposed to what *actually* happened. This tendency to skew our views towards a self-serving bias is known as 'hindsight bias' and this is where shared reflection can be useful in guarding against our natural instincts to see things as we would like them to be, as opposed to how they actually were. This is often the point about getting 'stuck' at a particular stage on the reflective cycle and the ability to take questioning further, perhaps in conjunction with another person, sometimes unlocks the next stage.

A further consideration in understanding more about how you see yourself and your practice is the notion of causal attributions. These relate to how individuals have a tendency to see events either positively or negatively as a combination of either luck (or bad luck) or due to their own actions. Being able to accurately attribute the causes of events is a key part of being an honest reflective practitioner, as it is often easy to attribute events that go well to ourselves, but excuse ourselves from the less successful actions as not being anything to do with us. In other words, since practice is personal and involves human agency, it is emotionally laden. Being able to accurately attribute the outcomes of our practice is a learned skill and is essential in unlocking our potential as practitioners.

Since much of the work of the sports and fitness practitioner is situational, being able to discern similarities and differences emerging about your practice and being able to identify the characteristics of them are key skills. This allows tangible alternatives to emerge if the respective knowledge bases are robust. Since much of sport and fitness practice is concerned with questioning perceptions, being able to recognise 'triggers for action' is one of the key roles of reflective practice. Thus reflection develops the capacity for practitioners to develop mental models of their practice and the associated conditions that enable these models to develop from principle to practice. In this sense, developing reflective judgement, according to King and Kitchener (1994), is the ability to work on practice that may be perceived as relatively loose, unstructured and relatively ill defined, and make sense of them; this is the essence of practice.

SUMMARY

Since coaching, managing and instructing are about cross-functional teamwork, being able to work with change in relation to how we think, order tasks and relate to people are essential. Being a good reflective practitioner therefore allows you to gain insight into your practice relative to the situation or indeed others. This process allows practitioners to be able to discern in which situations they have maximum effectiveness (other than simply measured through outcomes).

While this chapter has dealt with some of the basic concepts that will allow you to interrogate your thinking about yourself as a sport practitioner in order to validate your practice, it is important that you take small but relevant steps. Try simple things using some of the techniques suggested. Develop these techniques as you become more self-aware and establish and develop what works for you and your practice.

REFERENCES

Bolton, G. (2005) *Reflective Practice. Writing and Professional Development.* 2nd edition. London: Sage.

Côté, J., Salmela, J.H., Trudel, P., Baria, A. and Russell, S. (1995) The Coaching Model: a grounded assessment of expert gymnastic coaches' knowledge. *Journal of Sport and Exercise Psychology*, 17: 1–17.

Cross, N. and Lyle, J. (eds) (1999) *The Coaching Process: Principles and Practice For Sport.* Oxford: Butterworth Heinemann.

Fleishman, E.A. and Howell, W.C (1982) *Human Performance and Productivity.* Vol. 2. Hillsdale: Earlbaum.

Ghaye, T., Cuthbert, S., Danai, K. and Dennis, D. (1996) *Validation of Practice: Claims For Moving Practice Forward, Book 4.* Newcastle upon Tyne: Pentaxion.

Jasper, M. (2003) *Beginning Reflective Practice.* Cheltenham: Nelson Thornes.

Johns, C. (2004) *Becoming a Reflective Practitioner.* Oxford: Blackwell.

King, P.M. and Kitchner, K.S. (1994) *Developing Reflective Judgement.* San Francisco: Jossey-Bass.

Knowles, Z., Borrie, A. and Telfer, H. (2005) Towards the reflective sports coach: Issues of context, application and education. *Ergonomics*, 48: 1711–1720.

Lyle, J. (2002) *Sports Coaching Concepts. A Framework for Coaches' Behaviour.* Abingdon: Routledge.

Perry, W.G. (1970) *Forms of Intellectual and Ethical Development in the College Years: A Scheme.* Troy, MO: Holt, Rinehart, & Winston.

Saury, J. and Durand, M. (1998) Practical knowledge in expert coaches: on-site study of coaching in sailing. *Research Quarterly for Exercise and Sport*, 69: 254–266.

CHAPTER 5

EVALUATING PROFESSIONAL PRACTICE THROUGH REFLECTION
Professionalism in the workplace

Lindsey Dugdill

UNDERSTANDING PROFESSIONAL PRACTICE

This chapter aims to illustrate how sport and fitness practitioners can evaluate their own performance and professional practice through the use of reflection, and enhance the quality of their future practice in an iterative, ongoing manner.

In order to do this the concepts of professionalism and professional practice firstly need to be explored. Thinking about this for yourself:

■   Consider what the term 'professional' means to you.
■   Who do you come across in your own practice who you would deem to be a professional?
■   What is it that makes them professional?

According to Downie (1990) the key characteristics of a professional include:

1   Having skill and expertise underpinned by a broad knowledge base.
2   Providing a service which is delivered within a framework which considers all ethical, legal, and moral aspects relevant to that profession.
3   Having authority that is recognised by the public and may involve that professional in 'speaking out' in order to uphold standards of professional practice.
4   Having the independence to use this authority (this often results in self-regulation, e.g. in medical practice, where the State will delegate control of entry, standards, etc. to the body of practitioners themselves).

5 Having a perspective that values a philosophy of continuing educational development.
6 Working within a framework of 'legitimate authority' – characterised by its independence, evidence-based approach to development, regulation by professional authority – which results in that profession having a recognised value to the public.

Professional practice is often seen as the way a practitioner would go about doing their job whilst embracing the principles identified above. It would involve what they said and did with different clients (e.g. delivery of an exercise programme), their use of inter-personal skills (e.g. interviewing or practitioner–client conversations), their application of inter-professional working with other professionals and services (e.g. in onward referral for example), their use of existing evidence of 'what works' (e.g. from published guidelines), and their ongoing experience of doing the job in the 'real-world' setting. Professional knowledge of 'what works' is seen as equally important as the published evidence (from systematic reviews of research evidence) as exemplified by bodies such as the National Institute for Health and Clinical Excellence (NICE), UK, which uses a process whereby new public health guidance is tested out with practitioners prior to publication (NICE, 2006).

The advancement of a professional role requires that professionals be committed to the continual 'development of thinking'. Sometimes professional practice may involve trying new things, being innovative and challenging the boundaries of existing practice. This may be especially relevant when a client fails to respond to a tried-and-tested approach and the practitioner feels the need to try something different. The practitioner holds a pivotal role in the process of intervention with the client or group and can greatly influence the outcome by what they say and do at any time.

PROFESSIONAL DEVELOPMENT AND INTER-PROFESSIONAL WORKING

Reflective practice is a central tenet of both continuing professional development (CPD) and evidence-based approaches which are fundamental to high-quality professional practice. Evaluation is the process of judging the value of, or progress made towards predetermined goals, usually with respect to an intervention or programme. Evaluation should involve the systematical collection of relevant data that enables this judgement to be made. Evidence-based approaches refers to practice which is built on information – hopefully a consensus of 'what works' – derived from evaluation studies (and more broadly through research as well). Reflective practice can be a useful and integral part of evaluation studies, especially when working with novel contexts or teams where the knowledge of what works from the published evidence base is limited or non-existent.

Within the context of higher education, CPD implies:

> that staff are appointed not only for the knowledge, skills, and attitudes they have on appointment but also on account of the capacities to be flexible, adaptable, creative and amenable to change ... and the capability of learning throughout their careers.
>
> (Partington, 1999: p. 248)

Reflective principles, as described in earlier chapters can enable the practitioner to move the process of education and training outside of the formal education boundaries into everyday usage. Indeed, the process of 'honing' or refinement of practice is best done within the normal working environment of the practitioner – hence a system which allows continuous cycles of reflection is appropriate. Practitioners should be encouraged to operate within a framework which values self-evaluation and reflection in order to enhance the quality of practice and, hence, improve the effectiveness of service delivery. This will only become embedded in practice if the time to be reflective is built into delivery cycles; reflection is both practised (i.e. modelled) and explicitly valued by managers; staff are rewarded for delivery of a quality service (i.e. a performance management structure that recognises and measures quality is required) and practitioners are allowed to innovate and try out new ways of working as well as change the practices they no longer believe 'work well'.

Formal and informal mentorship may support these cycles of reflective practice, whilst sound management principles of planning and performance management can evaluate the progress a practitioner or team are making in terms of their effectiveness (Smith, 2001). Lack of direct endorsement for reflective/evaluative practice from managers is likely to discourage workers to such an extent that this practice will cease (even if practitioners have learnt the value of reflective practice during training).

It is becoming increasingly important for sport and fitness professionals to understand how to work together in inter-professional teams, and so reflection on team activities might also be an important part of service development (see case studies below). Embedding reflection within practice is probably more commonplace and accepted by health professionals when compared with sport/fitness professionals. Although many UK degree programmes now introduce students to reflect practice through the process of personal development planning (PDP), inter-professional working requires an understanding of the boundaries or limits within which any professional both could and should operate.

Ghaye (2005) identifies that through the practice of reflection within teams, professionals can be given a voice, where previously they may not have been heard. This may lead to the power relationships within teams being challenged (e.g. between managers and staff for instance) but also allows for differences of opinion to be resolved so a team can move forward together. Ideally, reflection which is done with a spirit of mutual respect can allow critical yet constructive voices to be heard which may lead to rationalisation and/or innovation within a service, which may then have a positive impact on its effectiveness.

Case study: Developing professional practice within exercise referral schemes

Exercise referral schemes (ERSs) are now commonplace in the UK. An ERS typically includes a series of steps. First, referral of a patient by a health professional (e.g. general practitioner; GP) to an exercise professional (exercise referral officer; ERO). Next, using medical information supplied by the GP and after other health screening procedures, a patient will be prescribed a programme of exercise (normally 12–14 weeks) which is often delivered within a controlled (usually leisure-based) setting (Dugdill et al., 2005). Effectiveness of delivery is heavily influenced by the quality of the working relationships and understanding shown between the health professional, exercise professional and patient.

The National Quality Assurance Framework for Exercise Referral Scheme (NQAF ERS), published in 2001 (Department of Health, 2001), aimed to improve the quality of practice and delivery of schemes in the UK and stated that practitioners should engage in CPD.

By embedding reflective practice within their work (through the use of a reflective diary, case notes, etc.) EROs are in an important position to be able to influence both:

a) The quality of a patient's ongoing structured programme of exercise, for example through the use of case notes based on factual information coming directly from the patient such as key motivators or barriers to exercise.

This would enable appropriate tailoring and support for the patient, which is more likely to result in successful adherence to the exercise programme.

b) The quality of the delivery of the overall scheme, for example meetings between GP practices (including GPs, practice nurses, physiotherapists) and the EROs can allow an interchange of information about the process of referral (e.g. what was said by the GP, how well the prescription to exercise was received by the patient) and the uptake and outcome of the exercise, from the ERO's perspective. This will help GPs to select the types of patients for whom the ERS is most likely to be effective.

LINKING REFLECTIVE PRACTICE AND EVALUATION

There is an increasing professional expectation in the fields of both sport and fitness, that practitioners will evaluate the programmes (services/interventions) that they are involved in both managing and/or delivering (Boutilier et al., 1997; Dugdill and Stratton, 2007).

As Dugdill and Stratton (2007) have previously described:

> Evaluation is made up of a number of progressive steps, the most important of which is the collection of appropriate data that is subsequently used to make a judgment about the value of an intervention. The evidence from an evaluation should enable practitioners to produce more effective interventions for participants. An evaluation should measure progress towards meeting the expressed aims and objectives of an intervention.
>
> (p. 3)

Evaluations often focus on impact and outcome measures but not on process measures. It is at this stage of an evaluation – the formative/process stages – when an intervention/service is being set up and tested, that reflective practice elements are of particular relevance. As described in the case study, regular reflection on the processes allows adjustments to be made to the delivery of the intervention in order to get a tailored model of intervention that works for the client. Process evaluation focuses on questions such as how and why an intervention is working and/or not working.

Practitioners can ask questions such as:

▪ How are we delivering the intervention?
▪ Is it working well for clients and how do we know?

- What is the skill mix of the delivery team? Is it enabling us to deliver the appropriate sessions within the intervention?
- Are there any gaps in the intervention?
- Are the processes of referral working well?
- What should we retain? What should we change in future?

All this information can help the refinement of the intervention design. Reflective practice can enable this process of intervention evaluation and development to become continuous and iterative. An evaluation process that informs practitioners of what is working and why, with respect to the intervention/service or practice, allows the practitioner to respond to the changing requirements of the clients, and also informs their own reflections. No one model of delivery will suit all and this process encourages the personalised tailoring which is more likely to lead to successful outcomes for the client.

Case study: Evaluation of the Getting Our Active Lifestyles Started (GOALS) programme

The GOALS project is a community-based, lifestyle change programme aimed at obese children and their parents, based in a major city in the north west of England (Stratton and Watson, 2009). As the evidence base of what interventions work in this area is almost non-existent in the UK, the intervention was designed using an action research evaluation framework with reflective practice embedded within it. The ethos of the project was to move away from a 'top-down' professionally led service to a more collaborative intervention which built directly on the needs of the participants (Nelson *et al.*, 2004). Ethical approval for the GOALS project was granted by the local NHS Paediatric Research Ethics Committee, and all the families provided written consent to take part in the research.

A series of data collection techniques (see Figure 5.1) including focus groups with children and parents, health behaviour discussions, reflective diaries completed by the multi-professional delivery team (consisting of a postgraduate exercise scientist [MSc], a probationary health psychologist [MSc] and a professional home economist [BSc]), anecdotal conversations and observations during intervention sessions, and worksheets were all used as part of the process of reflection by the delivery team. Based on their understanding of what was working well and why, the intervention sessions and overall intervention design was revised over time, retaining the most effective elements. The empowerment of GOALS staff

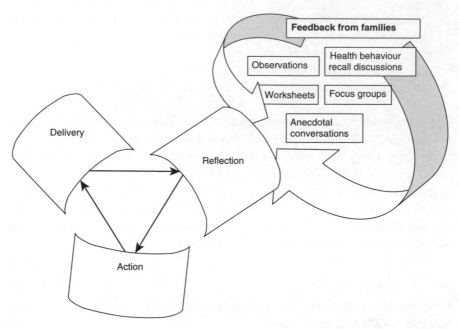

Figure 5.1 Action research model of GOALS intervention development

through the process of reflection is exemplified in the following quote taken from the evaluation:

> Evaluation is a central part of goals, staff are aware that their feedback is important and that their comments could help bring about changes to the programme. This helps staff feel more involved in the development of the programme.
>
> (GOALS staff member)

Reflection was particularly useful in the setting-up phase of the intervention when everything was new to the team and also when new members joined the team and processes changed.

CONCLUSION

In summary this chapter set out to show how reflective practice can influence professional practice in the workplace. It is vital for sport and fitness professionals to be aware of their current practice and know which skills and techniques to employ in order to further improve the way they 'do the job'. Reflective practice should take a central role in the CPD of all professionals, implemented within a supportive environment in which reflection is encouraged and endorsed by management. Reflective practice can also be a significant process in the evaluation of interventions or services (delivered by practitioners) which will lead to their improved development and delivery. Reflection is particularly useful at times of change or when practitioners are developing a new service where there is little or no evidence of 'what works' currently.

ACKNOWLEDGEMENTS

Thanks go to the Neighbourhood Renewal Fund for funding the GOALS project, all partners involved in the development of the GOALS project: Liverpool John Moores University, Liverpool City Council, Liverpool PCT, University of Salford and Alder Hey Children's Hospital, and all the participating families and staff that made the intervention possible.

REFERENCES

Boutilier, M., Mason, R. and Rootman, I. (1997) Community action and reflective practice in health promotion research. *Health Promotion International*, 12(1): 69–78.

Department of Health (2001) *Exercise Referral Systems: A National Quality Assurance Framework*. London: Department of Health.

Downie, R.S. (1990) Professions and professionalism. *Journal of Philosophy of Education*, 24: 2.

Dugdill, L. and Stratton, G. (2007) *Evaluating Sport and Physical Activity Interventions: A Guide For Practitioners*. University of Salford.

Dugdill, L., Graham, R. and McNair, F. (2005) Exercise Referral: the Public Health Panacea for Physical Activity Promotion? A critical perspective of exercise referral schemes; their development and evaluation. *Ergonomics*, 48: 11–14, 1390–1410.

Ghaye, T. (2005) *Developing the Reflective Healthcare Team*. Oxford: Blackwell Publishing Ltd.

National Institute of Health and Clinical Excellence (NICE) (2006) *Public Health Guidance: Development Process and Methods*. London: NICE.

Nelson, G., Poland, B., Murray, M. and Maticka-Tyndale, E. (2004) Building capacity in community health action research: Towards a praxis framework for graduate education. *Action Research*, 2(4): 389–408.

Partington, P. (1999) Chp 19, continuing professional development. In Fry, H., Ketteridge, S. and Marshall, S. (eds), *A Handbook for Teaching and Learning in Higher Education: Enhancing Academic Practice* (pp. 247–262). London: Kogan Page.

Smith P.A.C. (2001) Action learning and reflective practice in project environments that are related to leadership development. *Management Learning*, 32(1): 31–48.

Stratton, G. and Watson, P. (2009) Chp 8, young people and physical activity. In Dugdill, L., Crone, D. and Murphy, R. (eds), *Physical Activity and Health Promotion: Evidence-Based Approaches to Practice*. Oxford: Wiley Blackwells.

lindsey dugdill

CHAPTER 6

REFLECTIVE PRACTICE[1]

Neil Thompson

INTRODUCTION

The concept of reflective practice is one that is closely associated with the work of Donald Schön (Schön, 1983, 1987, 1992). It is an approach to professional practice that emphasises the need for practitioners to avoid standardised, formula responses to the situations they encounter. Reflective practice involves coming to terms with the complexity, variability and uncertainty associated with human services work.

WHAT IS REFLECTIVE PRACTICE?

Reflective practice begins from the premise that human problems cannot be solved by the simple application of technical solutions. People's problems are far too complex and 'messy' to be resolved in this way. Schön draws a distinction between the 'high ground' of theory and research and the 'swampy lowlands' of practice. He describes this as follows:

> In the varied topography of professional practice, there is a high, hard ground which overlooks a swamp. On the high ground, manageable problems lend themselves to solution through the use of research-based theory and technique. In the swampy lowlands, problems are messy and confusing and incapable of technical solution. The irony of the situation is that the problems of the high ground tend to be

[1] Edited from Thompson, N. (2005) 'Reflective practice', in Harrison, R. and Wise, C. (eds) *Working with Young People*, pp. 195–203, London: SAGE Publications. Originally published in Thompson, N. (2002) *People Skills* (2nd edition), Basingstoke: Palgrave Macmillan.

relatively unimportant to individuals or to society at large, however great their technical interest may be, while in the swamp lie the problems of greatest human concern.

(Schön, 1983: p. 54)

One significant implication of this is that practitioners cannot sit back and wait for 'experts' to provide them with solutions on a plate. Workers have to engage with the complexities of practice and navigate a way through them. That is, reflective practice is an active process of constructing solutions, rather than a passive process of following procedures or guidelines.

In order to do this, we must first undertake what Schön (1983) calls 'problem setting'. The messy situations workers encounter do not come with clearly defined problems ready made for the practitioner to start working on. Consequently, the first task the worker faces is to make sense of the situation, to develop a picture of the problem(s) to be tackled. This, then, is the process of 'problem setting'. As Schön (1983) puts it: 'Problem setting is a process in which, interactively, we *name* the things to which we shall attend and *frame* the context in which we will attend to them' (p. 40). Problem setting is part of the process of assessment and illustrates the point that assessment should not be seen as routine or mechanical – it is an active process of forming a picture, identifying problems and mapping out a way forward.

A reflective practitioner is a worker who is able to use experience, knowledge and theoretical perspectives to guide and inform practice. However, this does not mean applying ideas in a blanket form, unthinkingly and uncritically, regardless of the circumstances. Reflective practice involves cutting the cloth to suit the specific circumstances, rather than looking for ready-made solutions.

To inexperienced workers, this may sound very difficult and daunting. However, it is based on a set of skills that can be developed with experience, and offers a sound basis for high-quality practice and high levels of job satisfaction.

RELATING THEORY TO PRACTICE

Reflective practice involves being able to relate theory to practice, drawing on existing frameworks of ideas and knowledge so that we do not have to 'reinvent the wheel' for each new situation that arises. I shall therefore address some of the key issues relating to the application of theory to practice. I shall begin by outlining two common misunderstandings concerning the relationship between theory and practice.

58
neil thompson

First, we need to recognise that the relationship is not a simple or straightforward one. Theory influences practice in a number of subtle and intricate ways, but practice can also influence theory (Thompson, 2000). These are important points to recognise, as they help to dispel the myth that theory and practice are separate, unconnected domains. I shall discuss below the dangers of driving a wedge between theory and practice. Second, it is also important to realise that theory does not provide hard and fast answers or clear, simple solutions to problems. To see it otherwise is to misconceive the part that theory plays in guiding practice.

These two sets of issues represent the two extremes of a continuum. At one extreme, the tendency to separate theory from practice is problematic in terms of cutting off an important resource for understanding practice situations. At the other extreme, it is unhelpful to have unrealistic expectations of what theory can or should offer, as this too can have the effect of driving a wedge between theory and practice.

The middle ground between these two extremes is where reflective practice operates. It involves recognising the ways in which the general principles offered by theory can be adopted and 'tailored' to fit the specific circumstances of each situation dealt with. The tendency to divorce theory from practice is a dangerous one in so far as it leaves us open to a number of possible difficulties. These should become clear by considering why we should integrate theory and practice as effectively as possible.

FIVE REASONS FOR RELATING THEORY TO PRACTICE

1. Anti-discriminatory practice

Discrimination and oppression are inherent in the way society is organised. We therefore need to pay attention to theories of discrimination and oppression if we are to challenge their destructive effects. A reliance on 'common sense' is likely to reflect, rather than challenge, dominant discriminatory attitudes.

2. Evaluation

Evaluating our practice gives us useful opportunities to learn from our experience by identifying what worked well and what was problematic. In order to do this we have to draw on a theory base. For example, in evaluating a particular approach that was adopted, we need to have at least a basic understanding of the ideas on which that approach is based.

3. Continuous professional development

Commitment to continuous professional development depends on a theory base. The process involves avoiding 'getting into a rut' of unthinking, uncritical routines. Continuous professional development rests on our ability and willingness to adopt a reflective approach, to think creatively and critically about our work.

4. Professional accountability

As professionals, people workers are accountable for their actions. Consequently, we need to be able to explain and justify the decisions we make and the steps we take. It is difficult, if not impossible, to do this without reference to a theory base. Professional accountability demands reasoned arguments to justify our actions, and this, of course, involves drawing on a set of concepts that guide and inform our practice.

5. Inappropriate responses

If we rely on 'common sense' responses to the problems we encounter, there is a serious danger that our actions may not only prove ineffective but actually make the situation worse:

> A failure to draw on theoretical knowledge may lead to an inap-
> propriate response on the part of the worker. We may misinterpret
> what is happening and react in a way which is not helpful or which
> even makes the situation worse. For example, a person experiencing
> a bereavement may express considerable anger towards the worker.
> If the worker does not recognise such anger as a common part of
> the grieving process, he or she could easily misread the situation and
> interpret the anger as a rejection of the worker's help.
> (Thompson, 2000: p. 35)

Reflective practice, as these five examples illustrate, owes much to a purposeful application of theory to practice. This involves a proactive approach to using theoretical ideas and knowledge as a framework for maximising effectiveness.

This brings us to the question of how can we apply theory to practice – what needs to be done to draw on the benefits that theory can offer? This is a vast topic and so, in the space available, I shall limit myself to outlining the following six steps that can be taken to promote reflective practice:

- *Read*   For theory to be used to best effect it is important that we break down the barriers by challenging the assumption that reading is for students or staff in training and not for fully fledged practitioners. Unfortunately, it is commonly assumed by many people that reflecting on theory is a task for students but not for practitioners. For example, an experienced social worker once told me that he missed being a student as he had enjoyed reading widely on the subject of social work and related topics. When I asked him what was stopping him from continuing to do so, he struggled for an answer. In the end, he replied that it was because it was 'not the done thing' It is important, then, that such a 'reading is for students only' culture is broken down. Some may argue that they do not have enough time to read. However, there are two points that need to be made in response to this. First, time spent reading is an *investment* of time and can, by enhancing our practice, save time in the long-run. Second, reading can increase our levels of job satisfaction by giving us a broader perspective and greater insights into people work. In view of this, I feel it is worth devoting some of our own time, outside of working hours, to read about subjects related to our work.
- *Ask*   'Asking' can apply in two ways. First, in relation to reading, much of the people work literature base is written in a jargonistic academic style that makes it difficult to understand. It can be helpful to ask other people about such issues so that you can get past this barrier. The danger is that some people may give up on reading because they feel uncomfortable with the style of writing being used. Second, we can learn a great deal from other people's practice. Students often learn a great deal by asking questions like: 'Why do you do it that way?' or 'Have you any ideas how I might tackle this situation?' There is much to be gained from creating an open, inquiring, mutually supportive atmosphere in which all staff, not just students, can learn from each other.
- *Watch*   There is much to be learned from developing an enhanced level of awareness in terms of observational skills. Much of the time we may miss significant issues because we treat situations as routine and commonplace.

We need to remember that every situation is unique in some ways, and so we need to be attuned to what is happening and not make blanket assumptions. Practising in a routine, uncritical way can mean that we are, in effect, going around with our eyes closed, oblivious to significant factors that could be very important in terms of how we deal with the situation. Theoretical knowledge can help us understand and explain our experience, but if our experience is closed off by a failure to be sensitive to what is happening, then we will not notice that there is anything to be explained. Reflective practice relies on developing a sensitivity to what is happening around us.

- *Feel*   The emotional dimension of people work is a very important one. Our emotional responses can be painful and difficult to deal with. At the other extreme, using theory can sometimes be seen as cold and technical. However, this does not mean that the two – thinking and feeling – cannot be reconciled. Thought can help us understand (and therefore deal with) feeling, and feelings can help bring theory to life, turn concepts into working tools, and thereby develop a reflective approach.

- *Talk*   Sharing views about work situations and how these can be dealt with encourages a broad perspective. It provides opportunities for people to learn from each other's experience, to find common ground and identify differences of approach. Constructive dialogue about methods of work, reasons for taking particular courses of action and so on can be an excellent way of broadening horizons, deepening understanding and enhancing skills. Such dialogue also helps to create an open and supportive working environment, and this, in itself, can be an important springboard for reflective practice.

- *Think*   There are two main barriers to a thoughtful approach to practice. These are routines and pressure. A routinised approach amounts to working 'on automatic pilot' and is clearly a dangerous way of dealing with the sensitive issues. As I mentioned earlier, dealing with situations in a routine, unthinking way leaves us very vulnerable to mistakes. Pressure can also stand in the way of thinking about our practice. If we are very busy we have to be wary of allowing ourselves to be pressurised into not thinking about what we are doing. We need to remain in control of our workload so that we are able to think about our actions. Thinking time should be seen as an essential part of good practice, rather than a luxury that has to be dispensed with when the pressure is on.

These steps are not the only ones that can be taken to develop reflective practice but they should provide a good 'launch pad' for working out patterns of practice that can draw on the benefits of a reflective approach. One further important step towards reflective practice is the development of creative approaches, and it is to these that we now turn.

CREATIVE APPROACHES

Students training to enter the service industry are often anxious to be presented with ready-made techniques to use in practice, a toolbox of methods that can be applied in a simple or straightforward way. Such expectations, although understandable, are both unrealistic and unhelpful.

They are unrealistic because there are only a limited number of techniques that can be applied across a range of situations, and these will not be enough, in themselves, to provide an adequate repertoire for people workers. They are unhelpful because they are based on an inappropriate model of professional development. The worker should be seen not as a receptacle or storehouse to be 'stocked up' with methods and techniques, but rather as a generator of ideas and potential solutions.

There will be common themes across the situations encountered but there will also be features unique to each situation. People workers therefore have to be equipped to deal with novel situations by generating novel solutions. It is therefore worth considering, albeit briefly, how a creative approach can be developed.

A major barrier to developing creativity is an attitude that says: 'I can't. I'm not the sort of person who's creative'. This is a defeatist attitude that confuses skills with qualities. This is particularly significant with regard to creativity, as it is sometimes seen as having an almost magical quality, as if it were a 'special gift'.

Creativity can be learned; it can be developed through deliberate effort and experience. To promote this type of development, I shall present five strategies for stimulating a creative approach. These are:

- *Changing angle* Have you ever noticed how different a room looks if you sit in a different position from your usual one? Changing our 'angle' on a situation can give us a new perspective, with fresh insights. It can therefore pay dividends to switch position, metaphorically, so that we see the situations we are dealing with from different angles.
- *Developing a vision* Having clear objectives involves developing a vision of where we want to be, the point we want to reach. This type of vision

can also stimulate creativity. If we know where we are now and where we want to be in future, then we can map out the various routes for getting there, different 'modes of transport' and so on. By generating such options we are avoiding the narrow focus of seeing only one way forward.

- *Stepping back*   Sometimes we can get so close to a situation that we 'cannot see the wood for the trees', and we therefore get bogged down or lose our sense of direction. By 'stepping back', we can put some distance between ourselves and the situation that we are tackling. Stepping back from a situation gives us a breathing space and helps us develop a fresh perspective.

- *Letting go*   The technique of brainstorming can be a very helpful one by allowing people to make lots of suggestions without having to worry about whether they are sensible, logical or workable. In this way, the strait-jacket of conventional thinking can be thrown off and the potential for creative solutions is released. By 'letting go' in this way we generate a wide range of possibilities, many of which will have to be rejected as unsuitable. However, amongst these, there may well be a veritable nugget of gold.

- *Provocation*   Edward de Bono explains it in the following terms:

> A patterning system like the mind creates patterns which we then continue to use. Most of our thinking is concerned with fitting things into these patterns so that we can act usefully and effectively. But to change patterns and to unlock those 'insight patterns' which are readily available to us (only after we have found them) we need something entirely different. Provocation is the process. With provocation we do not describe something as it is or as it could be. With provocation we look at the 'what if' and 'suppose' ... Provocation creates an unstable idea so that we may move on from it to a new idea.
>
> (1983: p. 200)

CONCLUSION

Reflective practice involves drawing on theory, in so far as this represents the accumulated experience and expertise of others. In this way, we can use the theory base to avoid the need to 'reinvent the wheel'. However, theory does not come tailor-made for practice – the cloth has to be cut to fit the circumstances. The reflective practitioner therefore has to *engage* with theory, to use it and shape it creatively in a constructive and positive way, rather than simply wait passively for theory to provide ready-made solutions.

Reflective practice is, then, a creative and proactive practice, one that casts the practitioner in an active role. This is an approach to practice that is entirely consistent with people work, a form of work where the situations we deal with have many common themes, but are also, in some ways, special and unique. Reflective practice offers the use of a theory base to help us understand the common themes, and a focus on creativity to help us deal with the unique aspects of each situation we encounter.

REFERENCES

Bono, E. de (1983) *Atlas of Management Thinking*. Harmondsworth: Penguin.

Schön, D. A. (1983) *The Reflective Practitioner*. New York: Basic Books.

Schön, D. A. (1987) *Educating the Reflective Practitioner*. San Francisco: Jossey Bass.

Schön, D. A. (1992) The crisis of professional knowledge and the pursuit of an epistemology of practice. *Journal of Interprofessional Care*, 6(1).

Thompson, N. (2000) *Theory and Practice in Human Services*. 2nd edition. Buckingham: Open University Press.

CHAPTER 7

EXPERIENTIAL AND REFLECTIVE LEARNING[1]

Jenny Moon

INTRODUCTION

This is an account of an incident in a park. It is recounted by 'Annie' who was involved in the incident herself. It is written in different versions that demonstrate different levels of reflective writing. At the end of the accounts, there are notes on the criteria for the levels of reflection that each account portrays. You may not be given the notes until you have discussed your responses to the material.

THE PARK (1)

I went through the park the other day. The sun shone sometimes but large clouds floated across the sky in a breeze. It reminded me of a time that I was walking on St David's Head in Wales – when there was a hard and bright light and anything I looked at was bright. It was really quite hot – so much nicer than the day before, which was rainy. I went over to the children's playing field. I had not been there for a while and wanted to see the improvements. There were several children there and one, in particular, I noticed, was in too many clothes for the heat. The children were running about and this child became red in the face and began to slow down and then he sat. He must have been about 10. Some of the others called him up again and he got to his feet. He stumbled into the game for a few moments, tripping once or twice. It seemed to me that he had just not got the energy to lift his feet. Eventually he stumbled down and did not get up but he was still moving and he shuffled into a half-sitting and half-lying position watching the other children and I think he was calling out to them. I don't know.

[1] Edited from Moon, J. (2004) 'The Park: An exercise in reflective writing' in *A Handbook of Reflective and Experiential Learning*, pp. 196–209, London: RoutledgeFalmer.

Anyway, I had to get on to get to the shop to buy some meat for the chilli that my children had asked me to make for their party. The twins had invited many friends round for an end-of-term celebration of the beginning of the summer holidays. They might think that they have cause to celebrate but it makes a lot more work for me when they are home. I find that their holiday time makes a lot more work.

It was the next day when the paper came through the door – in it there was a report of a child who had been taken seriously ill in the park the previous day. He was fighting for his life in hospital and they said that the seriousness of the situation was due to the delay before he was taken to hospital. The report commented on the fact that he had been lying unattended for half an hour before someone saw him. By then the other children had gone. It said that several passers-by might have seen him looking ill and even on the ground and the report went on to ask why passers-by do not take action when they see that something is wrong. The article was headed 'Why do they "Walk on by"?' I have been terribly upset since then. James says I should not worry – it is just a headline.

THE PARK (2)

I went to the park the other day. I was going to the supermarket to get some meat to make the chilli that I had promised the children. They were having one of their end-of-term celebrations with friends. I wonder what drew me to the playground and why I ended up standing and watching those children playing with a rough old football? I am not sure as I don't usually look at other people's children – I just did. Anyway there were a number of kids there. I noticed, in particular, one child who seemed to be very over-dressed for the weather. I try now to recall what he looked like – his face was red. He was a boy of around 10 – not unlike Charlie was at that age – maybe that is why I noticed him to start with when he was running around with the others. But then he was beginning to look distressed. I felt uneasy about him – sort of maternal but I did not do anything. What could I have done? I remember thinking, I had little time and the supermarket would get crowded. What a strange way of thinking, in the circumstances!

In retrospect, I wish I had acted. I ask myself what stopped me – but I don't know what I might have done at that point. Anyway he sat down, looking absolutely exhausted and as if he had no energy to do anything. A few moments later, the other children called him up to run about again. I felt more uneasy and watched as he got up and tried to run, then fell, ran again and fell and half-sat and half-lay. Still I did nothing more than look – what was going on with me?

Eventually I went on. I tell myself now that it was really important to get to the shops. It was the next day when the paper came through the door that I had a real shock. In the paper there was a report of a child who had been taken seriously ill in the park the previous day. He was fighting for his life in the hospital and the situation was much more serious because there had been such a delay in getting help. The report commented on the fact that he had been lying, unattended, for half an hour or more. At first, I wondered why the other children had not been more responsible. The article went on to say that several passers-by might have seen him playing and looking ill and the report questioned why passers-by do not take action when they see that something is wrong.

The incident has affected me for some days but I do not know where to go or whom to tell. I do want to own up to my part in it to someone though.

THE PARK (3)

The incident happened in Ingle Park and it is very much still on my mind. There was a child playing with others. He looked hot and unfit and kept sitting down but the other children kept on getting him back up and making him play with them. I was on my way to the shop and only watched the children for a while before I walked on. Next day it was reported in the paper that the child had been taken to hospital seriously ill – very seriously ill. The report said that there were several passers–by in the park who had seen the child looking ill and who had done nothing. It was a scathing report about those who do not take action in such situations.

Reading the report, I felt dreadful and it has been very difficult to shift the feelings. I did not stop to see to the child because I told myself that I was on my way to the shops to buy food for a meal that I had to cook for the children's party – what do I mean that I *had to* cook it? Though I saw that the child was ill, I didn't do anything. It is hard to say what I was really thinking at the time – to what degree I was determined to go on with my day in the way I had planned it (the party really was not that important, was it?). Or did I genuinely not think that the boy was ill – but just over-dressed and a bit tired? To what extent did I try to make convenient excuses and to what extent was I being honest? Looking back, I could have cut through my excuses at the time – rather than now.

68

I did not go over to the child and ask what was wrong but I should have done. I could have talked to the other children – and even got one of the other children to call for help. I am not sure if the help would have been ambulance or doctor at that stage – but it does not matter now. If he had been given help then, he might not be fighting for his life now.

It would be helpful to me if I could work out what I was really thinking and why I acted as I did. This event has really shaken me to my roots – more than I would have expected. It made me feel really guilty. I do not usually do wrong, in fact, I think of myself as a good person. This event is also making me think about actions in all sorts of areas of my life. It reminds me of some things in the past, as when my uncle died – but then again I don't really think that that is relevant – he was going to die anyway. My bad feelings then were due to sheer sadness and some irrational regrets that I did not visit him on the day before. Strangely it also reminds me of how bad I felt when Charlie was ill while we went on that anniversary weekend away. As I think more about Charlie being ill, I recognise that there are commonalities in the situations. I also keep wondering if I knew that boy …

THE PARK (4)

It happened in Ingle Park and this event is very much still on my mind. It feels significant. There was a child playing with others. He looked hot and unfit and kept sitting down but the other children kept on getting him back up and making him play with them. I was on my way to the shop and only watched the children for a while before I walked on. Next day it was reported in the paper that the child had been taken to hospital seriously ill – very seriously ill. The report said that there were several passers–by in the park who had seen the child looking ill and who had done nothing. It was a scathing report about those who do not take action in such a situation.

It was the report initially that made me think more deeply. It kept coming back into my mind and over the next few days I began to think of the situation in lots of different ways. Initially I considered my urge to get to the shop – regardless of the state of the boy. That was an easy way of excusing myself – to say that I had to get to the shop. Then I began to go through all of the agonising as to whether I could have mis-read the situation and really thought that the boy was simply over-dressed or perhaps play-acting or trying to gain sympathy from me or the others. Could I have believed that the situation was all right? All of that thinking, I now notice, would also have let me off the hook – made it not my fault that I did not act at the time.

I talked with Tom about my reflections on the event – on the incident, on my thinking about it at the time and then immediately after. He observed that my sense of myself as a 'good person who always lends a helping hand when others need help' was put in some jeopardy by it all. At the time and immediately after, it might have been easier to avoid shaking my view of myself than to admit that I had avoided facing up to the situation and admitting that I had not acted as 'a good person'. With this hindsight, I notice that I can probably find it easier to admit that I am not always 'a good person' and that I made a mistake in retrospect rather than immediately after the event. I suspect that this may apply to other situations.

As I think about the situation now, I recall some more of the thoughts – or were they feelings mixed up with thoughts? I remember a sense at the time that this boy looked quite scruffy and reminded me of a child who used to play with Charlie. We did not feel happy during the brief period of their friendship because this boy was known as a bully and we were uneasy either that Charlie would end up being bullied, or that Charlie would learn to bully. Funnily enough, we were talking about this boy – I now remember – at the dinner table the night before. The conversation had reminded me of all of the agonising about the children's friends at the time. The fleeting thought/feeling was possibly something like this – if this boy is like one I did not feel comfortable with – then maybe he deserves to get left in this way. Maybe he was a brother of the original child. I remember social psychology research along the lines of attributing blame to victims to justify their plight. Then, it might not have been anything to do with Charlie's friend.

So I can see how I looked at that event and perhaps interpreted it in a manner that was consistent with my emotional frame of mind at the time. Seeing the same events without that dinner-time conversation might have led me to see the whole thing in an entirely different manner and I might have acted differently. The significance of this whole event is chilling when I realise that my lack of action nearly resulted in his death – and it might have been because of an attitude that was formed years ago in relation to a different situation.

This has all made me think about how we view things. The way I saw this event at the time was quite different to the way I see it now – even these few days later. Writing an account at the time would have been different to the account, or several accounts, that I would write now. I cannot know what 'story'

70

is 'true'. The bullying story may be one that I have constructed retrospectively – fabricated. Interestingly, I can believe that story completely.

THE PARK: COMMENTS ON THE QUALITY OF REFLECTION IN THE ACCOUNTS

The park (1)

This piece tells the story. Sometimes it mentions past experiences, sometimes anticipates the future but all in the context of the account of the story:

- There might be references to emotional state, but the role of the emotions on action is not explored.
- Ideas of others are mentioned but not elaborated or used to investigate the meaning of the events.
- The account is written only from one point of view – that of Annie.
- Generally, ideas are presented in a sequence and are only linked by the story. They are not all relevant or focused.

In fact, you could hardly deem this to be reflective at all. It is very descriptive. It could be a reasonably written account of an event that could serve as a basis on which reflection might start, though it hardly signals any material for reflection – other than the last few words.

The park (2)

In this account there is a description of the same events. There is very little addition of ideas from outside the event – reference to attitudes of others, or comments.

The account is more than a story though. It is focused on the event as if there is a big question to be asked and answered. In the questioning there is recognition of the worth of exploring the motives for behaviour but it does not go very far. In other words, asking the questions makes it more than a descriptive account, but the lack of attempt to respond to the questions means that there is little actual analysis of the events.

Annie is critical of her actions and, in her questions, signals this. The questioning of action does mean that Annie is standing back from the event to a small extent.

There is a sense that she recognises that this is a significant incident, with learning to be gained but the reflection does not go sufficiently deep to enable the learning to begin to occur.

The park (3)

The description is succinct – just sufficient to raise the issues. Extraneous information is not added. It is not a story. The focus is on the attempt to reflect on the event and to learn from it. There is more of a sense of Annie standing back from the event in order to reflect better on her actions and in order to be more effectively critical.

There is more analysis of the situation and an evident understanding that it was not a simple situation – that there might be alternative explanations or actions that could be justified equally effectively.

The description could be said to be slightly narrow (see The park (4)) as Annie is not acknowledging that there might be other ways of perceiving the situation – other points of view. She does not seem to recognise that her reflection is affected by her frame of reference at the time or now. It is possible, for example, that her experience with Charlie (last paragraph) – or her question about knowing the boy have influenced the manner in which she reacted. It might not just be a matter of linking up other events, but of going beyond and checking out the possibility that her frame of reference might have been affected by the prior experiences.

The park (4)

(You may not have been given the fourth part of The park)

The account is succinct and to the point. There is some deep reflection here that is self-critical and questions the basis of the beliefs and values on which the behaviour was based.

- There is evidence of standing back from the event, of Annie treating herself as an object acting within the context.
- There is also an internal dialogue – a conversation with herself in which she proposes and further reflects on alternative explanations.
- She shows evidence of looking at the views of others (Tom) and of considering the alternative point of view, and learning from it.

- She recognises the significance of the effect of passage of time on her reflection, for example, that her personal frame of reference at the time may have influenced her actions and that a different frame of reference might have led to different results.
- She notices that the proximity of other, possibly unrelated events (the dinner-time conversation) has an effect either on her actual behaviour and her subsequent reflection or possibly on her reflective processes only. She notices that she can be said to be reconstructing the event in retrospect – creating a story around it that may not be 'true'.
- She recognises that there may be no conclusion to this situation but that there are still things to be learnt from it.
- She has also been able to reflect on her own process of reflecting (acting metacognitively), recognising that her process influenced the outcome.

SECTION 2

ENCOURAGING AND MAINTAINING MOTIVATION

INTRODUCTION

The skill of developing motivation within the people we work with, whether they are athletes, customers or our colleagues, is an important factor in achieving maximum effectiveness. This could be an athlete achieving a certain performance, a fitness customer achieving their desired goal or a colleague achieving their targets. The development of a motivational climate to operate within is a subtle mix of getting the environment right, acting in a motivational way and understanding what motivates the individual. This section therefore examines what is meant by the term 'motivation', the dimensions of motivation, how to develop a motivational climate and techniques which can be used to promote motivation within the individual.

Chapter 8 is by Simon Rea, an academic at the Open University. This chapter uses a case study approach as a starting point to thinking about motivation. It considers how to define motivation before developing three different viewpoints of motivation that connect with sport and fitness environments.

Chapter 9 is an adapted version of a chapter written by K.B. Everard, Geoffrey Morris and Ian Wilson in their book *Effective School Management*. Bertie Everard was Company Education and Training Manager for ICI; he was also appointed as visiting fellow at the Polytechnic of Central London and visiting fellow at the University of London Institute of education. Geoffrey Morris is managing director of EMAS Business Consultants Ltd and was previously a teacher and head of department. Ian Wilson is headteacher at Rydens School in Croydon and an associate consultant with Surrey LEA. They examine the motivation of people in the workplace, in terms of how people are motivated to satisfy the differing needs they have and how this applies to two important theories in the subject of workplace motivation, including implications for leaders.

Chapter 10 is written by Caroline Heaney, an academic at the Open University. She examines the central topic of creating a motivational climate and addresses the role of the leader and their behaviour in influencing the climate. She goes on to consider the role other people around the individual play in influencing their motivation in a positive or negative way.

Chapter 11 is written by Steve Bull, a chartered psychologist, consultant and author in both sport and business. He has been the Great Britain Team Headquarters Psychologist at three Olympic Games as well as working with the 2005 Ashes winning England Cricket Team. This chapter uses his experience from sport and applies them to the business perspective to show how to develop a system for setting goals and the different types of goals that need to be set.

CHAPTER 8

THINKING ABOUT MOTIVATION IN THE WORKPLACE

Simon Rea

INTRODUCTION

James is a sports coach who runs after school sports sessions in a primary school. He notices that the same children are always ready first and always have the right training kit; these children also appear to show the most enthusiasm and have the most energy. He does become frustrated that the children always want to play football and don't put as much effort into other sports; so he ends up using football sessions as a bribe for the children who perform well in the other sessions.

Sammy is a fitness instructor who feels everyone should be as enthusiastic as she is about training in the gym. However, she finds that her customers will train hard for about six sessions and then start to make excuses about why they cannot come for their training sessions; she knows if they don't train in the gym they are probably not doing the exercises she asked them to do at home.

Kieran is the manager of a small sports centre and he finds that the same members of staff will volunteer to take on the challenging tasks he sets. They will always meet their objectives on time and to a high standard. He also has staff who will come in and do the work expected of them to a good standard but never put themselves out, or look for jobs which need to be done. Kieran finds that any changes he makes to motivate the staff will work for a short time but then start to lose their effect.

All of these professionals are aware that their issues are about motivating the people they work with and that developing and maintaining motivation is essential for their own success and the success of their business. However, they may not understand the concept of motivation fully, what affects motivation, and how motivation can be developed. They probably possess the technical skills and knowledge needed to coach, instruct and manage but their improved ability to motivate people would make them stand out from the crowd and achieve better results for all the people they work with. This chapter introduces the concept of motivation and examines three different approaches to motivation and will continue to draw on these three illustrative examples.

Sage (1977) has provided a classic definition of motivation:

> Motivation is the direction and intensity of effort
> (Weinberg and Gould, 2007: p. 52)

The direction of effort refers to the activities that we choose to direct our attention towards. For example, James (coach) finds that his primary school children direct their efforts towards football at the expense of other sports, whilst Kieran's staff are motivated to direct their effort into delivering their swimming lessons rather than scrubbing the poolside. The intensity of effort refers to how much effort the individual puts into each specific situation or towards a specific goal. Sammy (fitness instructor) finds that even her most committed customers will put different intensities of effort into their training and often this varies from day to day. While the direction and intensity of effort have been differentiated in this discussion you have probably experienced that those people who consistently attend their sessions and are well prepared (direction) will also expend most effort during the sessions (intensity). Conversely, those who often miss sessions, arrive late, and are poorly prepared will usually expend least effort. In reality the two, direction and intensity, tend to go together.

In our three differing exemplars each person has developed their own view of motivation and developed ways of motivating people accordingly. For example, Sammy (fitness instructor) feels that her enthusiasm should motivate other people and she shows enthusiasm because she is motivated herself. However, she finds it difficult to understand why other people are not as motivated to train like her and this does not fit in with her personal view of motivation and the factors which affect her motivation. Her understanding of motivation would be augmented by looking at different approaches that psychologists have taken to view motivation. This chapter will address three of the most accepted approaches to motivation: the trait centred view; the situation-centred view; and the interactional view.

THE TRAIT-CENTRED VIEW

The trait-centred view asserts that motivation is the result of an individual's personality and their individual characteristics. This suggests that motivation comes from within the individual, rather than from external sources. In developing the trait-centred view further psychologists would agree that motivated behaviour is largely determined by the personality, needs, and goals of the athlete, exerciser or employee (Weinberg and Gould, 2007). This would explain why some sportspeople are described as being 'highly driven' or 'a real competitor' to show that they are the type of person who is so motivated that they will work hard to achieve their goals. Conversely we may hear another sports person being described as 'a bit of a loser' as they lack direction and just let things pass them by. Individual success in maintaining an exercise programme for an extended period of time can be attributed to their drive and determination (Berger *et al.*, 2007). Kieran (manager) can see that his highly motivated group of staff members have the personality attributes that predispose them towards this type of behaviour. However, contrary to the trait view he also knows that his other staff members rely on him and his leadership to motivate them and if he is having a bad day then this affects the motivation of these staff members. This suggests that the climate or environment we are operating within has an influence on our motivation and thus motivation may be situation specific.

SITUATION-CENTRED VIEW

The situation-centred view proposes that it is the situation which is the primary determinant of motivation in an individual (Weinberg and Gould, 2007). This could explain why an individual is highly motivated on the sports field but less so in the workplace. In sporting environments it is often assumed that the coach (or teacher) plays a significant role in developing a motivational climate (Ames and Archer, 1988; Ames, 1992); however, athletes also consider that their team members' behaviour and how they worked as a group was of major importance (Pensgaard and Roberts, 2002).

Kieran (manager) believes that some of his staff members will be highly motivated irrespective of the situation or environment because their own motives are so strong. Likewise, Sammy (fitness instructor) sees a wide variation in motivation levels from her training customers in identical environments. While the environment and the climate created do play a role in motivation it would appear that the situation is not the only factor and thus sport and exercise

BOX 8.1: MYTHS ABOUT MOTIVATION

1. People are either motivated or not motivated

As described in the trait-centred view, some coaches and leaders believe that motivation is a stable personality characteristic and that an individual will either be motivated or not. They would say that motivation cannot be developed so would choose members for a team based on their personality. While some individuals will be more motivated than others the leader/coach can be influential in facilitating the development of goals and other measures of motivation (Weigand *et al.*, 2001).

2. Leaders give people motivation

Other coaches and leaders regard motivation as a quality they can instil into individuals as and when they need it; the situation-centred view would suggest this behaviour is part of developing a motivational climate. To give people motivation a leader would use motivational talks, quotes, slogans and images to fire people up. These techniques have a role to play but they may not be long-term strategies and will only address a small piece of the motivational jigsaw. Leaders cannot simply give motivation to individuals.

3. Motivation means sticks and carrots

A commonly held view of influencing motivation is that it involves using carrots (rewards) and sticks (punishments) to drive individuals on to achieve things they would not achieve on their own. This view suggests that individuals don't want to do something and that the leader will coerce them into it by punishing or rewarding them. Leaders who scream, shout, castigate and criticise often expend a lot of energy, meet resistance and negativity, and take the enjoyment out of the activity. Continually offering a carrot (reward) to an individual will eventually lose its power as well. To be effective as a coach or a leader you need to understand the needs of an individual and create an environment or culture which will allow motivation to thrive.

Source: Adapted from Burton and Raedeke (2008), pp. 124–125.

psychologists do not recommend the situation-centred view of motivation as being reliable for directing your practice (Weinberg and Gould, 2007). Box 8.1 looks at the issues associated with trait and situation-centred views in more depth.

INTERACTIONAL VIEW

The interactional view takes the perspective that personality traits, in this case drive and motivation, and the situation itself are individually weak predictors of performance (Cox, 2007). However, when they both interact they provide a much stronger predictor of performance and behaviour. This broader view of motivation, called the interactional view, suggests that you need to consider both the individual's personality and the situation they are operating within if you want to get the best performances out of people. This is important in both sport and workplace settings to get the right fit between the individual and the situation you are putting them in. Sammy (fitness instructor) may realise that the issue she has with her training customers is that their motivation may be affected by her style of leadership or by the activities she is making her customers take part in. Maybe one size does not fit all and she needs to vary activities to meet the personality and needs of her customers. James (coach) could look at his most successful coaching sessions, the sessions that create the highest motivation levels in his young players and transfer these qualities to the coaching of other sessions so that the group are more motivated to do other activities. Kieran (manager) may realise that some of his staff are not particularly motivated because of the way that he leads them and the motivational strategies he employs; in his case the situation they are operating in does not vary but their individual personality, values, interests and goals do vary.

CONCLUSION

Motivation is a difficult area for many managers, leaders, instructors or coaches to deal with because it is not a personality characteristic which remains stable in an individual and it is influenced by many factors. The customers, staff or young participants they deal with will experience fluctuations in motivation level dependent upon their mood, level of energy and their daily experiences and situation. However, by understanding that motivation is predominantly influenced by the interaction of the individual's personality and the situation

81

they find themselves in, you can start to influence the motivation of an individual in a positive way.

REFERENCES

Ames, C. (1992) Achievement goals, motivational climate and motivational process. In Roberts, G.C (ed.), *Motivation in Sport and Exercise* (pp. 168–176). Champaign, Illinois: Human Kinetics.

Ames, C. and Archer, J. (1988) Achievement goals in the classroom: Students learning strategies and motivational process. *Journal of Educational Psychology*, 73: 411–418.

Berger, G.B, Pargman, D. and Weinberg, R.S. (2007) *Foundations of Exercise Psychology.* 2nd edition. Morgantown, West Virginia: Fitness Information Technology.

Burton, D. and Raedeke, T.D. (2008) *Sport Psychology for Coaches.* Leeds: Human Kinetics.

Cox, R. (2007) *Sport Psychology: Concepts and Applications.* 6th edition. New York: McGraw-Hill.

Pensgaard, A.M and Roberts, G.C. (2002) Elite athletes' experiences of the motivational climate: The coach matters. *Scandinavian Journal of Medicine and Science in Sports*, 12: 54–59.

Sage, G. (1977) *Introduction to Motor Behaviour: A Neurophysiological Approach.* 2nd edition. Reading, Massachusetts: Addison-Wesley.

Weigand, D.A., Carr, S., Petherick, C. and Taylor, A. (2001) Motivational climate in sport and physical education: The role of significant others. *European Journal of Sport Science*, 1(4): 4.

Weinberg, R.S. and Gould, D. (2007) *Foundations of Sport and Exercise Psychology.* 4th edition. Leeds: Human Kinetics.

CHAPTER 9

MOTIVATING PEOPLE IN THE WORKPLACE[1]

K.B. Everard, Geoff Morris and Ian Wilson

MOTIVATION

'Motivation' can be defined as 'getting results through people' or 'getting the best out of people'. The second definition is slightly preferable, since 'the best' which people can offer is not necessarily synonymous with 'the results' which we might initially want from them, though it should be in line with the overall goals and ethos of the school or college.

As Peters and Waterman (1995) say: 'Management's principal job is to get the herd heading roughly west'. The head coach of a professional rugby club may have very definite ideas about the way he wants his teams to play, but it is essential for him to get the other coaches (defence, attack, forwards, backs, etc.) within the club to buy into his general game plan. He should also allow his coaches the flexibility of adopting whatever drills and practices they deem appropriate to the fulfilment of the plan once they've bought into it. A flexible but united front will benefit all teams and players being coached.

In motivating people we should be concerned with the needs and potential of three parties:

1 The group which we are managing or in which we manage.
2 The individuals who make up that group.
3 The 'clients' (athletes, players, etc.) of the school, college or other organisation in which we all work.

---

[1] Edited from Everard, K.B., Morris, G. and Wilson, I. (2004) 'Motivating people' in *Effective School Management* (4th edn), pp. 25–35, London: Paul Chapman Publishing/SAGE Publications.

A fundamental mistake is to forget that people are best motivated to work towards goals that they have been involved in setting and to which they therefore feel committed. If people do not feel committed towards a given result or activity, the only motivations at our disposal are those of the carrot and stick – reward and punishment. We therefore have to be prepared to modify our own initial perceptions of what is required. Some people have a strong 'internal' motivation – a sense of purpose or drive. Others do not.

WHOM DO WE NEED TO MOTIVATE?

In a hierarchical organisation, subordinates are obvious candidates for 'motivation'. However, it is even more important to be able to motivate equals and superiors. In the last resort, we can tell a junior member of our team what he or she is to do, but we have no such power with an equal and even less with a superior. Here we are in much more of a 'selling' role and, like all good salespeople, must be very aware of the benefits that will accrue to our customer.

A cynical – but often true – maxim is: 'There is nothing I cannot achieve provided that my boss gets the credit for it!'

SATISFYING NEEDS

People work in order to satisfy some need. The need may be to achieve fame or power, to serve other people or simply to earn the money to live. It may even be the rather negative need to avoid punishment.

Most motivational theorists have therefore concentrated their attention on:

- examining human needs
- considering how the needs are met and can be better met in work

People work at their best when they are achieving the greatest satisfaction from their work.

MASLOW'S HIERARCHY OF NEEDS

Maslow (1943) suggested that it was useful to think of human needs as being at different levels in a hierarchy (see Figure 9.1). The principle behind the hierarchy

Self-realisation	Achievement
	Psychological growth
Ego	Status
	Respect
	Prestige
Social	Friendship, group acceptance
	Love
Security	Freedom from danger
	Freedom from want
Physiological	Food, drink, shelter, sex,
	warmth, physical comfort

Figure 9.1 A hierarchy of needs, based on 'Hierarchy of needs', in Maslow, A.H. (1970) *Motivation and Personality*. 2nd edition, Copyright © by Abraham H. Maslow

is that, starting from the bottom, the needs at each level have to be satisfied to some extent before we think about needs at the next level up.

The physiological needs. Undoubtedly physiological needs are the most basic of all needs. For the person who is missing everything in life, it is most likely that the major motivation will be the physiological needs. A person who lacked food, security, love and esteem would probably hunger for food more strongly than for anything else.

The security needs. If the physiological needs are gratified, there then emerges a new set of needs, which are categorised roughly as the security needs. Robinson Crusoe's first thoughts on reaching his desert island were to find water, food and shelter. His second was to build a stockade and to get in reserves of food and water.

The social needs. If both the physiological and the security needs are fairly well satisfied, then there will emerge the needs for love and affection and belongingness. Now the person feels keenly the need for friends, a special relationship with one partner, or children. There is a hunger for affectionate relationships with people in general, for a place in the group.

The ego needs. Having established a base of friendship, acceptance and affection, most of us want to prove our worth within whatever group or groups we belong to. We seek to demonstrate to ourselves and others that we are as good as, or better than, other members of the group. We pursue promotion, influence, status, power, reputation, recognition, prestige, importance, attention.

The need for self-realisation.　Even if all these needs are satisfied, we may still be discontented and restless if we feel that we have talent and potential within us which we are not fully exploiting.

Why do people write poetry, plays, books and music, play sports, act in plays, take up hobbies, climb mountains? We have a need to achieve, fulfil ourselves, become what we are capable of becoming, meet new challenges.

In his later writings Maslow identified an even higher need, self-transcendence, to describe the inner grace of a person who feels called to serve a cause above and beyond him or herself, such as a deity.

THE RELEVANCE OF THE HIERARCHY

There are a number of important points to be made about the hierarchy:

1　If an individual is really deprived at a lower level, he or she may lose interest in the higher-level needs. How often do we hear someone who suddenly finds him or herself in pain in hospital make a remark like: 'To think that I was worrying yesterday because I hadn't been invited to … This puts things in perspective'? Serious financial hardship or threats of redundancy can take the mind off thoughts of achievement.

2　On the other hand, a 'satisfying' job at the higher levels will raise the level of tolerance or deprivation at the lower levels. Teachers, doctors and nurses are prepared to tolerate conditions of employment which would not be acceptable to someone with a boring job – though even they have their limits.

3　When a need at a given level is satisfied, the law of diminishing returns sets in. When I have eaten a meal, I do not wish to eat another immediately. While I may like friends and parties, too many become a nuisance. Even prestige can pall and those who courted publicity on their way to promotion and fame may seek, when they have 'arrived', to avoid the limelight.

4　'Oversatisfying' of a need may produce a sense of guilt and/or deliberate self-deprivation. Drop-outs are often the children of well-to-do families, and young people will undertake ventures which involve frugal living and risk in order to prove themselves.

5　Different people will feel needs with differing intensity. One person's social needs may only be satisfied when surrounded by friends, whereas another will be content simply to have the companionship and love of his or

k.b. everard, geoff morris and ian wilson

her partner. Very exceptionally, an individual will shun all company, but such 'hermits' are extremely rare. They may, like saints, have reached the level of self-transcendence.

The interesting thing is that when dealing with people with whom we work, *most of us have a tendency to behave as though the needs of others, particularly our subordinates, are at the lower levels*.

'I look for satisfaction in my job but the rest of the staff are concerned only about physical conditions, being treated kindly, not being asked to work hours which are unreasonable, being given appropriate recognition of their status'. The staff themselves often reinforce our beliefs by complaining about precisely those things we have just mentioned.

The two views of work – one asserting that people seek fulfilment through work, and the other suggesting that they seek only to satisfy lower-level needs – are neatly described by Douglas McGregor (1985). McGregor called the two conflicting assumptions about the nature of work Theory X and Theory Y.

THEORY X AND THEORY Y

Those managers who adopt 'Theory X' believe that:

1 Work is inherently distasteful to most people
2 Most people are not ambitious, have little desire for responsibility and prefer to be directed
3 Most people have little capacity for creativity in solving problems
4 Motivation occurs only at the physiological and security levels
5 Most people must be closely controlled and often coerced to achieve organisation objectives

'Theory Y' managers, on the other hand, believe that:

1 Work is as natural as play, if the conditions are favourable
2 Control of one's own work activities is often indispensable in achieving organisational gains
3 The capacity for creativity in solving organisational problems is widely distributed in the population
4 Motivation occurs at the social, ego and self-realisation levels as well as at the physiological and security levels
5 People can be self-directed and creative at work if properly led

motivating people in the workplace

FREDERICK HERZBERG

Herzberg (1975) put to the practical test, through a series of experiments conducted with widely differing groups of workers, the sort of thinking developed by Maslow and McGregor.

One of his best-known experiments consisted of asking people to think of three occasions when they had felt very satisfied in their work and three occasions when they had felt dissatisfied. He then asked them to categorise the causes of satisfaction and dissatisfaction under a number of headings. Finally he recorded for all the individuals in the group the frequency with which each category had been noted as a cause of satisfaction or dissatisfaction. A typical result is shown in Figure 9.2.

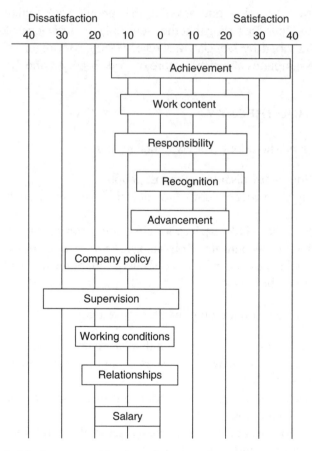

Figure 9.2 Motivators and hygiene factors

Source: Herzberg (1975)

From these findings, Herzberg drew some important conclusions:

1   The things which make people happy at work are not simply the opposites of the things which make them unhappy, and vice versa. The two sets of things are different in kind. You will not make people *satisfied*, therefore, simply by removing causes of *dissatisfaction*.
2   The things that make people dissatisfied are related to the job environment. The things that make people satisfied on the other hand are related to the job content.
3   While those who have a satisfying job may have a higher tolerance of dissatisfiers, the dissatisfying factors can be so strong that the job becomes intolerable.
4   Managers must therefore be concerned with ensuring both that causes of dissatisfaction are removed and that opportunities for satisfaction are increased – that, in Herzberg's terms, the job is 'enriched'. It is in this latter respect that managers usually fail. Instead of using the real 'motivation' which comes from a satisfying job, they use rewards and threats.

Herzberg calls the environmental factors which are capable of causing unhappiness the 'hygiene' factors because he believes that these have to be reasonably well 'cleaned up' as a prerequisite for satisfaction. Among the hygiene factors are:

- organisational policies and administration
- management
- working conditions
- interpersonal relationships
- money, status and security

The work content factors which lead to happiness Herzberg calls the 'motivators', and these are as follows:

- *Achievement*.   This is a measure of the opportunities for you to use your full capabilities and make a worthwhile contribution. It includes the possibilities for testing new and untried ideas.
- *Responsibility*.   A measure of freedom of action in decision-taking, style and job development.
- *Recognition*.   An indication of the amount and quality of all kinds of 'feedback', whether good or bad, about how you are getting on in the job.
- *Advancement*.   This shows the potential of the job in terms of promotion – inside or outside the organisation in which you currently work.

89

- *Work itself.* The interest of the job, usually involving variety, challenge and personal conviction of the job's significance.
- *Personal growth.* An indication of opportunities for learning and maturing.

Several jobs which score high on Herzberg's list – particularly where some form of teaching or coaching or development is concerned – can score low on recognition, which reflects a British or European cultural norm. We hesitate to tell people how they are getting on, though this knowledge is not only an element in job satisfaction but also essential for improvement and adjusting to the needs of the job. This should be the purpose of staff appraisal.

The relationship between the Herzberg 'motivators' and the top two levels of Maslow's hierarchy is self-evident.

INVOLVEMENT

Where staff at any level are 'involved' in decisions taken by their superiors, peers or even subordinates, all the motivators are brought into play. This is particularly the case where the decision under discussion will affect the person involved.

Involvement should produce the commitment to goals on which a sense of achievement depends. By involving people we show them recognition and increase their sense of responsibility. The interest of their job should be increased and we are providing them with the broader view which provides both a learning opportunity and experience which may be of use in seeking advancement.

THE SELF-MOTIVATED ACHIEVER

As with all needs, the intensity of the need for achievement varies greatly from person to person. In some pupils, particularly at secondary level, we may feel that it has almost disappeared! McClelland's (1985) interest is in those with very strong achievement needs who offer great potential, but can also pose problems where their own perception of goals may be different from our own.

McClelland would claim that most of us have a motivation to achieve something. He would also claim, however, that only in 10 per cent of the population is this a highly developed motivation. According to McClelland, the most convincing sign of a strong achievement motivation is the tendency of a person who is not being required to think about anything in particular, that is, who is free to relax or to let his or her mind wander, to think about ways of accomplishing something.

90

On a car journey the self-motivated achiever will typically set him or herself time targets or fuel-consumption targets. On the way to work he or she will try out new routes to cut mileage or time. He or she will work to achieve a standard in a sport, to take on new challenges in his or her job, to produce a play, to organise a new function.

Such tendencies emerge at a very early age. In a series of experiments McClelland provided young people with an upright pole and quoits. Some would throw the quoits aimlessly around, build towers, drop them with ease onto the pole or quickly lose interest. However, certain individuals would set themselves a challenge by attempting to hit the pole or throw the quoits over it from a distance chosen by them such that success would not come too easily nor be impossible or subject to pure luck. Following his subjects' careers, McClelland found that those who showed a strong achievement motivation in childhood tended to manifest the same drive in adult life.

Although only about 10 per cent of people are strongly motivated, the percentage in certain occupations is likely to be much higher. This is especially true of people in managerial positions, and independent entrepreneurs. A person with a strong achievement motivation is likely to surpass the accomplishments of equally able but less strongly motivated people, especially in one of the above occupations.

McClelland's studies have identified three major characteristics of the self-motivated achiever, and why supervisory tactics, which may be appropriate to other kinds of people, are often inappropriate when applied to a man or woman with a strong achievement motivation.

First, achievers like to set their own goals. They are nearly always trying to accomplish something. They are seldom content to drift aimlessly and let life happen to them. They are quite selective about which goals they commit themselves to and for this reason they are unlikely automatically to accept goals which other people, including their bosses or coaches, select for them. Neither do they seek advice or help except from experts or people who can provide needed skills or information. Achievers prefer to be as fully responsible for the attainment of their goals as it is possible to be. If they win they want the credit, if they lose they accept the blame. Either way they want the victory or defeat to be unmistakably theirs.

Second, achievers tend to avoid extremes of difficulty in selecting goals. They prefer moderate goals which are neither so easy that winning them would provide no satisfaction nor so difficult that winning them would be more a matter of luck than ability. They will tend to gauge what is possible and then select a goal that is as tough as they think they can fulfil, that is, the hardest practical challenge. This attitude keeps them continually straining their abilities to their realistic limits, but no further. Above all else they want to win and, therefore, they do not knowingly commit themselves to a goal that is probably too difficult to achieve.

Third, achievers prefer tasks which provide them with more or less immediate feedback, that is, measurements of how well they are progressing towards their goal. Because of the importance of the goal, they like to know how well they are doing at all times.

The effect of a monetary incentive on an achiever is rather complex. Achievers usually have a fairly high opinion of the value of their services and prefer to place a fairly high price tag on them: they are unlikely to remain for long in an organisation that doesn't pay them well. But it is questionable whether an incentive payment actually increases their output since they are normally working at peak efficiency anyway.

McClelland notes that monetary incentives are actually more effective with people whose achievement drives are relatively weak, because they need some kind of external reward to increase their effort. The main significance of additional income to achievers is as a way of measuring their success. McClelland emphasises that the achievement motive, as he defines it, is not the only source of success attainment. Other drives can also lead to high levels of attainment, but achievers have a considerable advantage.

Can the level of achievement motivation be increased in people whose achievement drives are not usually strong? McClelland believes this may be possible and indeed there are considerable reserves of latent untapped achievement motivation in most organisations. The key is to build more achievement characteristics into the job – personal responsibility, individual participation in the selection of targets, moderate goals and fast, clear-cut feedback on the results each individual is achieving, etc.

For achievers themselves, McClelland believes that many standard supervisory practices are inappropriate and in some cases may even hinder their per-formance. Work goals should not be imposed on achievers. They not only want a voice in setting their own goals but they are also unlikely to set them lower than they think they can reach. Highly specific directions and controls are unnecessary; some general guidance and occasional follow-up will do. But if the job does not provide its own internal feedback mechanism regarding the achiever's effectiveness, as is the case, for example, in some professional or administrative jobs, then it is vitally important to achievers that they be given frank, detailed appraisals of how well they are performing in their jobs.

MOTIVATION THEORY AND THE MANAGER

The key to effective management is the ability to get results from other people, through other people and in conjunction with other people. If the underlying psychology is wrong, the most carefully constructed system and techniques will fail. Efficient managers are not necessarily effective managers. But if relationships and motivation are good, people will readily accept and overcome some administrative or environmental flaws (but see Herzberg, 1975: p. 29).

Three basic rules should underlie management relationships and the application of any technique:

1   We should remember to use the 'motivators', that is, people's need for achievement, recognition, responsibility, job interest, personal growth and advancement potential. We tend to underestimate the needs of other people in these areas. Involving others in decisions which affect them is one way of meeting all or most of these needs.
2   The relative intensity of psychological needs will vary greatly from person to person and from time to time. There are people who simply are not interested in motivators, or who do not wish to have these needs satisfied at work. If an instructor's spouse loses his or her job, security needs may well be the most important need. If there is a marriage break-up, both security and social needs may surface, though these may be followed later by a need to find renewed interest and achievement in the job.
    These are predictable and often recognisable behavioural phenomena. However, when symptoms and causes are less obvious, the risk is that we misjudge the needs of colleagues or friends. Some of us have a tendency to assume that the needs of others are the same as our own; others tend to assume the opposite.
3   We should try to suit our management behaviour to both the personalities and the needs of the situation. Our automatic behavioural reaction may not be the right one. Think about the alternatives.

Despite every effort there will remain individuals who have no wish to be 'motivated' and who view with suspicion any attempt to increase their responsibilities, job interest or involvement. Such attitudes may typically be found in caretakers, ancillary staff or teachers who are frustrated. However, the danger is always that we give up too easily. The right approach may prompt a surprisingly warm response.

REFERENCES

Herzberg, F. (1975) *Work and the Nature of Man*. Reading: Crosby Lockwood.
Maslow, A.H. (1943) A theory of human motivation. *Psychological Review*, 50: 370–396.
McGregor, D. (1985) *The Human Side of Enterprise*. New York: McGraw-Hill.
McClelland, D.C (1985) *The Achieving Society*. London: Simon and Schuster.
Peters, T.J. and Waterman, R.H. (1995) *In Search of Excellence*. New York and London: Harper Collins.

CHAPTER 10

CREATING A MOTIVATIONAL CLIMATE

Caroline Heaney

Being able to motivate those around you is an important skill in the sport and fitness industry. In order to perform their roles effectively, fitness instructors and sports coaches need to be able to motivate their charges, whilst managers need to be able to motivate their staff. This chapter will consider what those who need to motivate others can do to create a *motivational climate*. In the context of this chapter we will refer to those who need to motivate others as 'leaders'.

The creation of a motivational climate will be considered from three perspectives: the behaviour of the leader (i.e. the coach, instructor or manager), the environment, and the influence of others.

BEHAVIOUR OF THE LEADER

How the leader behaves can have a significant impact on the motivation of others. For example, a manager who is perceived as not caring about their own performance is unlikely to inspire and motivate their staff. Therefore, those who wish to motivate others need to pay close attention to their own behaviour and consider its impact on the motivation of others.

The perceived attitude of the leader is important in determining the motivation levels of others. A leader who behaves in what is perceived as a positive way will encourage greater levels of motivation than one who is perceived to behave in a negative way. For example, Peterson (1993) found that exercise class participants rated the ability to stay focused and to be energetic as important and influential behavioural characteristics present in good exercise class leaders.

A 'personal' approach by the leader is also thought to be of benefit in enhancing motivation. Fox *et al.* (2000) found that exercise leaders who used participants' names and engaged in conversations with participants before, during and after exercise classes encouraged greater levels of *exercise adherence*. Exercise adherence refers to an individual's ability to stick to a programme of regular exercise, which is clearly closely related to motivation.

This personal approach also works in a workplace setting. Thompson (2002) suggests that a manager who is perceived as personable and takes the time to speak to their employees will foster a greater level of motivation amongst his/her staff.

Motivation to persist at a specific task is strongly linked to self-confidence or *self-efficacy*. Self-efficacy can be defined as situation-specific self-confidence (Cox, 2002). According to self-efficacy theory, which was developed by Albert Bandura (1977), there are four main factors that influence self-efficacy (see Table 10.1). Those who have high levels of self-efficacy about their ability to perform a specific task will be more motivated to attempt and persist at the task

Table 10.1 Bandura's sources of self-efficacy

Source	Definition	Application
Performance Accomplishments	Previous performance experiences.	Previous successful attempts at a task will increase self-efficacy.
Vicarious Experience	Information derived from seeing others perform the task/activity.	Seeing a role model perform a task can increase self-efficacy as it allows the individual to build a mental picture of how to perform the task.
Verbal Persuasion	The persuasive techniques used by self or others.	Encouragement from a coach, instructor or manager can increase self-efficacy.
Emotional Arousal	The emotional reaction to potentially stressful and taxing situations and its interpretation.	People generally have higher levels of self-efficacy when their levels of emotional arousal are not excessively high. It is necessary to be emotionally ready and optimally aroused in order to perform a task effectively and thus develop self-efficacy.

Source: Adapted from Bandura (1977), pp. 195–200 and Cox (2002), pp. 19–20

(Weinberg and Gould, 2007). Therefore, interpersonal communications with those we are trying to motivate should reflect this, that is communications aimed at improving motivation and performance should aim to enhance self-efficacy. The way in which feedback is presented provides a good example of this.

Providing feedback is an essential part of the leader's role. According to Weinberg and Gould (2007) the two main functions of feedback are to motivate and instruct. We often concentrate on verbal forms of feedback, but it is worth noting that feedback can be both verbal and non-verbal. Sometimes saying nothing at all provides the individual with feedback (e.g. 'she hasn't said anything so I must have done it right' or 'she hasn't said anything so she must be really disappointed'). Likewise our body language often speaks louder than our verbal messages. For example, a roll of the eyes may communicate far more information than the verbal message that follows it.

To enhance self-efficacy and therefore motivation, we should aim to give predominantly positive feedback (Weinberg and Gould, 2007; Weiss and Ferrer-Caja, 2002). Fox et al. (2000) found that greater levels of exercise class adherence were associated with leadership styles where the instructor gave reinforcement for positive behaviours, focused on positive comments during instruction, rewarded effort and gave encouragement.

However, there will inevitably be some instances when feedback needs to convey a potentially difficult message, for example where someone is doing something incorrectly. The way in which this feedback is delivered can have differing effects on an individual's self-efficacy. Ideally we need to deliver the message in a way that it is received and understood, but without decreasing self-efficacy and thus motivation. First, it is important that negative feedback is constructive and that it is targeted at the behaviour and not the individual (Cabral and Crisfield, 2000). Second, the impact of negative feedback on self-efficacy can be lessened if it is accompanied by positive feedback. This method is often referred to as the 'sandwich technique' as it involves sandwiching a piece of negative feedback between two pieces of positive feedback (Wrisberg, 2007). Box 10.1 gives two examples of how the same corrective feedback could be delivered. The first example could be interpreted as a criticism, whilst the second example is more likely to be interpreted positively.

A discussion of leader behaviour would not be complete without a brief mention of leadership styles and how they might impact on motivation. There are broadly two extremes of leadership style: an autocratic style in which the leader stresses their authority and makes decisions on their own, and a democratic style in which the leader consults team members when making decisions (Weinberg and Gould, 2007). Cox (2002) suggests that a controlling or autocratic style can decrease an individual's intrinsic motivation by removing their perception of being in control. This would suggest the efficacy of a more democratic style of leadership in enhancing motivation. The extract below, which is an adaptation of a famous poem called 'Children live what they learn', by Dorothy Law Nolte, also indicates how other aspects of leadership style may impact on the individual.

> If an athlete is coached with criticism, she learns to condemn;
> If an athlete is coached with hostility, he learns to fight;
> If an athlete is coached with ridicule, she learns to hate;
> If an athlete is coached with shame, he learns to feel guilty;
> If an athlete is coached with tolerance, she learns to be patient;
> If an athlete is coached with encouragement, he learns to be confident;
> If an athlete is coached with praise, she learns to appreciate;
> If an athlete is coached with fairness, he learns justice;
> If an athlete is coached with consistency, she learns to trust;
> If an athlete is coached with respect, he learns to respect himself.
>
> (Martens, 2004: p. 145)

Moving on from this recognition of the importance of leadership style, Epstein developed a framework which identified six areas that a leader should take into consideration when developing a motivational climate (Treasure, 2001). This framework is known by the acronym 'TARGET', which stands for task, authority, recognition, grouping, evaluation and timing (Duda and Balaguer, 2007). Table 10.2 summarises these six areas and considers the strategies that can be put in place to modify each area. Whilst the components of the table refer to athletes and sport, they can equally be applied to exercise participants or members of staff in exercise or workplace settings.

caroline heaney

Table 10.2 Using 'TARGET' to create a motivational climate

TARGET Structure	Strategies
Task. What athletes are asked to learn and what tasks they are given to complete (e.g., training activities, structure of practice conditions).	Provide the athlete with a variety of moderately demanding tasks that emphasise individual challenge and active involvement. Assist athletes in goal setting. Create a developmentally appropriate training environment by individualising the demands of the tasks set.
Authority. The kind and frequency of participation in the decision-making process (e.g., athlete involvement in decisions concerning training, the setting and enforcing of rules).	Encourage participation by your athletes in the decision-making process. Develop opportunities for leadership roles. Get athletes to take responsibility for their own sport development by teaching self-management and self-monitoring skills.
Recognition. Procedures and practices used to motivate and recognise athletes for their progress and achievement (e.g., reasons for recognition, distribution of rewards, and opportunities for rewards).	Use private meetings between coach and athlete to focus on individual progress. Recognise individual progress, effort, and improvement. Ensure equal opportunities for rewards to all.
Grouping. How athletes are brought together or kept apart in training and competition (e.g., the way in-groups are created during practices).	Use flexible and mixed ability grouping arrangements. Provide multiple grouping arrangements (i.e., individuals, small group, and large group activities). Emphasise cooperative solutions to training problem set.
Evalution. Standards set for athletes' learning and performance and the procedures for monitoring and judging attainment of these standards.	Development evaluation criteria based on effort, improvement, persistence, and progress toward individual goals. Involve athletes in self-evaluation. Make evaluation meaningful. Be consistent.
Timing. Appropriateness of the time demands placed on learning and performance (e.g., pace of learning and development, management of time and training schedule).	Training programmes should recognise that athletes, even at the elite level, do not train, learn, or develop at the same rate. Provide sufficient time before moving on to the next stage in skill development. Spend equal time with all athletes. Assist athletes in establishing training and competition schedules.

Source: Reproduced from Duda and Treasure (2006), p. 73

THE ENVIRONMENT

The role of the environment in enhancing motivation is often underestimated. However, both the situational and interactional views of motivation suggest that the environment is important (Weinberg and Gould, 2007). The environment is a rather general term that can include a wide range of motivational influences external to the individual, such as the structure of a training session or management meeting, the competition season, the provision of external rewards or the physical environment. It can also include the factors that we are discussing under separate headings in this chapter (leader behaviour and the influence of others).

The following citation taken from Carron *et al.* (2003) illustrates how the environment can motivate our behaviour.

> George Orwell's classic novel '1984' describes a dark picture of a futuristic society in fear of the ever-present, watchful eye of Big Brother. Members of the party in 1984 were awakened with a whistle every morning at the same time. Three minutes after the sound of the whistle, a fitness instructor would appear on the telescreen. Party members did not think about having time for exercise; they did not consider if they had the confidence to complete the exercise; nor did they have intentions regarding frequency, duration, intensity, or type of physical activity. They simply did it. Why? Because their **environment** was structured so that each day they would do it. No questions, no options. And if they did attempt to miss the physical activity, they would be quickly chastised and bought back into behavioural conformity.
>
> (Carron *et al.*, 2003: p. 118)

Clearly, to use such methods to motivate our staff or customers would be a rather draconian infringement of human rights. However, whilst it is an extreme example, it does illustrate that we can manipulate the environment to encourage motivation. Environments with cues or prompts to encourage a specific behaviour, aesthetically pleasing surroundings, easily accessible facilities and limited real or perceived barriers are more likely to encourage motivation (Howley and Franks, 2003).

Environmental prompts or reminders are one strategy for adapting the environment to motivate people to perform a specific behaviour. Environmental prompts can take several different forms (e.g. a poster, text message or email message), and can be as simple as a sign on a wall. Blamey *et al.* (1995) investigated the effect of an environmental prompt on physical activity levels. They placed a sign which read 'stay healthy, save time, use the stairs' close to a set of stairs next to an escalator in Glasgow. It was found that the sign led to an increase in stair usage from 12% to 22% in males and 5% to 14% in females over a two-week period. Whilst such environmental prompts are beneficial, there is evidence to suggest that their effectiveness is only short term and that they are not so effective for changing complex behaviours (Carron *et al.*, 2003). In Chapter 19 the concept of 'organisational culture' is discussed, which has resonance with the above examples of the environment encouraging motivation.

Another way of creating a motivational climate is to encourage *cohesion* within your team. Cohesion can be defined as the tendency for a group to stick together and remain united (Carron *et al.*, 1998). It has been suggested that sport and fitness teams and groups who have high levels of cohesion have higher levels of motivation towards achieving their goals and higher levels of adherence (Carron *et al.*, 2003). The same is also true of workplace teams (Michalisin *et al.*, 2007).

Strategies that have been found to enhance cohesion in sport and fitness settings include the setting of team goals, using team uniforms to give feelings of distinctiveness, encouraging communication between group members (e.g. by having individuals in close proximity), keeping group membership consistent, avoiding overly large groups, giving groups names, team-building activities, and holding regular meetings (Carron *et al.*, 1999; Cox, 2002; Carron *et al.*, 2003; Hodge, 2004; Weinberg and Gould, 2007).

THE INFLUENCE OF OTHERS

As well as recognising the influence of their own behaviour on others, leaders should also recognise the influence of other people on the motivation of their team members. These other people can include colleagues, parents/carers, peers, friends, siblings and other leaders.

Carron *et al.* (1999) refer to these influences as *social influences*. Social influence can be described as 'an individual's perceptions of comfort/discomfort, assistance, information, approval/disapproval, and/or pressure from formal or informal contacts with individuals, groups or collective others' (Carron *et al.*, 1999: p. 3). In short it can be said that our attitudes, opinions and behaviours are strongly affected by others, whether consciously or unconsciously.

The influence of other group members has been found to be significant. For example, in exercise settings it has been found that exercising in a group often leads to greater adherence than exercising alone (Carron et al., 1999). This relates in part to the aspects of team cohesion discussed in the previous section, but also to factors such as the effect of an audience on our behaviour and motivation. Similarly, Ntoumanis and Vazou (2005) suggest that achievement motivation may be influenced by the peer group in youth sport.

Family and significant others (e.g. partner, friends, parents/carers) are also highly influential. Several studies have found that people who receive support and encouragement from family members and significant others have higher levels of exercise adherence than those who don't, and are more confident about their abilities (Howley and Franks, 2003; King and Castro, 2006). It has been suggested that parents influence children's participation in sport and exercise through role modelling, social influence and social support (Taylor and Wilson, 2005). Therefore, if you are trying to motivate people to participate in sport or exercise, you should encourage them to exercise with a friend or family member, or try to educate the family and friends about the benefits of exercise (King et al., 2006).

The theory of planned behaviour (Ajzen, 1991) recognises the importance of social influence by identifying 'subjective norm' as one of the predictors of intention and behaviour; both concepts that are strongly related to motivation. Subjective norm can be defined as 'the perceived social pressure to perform or not perform the behaviour' (Ajzen, 1991: p. 188) and is the product of the perceived expectation of significant others and the individual's motivation to comply with these expectations (Carron et al., 2003).

CONCLUSION

It is important to recognise that motivation towards a particular task, role or activity can be influenced by a multitude of factors. Successful motivators are therefore those who recognise this and seek to develop a motivational climate by addressing a wide range of influences. Whilst this chapter has focused primarily on external factors influencing motivation, the importance of internal factors should not be forgotten. The intrinsic motivation of the individual can be influenced by some of the external factors discussed in this chapter, but it should also be remembered that the intrinsic motivation of the individual can influence the effectiveness of these external factors.

For example, a highly intrinsically motivated individual will thrive even in a low motivation environment. In contrast an individual with low intrinsic motivation will not.

REFERENCES

Ajzen, I. (1991) The theory of planned behavior. *Organizational Behavior and Human Decision Processes*, 50: 179–211.

Bandura, A. (1977) Self-efficacy: toward a unifying theory of behavioral change. *Psychological Review*, 84(2): 191–215.

Blamey, A., Mutrie, N. and Aitchison, T. (1995) Health promotion by encouraged use of stairs. *British Medical Journal*, 311: 289–290.

Cabral, P. and Crisfield, P. (2000) *Motivation and Mental Toughness*. Leeds: National Coaching Foundation.

Carron, A.V., Brawley, L.R. and Widmeyer, W.N. (1998) The measurement of cohesiveness in sport groups. In Duda, J.L. (ed.), *Advances in Sport and Exercise Psychology Measurement* (pp. 213–226). Morgantown: Fitness Information Technology.

Carron, A.V., Hausenblas, H.A. and Estabrooks, P.A. (1999) Social influence and exercise involvement. In Bull, S. (ed.), *Adherence Issues in Sport and Exercise* (pp. 1–17). Chichester: Wiley.

Carron, A.V., Hausenblas, H.A. and Estabrooks, P.A. (2003) *The Psychology of Physical Activity*. London: McGraw-Hill.

Cox, R.H. (2002) *Sport Psychology – Concepts & Applications*. 5th edition. London: McGraw-Hill.

Duda, J.L. and Balaguer, I. (2007) Coach-created motivational climate. In Jowett, S. and Lavallee, D. (eds), *Social Psychology in Sport* (pp. 117–130). Leeds: Human Kinetics.

Duda, J.L. and Treasure, D.C. (2006) Motivational processes and the facilitation of performance, persistence, and well-being in sport. In Williams, J.M. (ed.), *Applied Sport Psychology* (pp. 57–81). London: McGraw-Hill.

Fox, L.D., Rejeski, W.J. and Gauvin, L. (2000) Effects of leadership style and group dynamics on enjoyment of physical activity. *American Journal of Health Promotion*, 14: 277–283.

Hodge, K. (2004) *Sport Motivation*. London: A&C Black.

Howley, E.T. and Franks, B.D. (2003) *Health Fitness Instructor's Handbook*. 4th edition. Leeds: Human Kinetics.

King, A.C. and Castro, C. (2006) Factors associated with regular physical activity participation. In *American College of Sports Medicine, ACSM's Resource*

Manual for Guidelines for Exercise Testing and Prescription (pp. 565–571). 5th edition. London: Lippincott, Williams & Wilkins.

King, A.C., Martin, J.E. and Castro, C. (2006) Behavioral strategies to enhance physical activity participation. In *American College of Sports Medicine, ACSM's Resource Manual for Guidelines for Exercise Testing and Prescription* (pp. 572–580). 5th edition. London: Lippincott, Williams & Wilkins.

Martens, R. (2004) *Successful Coaching*. 3rd edition. Leeds: Human Kinetics.

Michalisin, M.D., Karau, S.J. and Tangpong, C. (2007) Leadership's activation of team cohesion as a strategic asset: An empirical simulation. *Journal of Business Strategies*, 24: 1–26.

Ntoumanis, N. and Vazou, S. (2005) Peer motivational climate in youth sport: Measurement development and validation. *Journal of Sport & Exercise Psychology*, 27: 432–455.

Peterson, S.L. (1993) Qualities to look for in an exercise leader. *Fitness Management*, 52: 32–33.

Taylor, J. and Wilson, G. (2005) *Applying Sport Psychology – Four Perspectives*. Leeds: Human Kinetics.

Thompson, N. (2002) *People Skills*. 2nd edition. Basingstoke: Palgrave Macmillan.

Treasure, D.C. (2001) Enhancing young people's motivation in youth sport: An achievement goal perspective. In Roberts, G.C. (ed.), *Advances in Motivation in Sport and Exercise*. Leeds: Human Kinetics.

Weinberg, R.S. and Gould, D. (2007) *Foundations of Sport & Exercise Psychology*. 4th edition. Leeds: Human Kinetics.

Weiss, M.R. and Ferrer-Caja, E. (2002) Motivational orientations and sport behavior. In Horn, T. (ed.), *Advances in Sport Psychology* (pp. 101–183). Leeds: Human Kinetics.

Wrisberg, C.A. (2007) *Sport Skill Instruction for Coaches*. Leeds: Human Kinetics.

CHAPTER 11

OUTCOME, PERFORMANCE AND PROCESS GOALS[1]

Steve Bull

Let me introduce you to a simple framework used by athletes but about which I have had much positive feedback in my consulting. It is a goal focusing framework which distinguishes between *outcome, performance* and *process* goals. Outcome goals relate to beating the opposition. Performance goals refer to the numbers (in sport that is points, times or distances; in business it could be targets for turnover, sales, waste reduction, staff retention rates, etc.) required to achieve the outcome. Process goals are the controllable behaviours you need to engage in to deliver the performance goals. This could include tactics and strategy processes as well as attitude and thinking processes.

Table 11.1 Examples of outcome, performance and process goals from sport and business

Goal type	Sport (long jumper)	Business (junior sales executive)
Outcome goal *The WHY*	Win Gold Medal at the National Championships	Win National Sales Award
Performance goal *The WHAT*	Jump 8.25 m in the Finals	Improve my sales by 8% from last year
Process goals *The HOW*	Drive with arms in run-up High knee lift Reach long in jump	Get to sales meetings 10 minutes earlier to allow more time to prepare Ask more questions in the first 5 minutes of the meetings Maintain more eye contact during client conversations

[1] Edited extract from Bull, S. (2006) *The Game Plan: Your Guide to Mental Toughness at Work*, Chapter 4 pp. 54–61, Chichester: Capstone Publishing/Wiley.

I have used this simple framework successfully with business leaders who are putting annual business plans together and the principles within the structure can easily apply to organisational goal setting. However, for the purposes of this chapter, I shall focus on the individual. The example of an elite long jumper illustrates how the system works. First, we identify the *outcome* goal which in this case is to win the Gold Medal at the National Championships. This is an incredibly challenging goal and although realistic it does not tell us 'what' we need to do to achieve that dream goal. So, we do some analysis and figure out that a jump of 8.25 metres will be enough to beat the rest. We now have a *performance* goal which we have figured out by examining previous results, current form of the opposition and our own capabilities. Focusing on 8.25 metres immediately becomes a more specific target – and a more controllable one. However, we need to go one stage further. 'How' are we going to jump 8.25 metres? Working with our coach we now focus on three 'processes' which are entirely within our personal control and which, if executed correctly, will give us the best possible chance of landing the 8.25 metre jump. When getting ready to perform in the 'critical moment' where should our focus be? Not on winning the Gold Medal (despite it being the reason for us being there!). Nor on the actual 8.25 metres. We should be focused on our *process* goals – that is, the three controllable processes that we know will impact on our performance. These processes give us confidence and help us to avoid getting carried away with the intensity and pressure of the moment. It's sort of like 'going back to basics'. Get the basic performance processes right and the outcome will look after itself.

> I tried not to think about the outcome and to concentrate on the performance.
>
> Nicola Benedetti, 16-year-old violinist,
after winning the BBC's Young Musician of the year

So for our junior sales executive who is desperate to win the national sales award (and secure the fantastic holiday which is on offer as an incentive!), he or she needs to do the analysis and figure out exactly what kind of numbers will need to be delivered to win the award – above and beyond the annual improvement target which will be imposed by the company anyway. Getting together with their boss or the National Sales Manager might be necessary to ascertain exactly what an appropriate extra target might be. In the example cited it is 8%. Then it is a case of identifying the controllable processes which need to be focused on during the critical performance moments – that is, during sales meetings with customers. And it is those processes that should be focused on when the

Table 11.2 The breakdown of outcome and performance goals to process goals

Goal type	HR middle manager	Retail store manager
Outcome goal *The WHY*	Get appointed to the senior manager position which is coming up in November	Win Regional Store of the month award
Performance goal *The WHAT*	Improve my client evaluations by an average of 0.5 points	Increase 'like for like' sales by 4% Reduce waste by 11%
Process goals *The HOW*	Respond to requests for information much quicker Spend 5 minutes extra preparing for client meetings Create a Confidence Peaks Chart and read it once per week for the next 3 months updating it as appropriate	Implement an extra 1–1 meeting with each of my top team members Do an extra store walk per day and engage more with staff when doing so Devote two quality half-days to coaching the warehouse team on the 3 new initiatives agreed last week

performance is taking place. As indicated in the Table 11.2 this individual needs to focus on arriving at sales meetings 10 minutes earlier than usual so as to be better prepared, asking more questions in the first five minutes and maintaining more eye contact during conversations.

To broaden your thinking, Table 11.2 presents two further examples. These are merely presented to encourage you to always seek to work towards having real clarity around the key 'processes' in your performance – whether it be an individual, team or organisational performance. When perform-ing in critical moments this is where your attention has to be – on the processes.

When marathon record holder, Paula Radcliffe, was asked once about how she stays mentally tough her reply was related to having a 'process focus' although like many athletes she uses a little mind game to keep her attention in the here and now.

> I count … I count to 100 three times – that's a mile. That's how I count the miles off. I think about the minute I'm in now rather than what's left to come.
> Paula Radcliffe, after winning the 2003 London Marathon in world record time

ENGLAND'S ASHES 2005 GOALS APPROACH

In his book, *Ashes Regained: The Coach's Story*, Duncan Fletcher outlines the approach to goal focusing which I had introduced to him prior to a previous tour of the West Indies and which provides an illustration of the *outcome, performance, process* structure as it related to the Ashes victory of 2005.

> We always determine our goals by the use of a definitive structure, a series of building blocks divided into three main processes: the why, the what and the how ... the why is the outcome goal ... the what is the performance goals in four disciplines: batting, bowling, fielding and the mental aspect of the game. Thus with batting, it was our goal to make at least 400 in the first innings of each Test in no more than 130 overs (we did that three times against Australia – they did not do it once) ... The how is obviously the actual procedure; the physical actions which need to take place for all this to come together. We emphasise key words such as concentration, communication and confidence in respect of this, but a common thread is to ensure that we replicate match conditions as closely as we can in practice. It is important to realise that each individual then has to undergo the same process, using the same structure (the why, the what and the how) in order to determine their own personal goals. That is entirely self-motivated. Each player is then given a sheet on which they lay out their own goals. They then hand that back to me before the First Test of the summer.
>
> Duncan Fletcher, Coach of the 2005 Ashes winning
> England Cricket Team

Figure 11.1 presents a blank version of the type of Goal Chart to which I introduced Duncan Fletcher.

In Figure 11.1, you'll see that there are three boxes for the performance goals. This is not unusual as it is commonplace for people to focus on more than one area of the performance as being important in contributing to the outcome. As Fletcher himself pointed out, the England cricket team had four – one each for batting, bowling, fielding and the mental game. Likewise there are multiple boxes for the process goals. You'll need to adapt this chart to meet your own personal circumstances by merely choosing how many boxes you think you need at each of the three levels. As I keep pointing out, ultimately, what you're looking

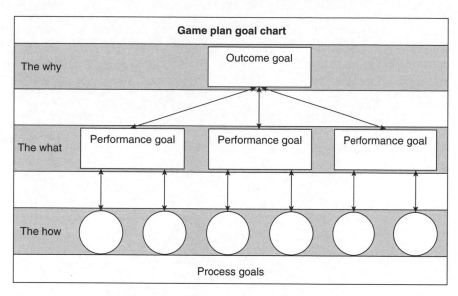

Figure 11.1 Game plan goal chart

for is something that will assist you in focusing on the processes involved in yours or others' performance.

REFERENCES

Benedetti, Nicola (2004) *The Daily Telegraph*, 4.5.04.
Fletcher, Duncan (2005) *Ashes Regained: The Coach's Story*. London: Simon & Schuster.
Radcliffe, Paula (2003) BBC TV, 13.4.03.

SECTION 3

COMMUNICATING EFFECTIVELY

INTRODUCTION

Effective communication is a vital component of working successfully in the field of sport and fitness. Those working in sport and fitness need to be able to communicate effectively with colleagues and customers alike, but what is it that makes communication effective? This section seeks to address this question by examining the components of, and influences upon, effective communication. It begins by addressing some of the core components of successful interpersonal communication before examining the more specific issues of ethics, group communication and diversity.

Chapter 12, which is written by Caroline Heaney of the Open University, addresses two of the most important aspects of effective communication for those working in sport and fitness: active listening and effective questioning. As well as describing and analysing these important strategies, the chapter considers how sport and fitness professionals can demonstrate these skills in practice.

Chapter 13 is also written by Caroline Heaney of the Open University. It examines some of the ethical considerations of working in the sport and fitness industry. This topic is not necessarily what you would expect to see in a section on effective communication. However, as you will begin to appreciate when you read the chapter, ethical issues impact significantly on our communications with others.

Chapter 14 by David Yukelson of Pennsylvania State University examines group communication. David is a renowned sport psychologist and professor of sport and exercise science, with a special interest in group cohesion and team building. Whilst the focus of the chapter is on team communication within a competitive sport environment, the concepts and principles discussed can easily be applied to team communication within many other environments, such as between colleagues in the workplace and exercise class participants.

Chapter 15, *Valuing Diversity*, is written by Neil Thompson. Neil is a director of Avenue Consulting and has authored many books dealing with a range of social issues. The chapter considers several aspects of diversity including class, race, gender, disability and age. It is important to consider diversity in relation to communication as it can impact on our interactions with others. Awareness of issues of diversity can help us to take more of an equal opportunity approach to our professional interactions with others.

CHAPTER 12

ACTIVE LISTENING AND EFFECTIVE QUESTIONING IN SPORT AND FITNESS

Caroline Heaney

For those working in sport and fitness, effective communication skills are an essential part of their repertoire. For communication to be effective it requires that both parties in the communication process understand each other and feel understood (Yukelson, 2006). This can be facilitated through two important components of effective communication: active listening and effective questioning.

Active listening suggests that listening is not a one-way passive experience: there are actually quite a lot of active characteristics that those listening can contribute in order to make the speaker feel listened to. Effective questioning allows those involved in sport and fitness to elicit information that will allow them to develop a more sophisticated awareness of others' perspectives. This chapter will examine the strategies of active listening and effective questioning and consider how they can be used to enhance interpersonal communication, drawing on practical work-based examples wherever possible.

ACTIVE LISTENING

Active listening can be defined as 'a process whereby listeners make deliberate responses to the speaker to communicate clearly that they are attending to what the speaker is saying' (Gavin, 2005: p. 100). This is often referred to as listening with a purpose. The aim of active listening is to make the speaker feel listened to and understood. This is important in sport and fitness where, for example, a client or athlete may fail to divulge important information to an instructor or coach who they perceive to be not listening properly. Failure to divulge such information may impact on the quality of service that can be provided by the coach or instructor.

A primary goal of the sport or fitness professional, then, is to demonstrate to the speaker that they are actively listening. How is this achieved? Perhaps you can begin to answer this question by considering your own experiences as a speaker in interpersonal communication. What is it that makes you feel listened to? Conversely, what might a listener do that would make you feel that you are not being listened to? The following scenario may help you to answer these questions.

Imagine you have recently joined a gym and are undergoing a one-to-one consultation with a fitness instructor. The fitness instructor has asked you to describe your previous experiences of exercise. In response to this you deliver a fairly detailed account of your previous experiences. Consider how you would feel if the instructor (listener) responded in the following ways whilst you were speaking.

1   He or she looked out of the window the entire time you were speaking.
2   He or she made regular eye contact with you and nodded in appropriate places.
3   He or she made no comment at all when you finished speaking and moved on to a different topic.
4   He or she summarised the main points when you finished speaking before moving onto a different topic.

In response 1, the instructor looking out of the window and not making any eye contact with you could signal a lack of interest and make it unlikely that you would feel attention was being paid to you. Response 2, where regular eye contact is accompanied by appropriate nodding, is much more likely to make you feel listened to. Similarly, in responses 3 and 4, an instructor who makes no acknowledgement of what has just been said (response 3) is less likely to reassure you that your points have been noted than one who effectively summarises what you have said (response 4). An active listener, then, needs to emulate the type of behaviour seen in responses 2 and 4 in order to indicate to the speaker that they are listening. Two key active listening techniques are the use of 'minimal encouragers' and reflective statements.

Minimal encouragers

Minimal encouragers are described by Young (2001: p. 85) as 'brief supportive statements that convey attention and understanding'. They can be both verbal and non-verbal. Verbal minimal encouragers include the use of words, statements or noises such as 'Mmm-hmm', 'uh-huh', 'okay', 'yes' or 'I see what you mean'. Non-verbal minimal encouragers include nodding and various facial expressions such as smiling. These minimal encouragers provide support to the speaker without interrupting the flow of their conversation.

Gavin (2005) suggests that, in order to be effective, minimal encouragers should be used with awareness and in synchrony with the information being delivered by the speaker. He suggests that the too frequent or untimely use of minimal encouragers can convey an impression of boredom or impatience to the listener – the opposite of what active listening seeks to express.

Reflective statements

The instructor in response 4 above used reflective statements – summarising or reflecting back to the speaker the key points of what they said (Whiteley et al., 2006). This not only ensures that the speaker feels listened to, but also reassures them that they have been accurately understood. Reflective statements can reflect the direct content of the message or the underlying emotional content of the message. Gavin (2005) refers to these types of statements as reflection of content and reflection of feeling, respectively. Both types can be useful to a sport or fitness professional. Box 12.1 gives examples of how they might be used.

BOX 12.1: THE DIFFERENCE BETWEEN REFLECTION OF CONTENT AND REFLECTION OF FEELING

EXAMPLE 1: REFLECTION OF CONTENT

CLIENT: 'I've tried everything – swimming, Pilates, gym, running, spinning classes, but it's always the same. I start off really keen for a couple of months and go all the time, but gradually as time goes on I get less and less keen and eventually I stop going. I make every excuse under the sun not to go'.

INSTRUCTOR: 'So you've tried several different types of exercise before, but whilst you always start off keen, your enthusiasm drops off after a couple of months'.

115

Reflective statements can be thought of as a collective term for a wide range of techniques, including paraphrasing, re-stating and summarising. Whilst these share a common theme of reflecting back the speaker's message they vary slightly in technique.

Paraphrasing involves rephrasing in your own words what you perceive to be the core message of someone's communication. It allows you to check your understanding of what you have heard and to communicate to the listener that you have understood them. Paraphrasing can also help to feed back the message in a clearer form. Ivey and Ivey (2003) suggest that ideally a paraphrase should comprise four elements:

1   Sentence Stem: The paraphrase should begin with a lead-in such as 'It seems that what you're saying is …'
2   Key Words: The paraphrase should include some key words used by the speaker.
3   Expressing Content: The paraphrase should summarise the content of what has been said.
4   Verification: The listener should check that their paraphrase is accurate by using questions such as 'Is that correct?'

Re-stating involves repeating back significant words or phrases that the speaker has used. Repetition of these significant elements can encourage further discussion, as indicated in the example below.

■   ATHLETE: 'I feel so pressured'
■   COACH: 'Pressured?' (restating)
■   ATHLETE: 'Yes, I feel like I have to do well in this competition …'

Summarising is a form of paraphrasing that aims to bring together the different features or issues of a session in a brief and succinct fashion. It is essentially an overview or review of the core points and feelings presented. It can be useful to begin or end a session, clarify content or feeling, emphasise understanding, move the discussion on, or help prioritise and focus. An instructor may conclude a one-to-one consultation with a summary such as the one below.

> 'From what you have told me today it seems that on the one hand you feel that you are making good progress on some of your goals, but you still feel that you are not making enough progress on your weight loss goal and that is making you lose heart. However, you feel confident that if you cut back on your mid-morning snacks you will start to see a bit more progress, which will re-motivate you. Is that an accurate summary?'

Whilst active listening, facilitated through the use of techniques such as minimal encouragers and reflective statements, is an important skill for sport and fitness professionals, its effectiveness can be boosted by teaming it with effective questioning. For example, our reflective statements can include questions to encourage further discussion of important points. Next we consider what constitutes effective questioning.

EFFECTIVE QUESTIONING

In order to provide an effective sport or fitness service it is often necessary to elicit specific important information from clients and athletes. For example, a fitness instructor or coach needs to know the medical background, goals and expectations of those they instruct. Asking questions is a tool in gaining this information. Asking questions may seem a simple task, though in practice it requires considerable skill. The way in which questions are asked can have a significant impact on the type and level of information given, whilst the excessive use of questions can cause people to be defensive and therefore hinder the development of rapport between professional and customer (Gavin, 2005).

Questions can be used for several purposes within sport and fitness professions. Gavin (2005) states that the most common reasons are:

1   To initiate interviews and find out relevant information about a client's background and previous experiences.
2   To encourage communication.

3   To assess client issues.
4   To clarify meaning.
5   To express interest.
6   To discover deeper meaning.
7   To create focus within a discussion.
8   To guide discussions back onto the appropriate topic.

Questions can also be used to help an individual to understand their own situation and develop their decision-making skills (Wrisberg, 2007). For example, questions such as 'what are your options in this situation?' or 'why did you respond in this way?' may help an athlete to develop strategies for dealing with different situations that may arise within their sport. The types of question used in a professional context fit broadly into the categories of closed and open questions.

Closed questions

Closed questions are those which require only a single-word or short-phrase answer, such as 'yes' or 'no'. Examples include: 'how old are you?', 'do you have high blood pressure?' and 'on a scale of 1–10 how difficult did you find that exercise?' These types of question can be useful, for example, to obtain facts or verify information, but may not be suitable in other contexts due to the limited amount of information they yield.

Open questions

Open questions require a more detailed answer than closed questions. They tend to start with words such as 'what', 'where', and 'how'. Open questions are useful for generating discussion, eliciting more detailed information and encouraging the other person to speak. They are also far less rigid than closed questions and provide opportunities for people to explore thoughts and feelings. As open questions can generate a large volume of information, they are often followed by reflective statements to summarise the content.

Below are some examples of open questions:

■   'How did that make you feel...?'
■   'Can you give me an example?'
■   'If you were put in that situation again, how would you respond?'

caroline heaney

The final question above is an example of a hypothetical question. This type of question can be useful in sport and fitness settings to encourage clients to explore their thoughts, feelings and behaviours and to develop strategies.

Some professionals feel that 'why' questions should be avoided as they can be interpreted as interrogative and judgemental (Weinberg and Gould, 2007), though in practice this would probably depend on the context. Nevertheless, it does highlight the potential for questioning to be perceived as interrogative. In light of this, Gavin (2005) advocates the use of indirect questioning to break the pattern of serial questioning. Indirect questions are statements rather than questions, but yet they do invite a response, for example, 'I'd be interested to hear how you responded to this situation'.

Questions to avoid

Whilst effective questioning can help to facilitate working relationships in sport and fitness, ineffective questioning can have the opposite effect. Below is a list of some of the questioning practices that should be avoided.

- Leading questions: Those that are worded in such a way that they aim to influence the response, such as 'you prefer cycling to running, don't you?'
- Multiple questions: Those that include more than one question, such as 'So how long have you been playing rugby, what are your goals and what might stop you from achieving your goals?'. These are confusing and may only elicit a response to one question.
- Too many questions: Questions should ideally be kept to a minimum and only used when necessary. A barrage of successive questions can make people defensive.

As well as avoiding the questioning practices above, the guidelines in Box 12.2 will help to ensure that you ask effective questions.

CONCLUSION

Effective interpersonal communication skills are essential for any sport or fitness professional to master. In this chapter we have investigated two key aspects of successful communication: active listening and effective questioning. Only when we are listening with full attention and purpose, and asking the right questions at the appropriate time, are we able to fully understand and deliver to those we work with.

REFERENCES

Gavin, J. (2005) *Lifestyle Fitness Coaching*. Leeds: Human Kinetics.

Ivey, A.E. and Ivey, M.B (2003). *Intentional Interviewing and Counseling*. 5th edition. Pacific Grove, California: Brooks/Cole.

Weinberg, R.S. and Gould, D. (2007) *Foundations of Sport and Exercise Psychology*. 4th edition. Leeds: Human Kinetics.

Whiteley, J.A., Lewis, B., Napolitano, M.A. and Marcus, B.H. (2006) Health counseling skills. In L.A. Kaminsky (ed.), *ACSM's Resource Manual for Guidelines for Exercise Testing and Prescription*. 5th edition (pp. 588–587). London: Lippincott, Williams & Wilkins.

Wrisberg, C.A. (2007) *Sport Skill Instruction for Coaches*. Leeds: Human Kinetics.

Young, M.E. (2001) *Learning the Art of Helping: Building Blocks and Techniques*. Upper Saddle River, New Jersey: Prentice Hall.

Yukelson, D.P. (2006) Communicating effectively. In J.M. Williams (ed.), *Applied Sport Psychology: Personal Growth to Peak Performance*. 5th edition (pp. 174–191). New York: McGraw-Hill.

CHAPTER 13

ETHICAL AND PROFESSIONAL ISSUES IN SPORT AND EXERCISE

Caroline Heaney

> All good people who have power over others, even just a little power, and even just for a little while, need access to an ethic that can guide their use of that power
>
> (Thompson, 1983, cited in Makarowski, 1999: p. 36)

Working in the sport and fitness industry, and the close contact with members of the public that brings, leaves the potential for ethical and professional challenges. In this chapter we shall discuss ethical and professional principles, boundaries and guidelines as they relate to sport and fitness professionals.

We begin by defining professional ethics. Loubert (1999) defines ethics as 'the study of rules, standards and principles that dictate right conduct among members of a society. Such rules, standards and principles are based on moral values which serve as a basis for what is considered right' (p. 162). An ethical issue would thus involve a situation that could potentially fall foul of these moral values. Ethics are based on what a society deems as acceptable and provide guidance on what is appropriate behaviour (see box 13.1).

Professions, such as those in the field of sport and fitness, are associated with specific characteristics that set them apart from other workers. One of these professional characteristics is a commitment to high standards of ethical behaviour. Various professional codes exist to govern professional ethics. For example, the Register of Exercise Professionals (REPs) states that their register 'encourages a properly qualified base of exercise professionals who demonstrate commitment to the industry Code of Ethical Practice' (REPs, 2008a). Sports coaches will be governed by the code of conduct and/or ethics of their governing body. Other professionals within sport and exercise will be governed by the code of any relevant professional body of which they are a member, for example the British Association of Sport and Exercises Sciences.

The kinds of areas covered by a Code of Ethics/Conduct are shown in the example Box 13.2 below. This example is a Code of Code of Conduct for Sports Coaches from Sports Coach UK. In essence professional ethics seek to prevent professionals from doing things that will harm the client or society (Ivey *et al.*, 1997). They are naturally often associated with upholding the law.

BOX 13.2: THE SPORTS COACH UK CODE OF CONDUCT FOR SPORTS COACHES

The Sports Coach UK Code of Conduct identifies four key principles inherent in good coaching practice. These four principles are mirrored in the Codes of Ethics/Conduct of many sports governing bodies and the Register of Exercise Professionals Code of Ethical Practice (REPs, 2008b).

1   *Rights*
    Coaches must respect and champion the rights of every individual to participate in sport.
2   *Relationships*
    Coaches must develop a relationship with athletes (and others) based on openness, honesty, mutual trust and respect.
3   *Responsibilities – personal standards*
    Coaches must demonstrate proper personal behaviour and conduct at all times.

Sport and fitness professionals should work within any relevant professional
codes of conduct and/or ethics in order to minimise the potential harm that
non-ethical behaviour could bring.

In addition to professional ethics, our personal values also impact upon our
professional work. Our personal values (attitudes and beliefs) are shaped by our
experiences and upbringing (Gavin, 2005). These, coupled with guidelines on
professional ethics, will influence the decisions we make in specific situations.

Meara *et al*. (1996) identified six moral principles that should form the foundations of ethical professional behaviour. These principles and their application to
sport and exercise professionals are summarised in Table 13.1.

Table 13.1 Principles of ethical professional behaviour in sport and exercise

Principle	Application
Autonomy	Sport and exercise professionals should encourage independence rather than dependency amongst their clients.
Non-maleficence	Sport and exercise professionals should not harm their clients and should identify and avoid possible risks.
Beneficence	The actions of the sport and exercise professional should be of benefit to the client. If the professional cannot provide benefit to the client they should refer them to another person.
Justice	Sport and exercise professionals should strive to provide equal treatment and opportunities to all of their clients.
Fidelity	Sport and exercise professionals should honour the commitments they make to their clients and be trustworthy.
Veracity	Sport and exercise professionals should always be truthful and fully inform their clients.

Source: Adapted from Gavin (2005), p. 68

POTENTIAL ETHICAL ISSUES IN SPORT AND FITNESS PROFESSIONS

According to Loubert (1999) there are four primary categories of potential ethical situation that can arise: exploitation, breach of confidentiality, conflict of interest, and dependency. We will examine each of these in turn in relation to sport and fitness.

1. Exploitation

Exploitation refers to the intentional use of another person or group to achieve some selfish objective (Loubert, 1999). Clients or athletes could potentially become vulnerable to exploitation for money, sex or goods by an unscrupulous sport or exercise professional. Clearly such a scenario would be unethical and often in breach of the law. The professional penalties for such a situation would be severe.

Ethical issues involving exploitation are a risk in interpersonal relationships where there is a power differential (Lyle, 2002). Those in positions of power, such as coaches or instructors, have the capacity to abuse that power, thus making their clients or athletes vulnerable. Children are a particularly vulnerable group and there have been documented cases of child sexual abuse by coaches in recent years (Brackenridge, 1997, 2001; Burke, 2001; Lyle, 2002). In light of this the Child Protection in Sport Unit (CPSU), a partnership between the National Society for the Prevention of Cruelty to Children (NSPCC), Sport England, Sport Scotland, the Sports Council for Northern Ireland and the Sports Council for Wales was set up in 2001 to coordinate and support sports organisations' implementation of the 2000 National Action Plan for Child Protection in Sport (CPSU, 2008).

2. Breach of confidentiality

Confidentiality is the cornerstone of ethical principles. Sport and fitness pro-fessionals often engage in communication of a personal nature with clients. Professionals have a duty of care to maintain the confidentiality of such personal information for both ethical and legal reasons (e.g. Data Protection Act). A potential ethical situation occurs when this confidentiality is breached. Legitimate breaches of confidentiality might include sharing information about a client with a colleague who will also be working with the client. Whilst this is completely acceptable, it is important that the client is informed who the information will be shared with and why. If the client is made aware of this from the start (before disclosing personal information) then there has been no ethical breach.

Confidentiality issues become more complicated in a situation where a client divulges information that you may not feel comfortable keeping confidential. For example, an athlete may divulge to you in confidence that they are using performance-enhancing drugs. You are then faced with the question of whether to maintain the athlete's confidentiality or report them. In the thick of such a situation, the answer to this question may not be as clear cut as it seems. As a guide, Loubert (1999) suggests that there are three instances in which it is acceptable to breach confidentiality:

- When there is clear and imminent danger to the client.
- When there is clear and imminent danger to other persons.
- When legal requirements demand that confidential information is released.

Makarowski (1999) suggests that the clients or athletes that you work with should be informed that the information they give you will be kept confidential unless there is a risk of harm to them or others, or if there is a legal issue, assuming that this is your organisational policy.

3. Conflict of interest

Ethical issues often occur when an individual is performing multiple roles. A coach for instance might also be a sports therapist or parent, roles which may have conflicting requirements. Consider a situation where a sports therapist has diagnosed an injury in a footballer that could be aggravated by participating in a game. As a sports therapist the individual would prevent the footballer from playing. However, if the individual is also the coach of the team and the footballer is the team's star player, the individual may want the footballer to play. The two roles create conflicting objectives and thus an ethical conflict or dilemma for the individual to address.

4. Dependency

Sport and exercise professionals often act in 'helping' roles. When acting in such roles it is possible for clients to become dependent on the professional.

The occurrence of dependency is not in itself an ethical issue. However, failure of the professional to take action to deal with the dependency would be (Loubert, 1999). High levels of dependency can also make individuals vulnerable to exploitation (Burke, 2001). Therefore, sport and exercise professionals should aim to nurture and develop independent individuals capable of making their own decisions and resilient to exploitation (Burke, 2001).

In addition to these four categories of potential ethical dilemma, there are many other potential ethical dilemmas which you may face in your day-to-day work. In the next section we will consider some situations that you should try to avoid due to the ethical issues involved.

ETHICAL SITUATIONS TO AVOID

Makarowski (1999) and Ray *et al.* (1999) recommend that from an ethical perspective, professionals should avoid situations where:

1   There is a conflict of interest.
2   Dependency may occur.
3   A lack of training or resources make the situation difficult to deal with.
4   We will feel uncomfortable.

We have already considered 1 and 2, so this section will focus on the remaining situations.

Lack of training

We should not work with people who have specific problems which we have not been trained to deal with; neither should we attempt specific skills which we have not been trained to use. For example, a fitness instructor should not provide sports massage unless they are qualified to do so. It would be unethical for the instructor to do this as they could potentially harm the client.

Lack of resources

If you do not have the necessary resources (e.g. time and energy) to provide a particular service to a client, then you should not volunteer to provide it. For example, an athlete may request a coach who can train them five times per week. It could be considered unethical for the coach to agree to coach this athlete knowing that they only have the time available to coach the athlete twice a week.

Lack of comfort

You should avoid committing to situations that you feel uncomfortable with. For example, you may feel uncomfortable working with a jockey who you are aware uses extreme weight loss practices. These extreme practices may go against your morals and ethics, and consequently you might feel uncomfortable being a part of the jockey's support team. If this were the case it would be unwise for you to become involved.

DEALING WITH AN ETHICAL DILEMMA

When faced with an ethical dilemma, Loubert (1999) suggests that we should follow the three-step process outlined below.

1   Identify the greatest variety of choices possible, including those which may seem extreme.
2   Investigate each of the possible choices identified.
3   Judge your choices from an 'other-centred' perspective rather than a 'self-centred' perspective. If possible discuss the situation with other people (e.g. a supervisor). However, ensure that you do not breach confidentiality whilst doing this.

This process allows us to think through the situation and make an informed decision about the ethical issue, rather than making a rash decision that we could later regret. Once we have made a decision about how to deal with an ethical dilemma, a final check should be evaluating the decision against the criteria listed below (Makarowski, 1999).

- Is my decision/action compatible with my goals, values and expectations?
- Does it feel right?
- Where does my decision/action ultimately lead?
- What is the track record of others when making a similar decision? What is my track record when making a similar decision?
- By doing this, what am I saying about myself?

Prevention

The best way of dealing with an ethical dilemma is to have systems in place that prevent it from happening. Various preventative measures can be put in place, but one that is particularly pertinent is the use of *informed consent*.

Informed consent is commonly used in sport and exercise. Informed consent can be verbal (e.g. before measuring a client's body fat percentage) or written (e.g. a signed pre-exercise test consent form). Informed consent involves fully informing the client about what will happen, ensuring they understand that information and gaining their consent before continuing.

An informed consent form can be useful in formally clarifying potentially ethically related information to your client. Information that could be included in an informed consent form includes information about your qualifications (e.g. what level of coach or instructor you are), the roles and responsibilities of you and the client, details about confidentiality (e.g. who will have access to information, clauses about when you will breach confidentiality), and a statement about freedom of consent (i.e. the client is free to give their consent or not).

PROFESSIONAL BOUNDARIES

An ethically competent professional is aware of professional boundaries and does not cross them. Professional boundaries relate to two main areas: competency and relationships.

In relation to competency, professional boundaries dictate that you should only carry work-related tasks in areas where you have been trained to do so. This is of particular importance in the sport and fitness industry where instructing physical activities in an incorrect way can potentially cause serious injury.

Sport and fitness professionals often develop close relationships with their clients or athletes. This is a normal progression and aids interpersonal communication and client satisfaction. However, it is important that professionals set boundaries on what is an acceptable close relationship with a client and what is unacceptable or unprofessional. For example, most organisations would consider it inappropriate for a professional to have a sexual relationship with a client. Difficult ethical dilemmas can occur when a sexual attraction develops between a professional and a client. The professional may have to make a decision about whether they should continue to work with the client or not. In relation to this issue the Sports Coach UK Code of Conduct for Sports Coaches states that 'coaches must avoid sexual intimacy with athletes either while coaching them or in the period of time immediately following the end of the coaching relationship' (Sports Coach UK, 1996). The code also recommends that a coach refers an athlete to another coach if it becomes clear that an intimate relationship is developing.

Professional boundaries are important in protecting both professionals and their clients. Failure to set such boundaries can lead us into difficult ethical situations.

CONCLUSION

Ethical issues are an important consideration for sport and fitness industry professionals. It is important that we work within an ethical code and within our professional boundaries. The following is a summary of guidelines to help you avoid difficult ethical situations.

- Study the relevant professional codes of ethics and conduct.
- Learn to recognise situations where ethical concerns may be present or appear to be present.
- Increase your sensitivity to situations where ethical concerns are present.
- Consult others whenever there are ethical questions, especially when the answers are not clear or not clearly defensible.
- Refer clients to other practitioners when their needs are beyond your professional boundaries, or if you become a primary party in an ethical dilemma.
- Document carefully and often.
- Follow your conscience.
- Fully disclose to clients/athletes all of your roles that might involve them directly or indirectly.
- In dealing with an ethical dilemma consider the possible courses of action carefully.

(Loubert, 1999)

REFERENCES

Brackenridge, C.H. (1997) 'He owned me basically…' Women's experience of sexual abuse in sport. *International Review for the Sociology of Sport*, 32(2): 115–130.

Brackenridge, C.H. (2001) *Spoilsports: Understanding and Preventing Sexual Exploitation in Sport*. London: Routledge.

Burke, M. (2001) Obeying until it hurts: Coach-athlete relationships. *Journal of the Philosophy of Sport*, 28: 227–240.

Child Protection in Sport Unit (2008) *About the CPSU* [online]. Available online: www.thecpsu.org.uk/Scripts/content/Default.asp?Page=AboutUs&MenuPos=Top&Menu=01&Sel=00 (accessed 13 May 2008).

Gavin, J. (2005) *Lifestyle Fitness Coaching*. Leeds: Human Kinetics.

Ivey, A.E., Ivey, M.B. and Simek-Morgan, L. (1997) *Counseling and Psychotherapy: A Multi-Cultural Perspective*. Boston: Allyn & Bacon.

Loubert, P.V. (1999) Ethical perspectives in counseling. In R. Ray and D.M. Wiese-Bjornstal (eds), *Counseling in Sports Medicine* (pp. 161–175). Leeds: Human Kinetics.

Lyle, J. (2002) *Sports Coaching Concepts – A Framework for Coaches' Behaviour*. London: Routledge.

Makarowski, L.M. (1999) Ethical and legal issues for sport professionals counseling injured athletes. In D. Pargman (ed.), *Psychological Bases of Sport Injuries* (pp. 29–47). Morgantown, West Virginia: Fitness Information Technology.

Meara, N.M., Schmidt, L.D. and Day, J.D. (1996) Principles and virtues: A foundation for ethical decisions, policies and character. *Counseling Psychologist*, 24(1): 4–77.

Ray, R., Terrell, T. and Hough, D. (1999) The role of the sports medicine professional in counseling athletes. In R. Ray and Wiese-Bjornstal, D.M. (eds.), *Counseling in Sports Medicine* (pp. 3–20). Leeds: Human Kinetics.

Register of Exercise Professionals (2008a) *About REPs* [online]. Available online: www.exerciseregister.org/custom/REPsAbout.htm (accessed 7 March 2008).

Register of Exercise Professionals (2008b) *The Register of Exercise Professionals of the United Kingdom Code of Ethical Practice*. London: Register of Exercise Professionals.

Sports Coach UK (1996) *Code of Conduct for Sports Coaches*. Leeds: Sports Coach UK.

CHAPTER 14

COMMUNICATION AND GROUPS[1]

David Yukelson

One of the most gratifying experiences a coach or athlete can have is to be a member of a team that gets along well and works together efficiently in a cohesive, harmonious, task-oriented manner (Orlick, 2000; Yukelson, 1984).

When individuals work together in groups, communication, coordination, and interaction are essential (Carron and Hausenblas, 1998). In fact, communication lies at the heart of group process. If a group is to function effectively, members must be able to communicate easily and efficiently with one another (Shaw, 1981). Communication directly affects group solidarity, collective efficacy, and team performance (Zaccaro *et al.*, 1995). Team building comes from a shared vision of what the group is striving to achieve and is tied to commitment, individual and mutual accountability, collaboration, communication, and teamwork. A shared vision that has meaning and purpose creates synergistic empowerment. Likewise, in successful teams, coaches and athletes talk openly and honestly about interpersonal and task-related issues that affect them directly, and everyone works together to develop a positive group atmosphere/team culture conducive for team success (Cannon-Bowers and Salas, 2001; Janssen, 1999; Katzenbach and Smith, 1993; Yukelson, 1997).

Unfortunately, not every group functions cohesively. Many interpersonal problems on teams stem from poor communication. Interpersonal conflict is often the result of misunderstanding or miscommunication of feelings. Henschen and Miner (1989) have identified five types of misunderstandings that often surface within groups: (1) a difference of opinion resolvable by common sense; (2) a clash of personalities in the group; (3) a conflict of task or social roles among group members; (4) a struggle for power between one or more individuals;

---

[1] Edited extract from Yukelson, D. (2006) 'Communicating effectively' in Williams, J.M., *Applied Sport Psychology* (5th edn), pp. 178–91, New York: McGraw-Hill.

and (5) a breakdown of communication between the leader and the group or among members of the group itself. Misunderstandings are also the result of inaccessibility to relevant information (not being privy to certain sources of information); inattentiveness (failing to listen, not paying attention, being distracted); lack of assertiveness (failure to speak up) or misperceiving someone's motives, intentions, or behaviour (inference mind reading). Similarly, people are often afraid to express how they truly feel for fear of being ridiculed or rejected for saying what is truly on their minds (Orlick, 1986).

Several teams I have worked with have had their fair share of interpersonal communication problems and conflict. Problems have ranged from interpersonal jealousies within the team to power struggles, control issues, perceived injustices, and coach–athlete as well as athlete–athlete inequities. Learning how to express oneself in a constructive manner and communicate effectively is an important initial step in preventing and solving problems.

It has been stated that the more open you can be with each other, the better are your chances of getting along and achieving both individual and team goals (Orlick, 1986). Thus, it is important for coaches and athletes to learn how to express their thoughts and feelings about various issues that affect them directly. Team building requires a group climate of openness in which airing problems and matters of concern is not just appropriate but encouraged. Orlick expounds by saying, 'Harmony grows when you really listen to others and they listen to you, when you are considerate of their feelings and they are considerate of yours, when you accept their differences and they accept yours, and when you help them and they help you' (Orlick, 2000: p. 143).

TEAM COMMUNICATION DYNAMICS

As already mentioned, many communication problems on teams are the result of misunderstanding or miscommunication between the coach and the team or among athletes themselves. Harris and Harris (1984) offer an interesting framework to examine communication processes in athletic teams. The framework consists of coach–team, coach–athlete, athlete–coach, and athlete–athlete interactions.

Coach–team communications

From a coach–team perspective group synergy and team chemistry are of vital importance. According to DePree (1989), group synergy comes from leaders (in this case coaches) sharing a vision of what could be if everyone puts his or her skills and resources together to achieve team goals and objectives. Individual and mutual accountability, passion and belief, and a genuine commitment to a common team goal are needed. Athletes unite behind common goals, so it is important to get athletes to think in terms of the philosophy, operating procedures, and values that govern the team (Yukelson, 1984). Similarly, homogenous attitudes and expectations (e.g. unity of purpose) as well as shared ideals and covenants to live by are required (Riley, 1993; Walsh, 1998). In terms of shared ideals, it is important to obtain *consensus and commitment* from the team regarding team goals, operating procedures, rules of engagement, and normative behaviours, including appropriate methods for achieving them (Carron and Hausenblas, 1998; Martens, 1987). To this end, the coach should solicit input from team members regarding their perceptions of what needs to be done for everyone to come together and be an effective team (Janssen, 1999; Katzenbach & Smith, 1993; Kouzes & Posner, 1995; Yukelson, 1997). Everyone on the team must be on the same page, working together with a collective desire to be successful.

To achieve these ends, a coach may find the communication principles outlined Box 14.1 in useful.

BOX 14.1: COMMUNICATION PRINCIPLES

- *Impart* relevant information regarding team rules, expectations, operating procedures, and goals the group is striving to achieve. Clarify the team's mission, outline strategies and action plans to reach team goals and objectives, and involve staff and athletes in decisions that affect them directly.
- *Inspire* athletes to reach for their best. Communicate with a sense of inspired enthusiasm. Be honest, direct, and sincere. Instill a sense of pride, passion, belief, and team spirit. Strive to make everyone on the team feel valued and significant.
- *Monitor the progress the team is making*. Set up a goal-setting programme (e.g. goal boards are often very helpful), monitor, evaluate, and adjust goals as needed. Give athletes feedback on how they are doing in relation to individual and team goals; challenge everyone involved to become better.
- *Clarify* how things are going. Talk openly about the commitment that is required to achieve team goals and what needs to be done to

---

keep things on task. Challenge everyone to take responsibility for their own actions and to work with continued effort, purpose, and focus.

■ *Reinforce* behaviour that you want repeated. Catch people doing things right; provide lots of support, encouragement, and positive reinforcement; discipline athletes according to your coaching philosophy and team mission statement; correct errors in a positive way.

Coach–athlete communications

As for coach–athlete lines of communication, coaches should build a psychological and social environment conducive to goal achievement and team success. They should take the time to get to know their athletes as unique goal-oriented individuals and find out what their strengths, interests, and needs are. Martens' (1987) ideas regarding transformational leadership and reciprocal influence are applicable in the context of athletes and coaches working together to meet each other's needs and goals. Coaches should be open, honest, and upfront with athletes about various decisions that affect them directly. This will ease many misunderstandings that can often lead to hurt feelings, dissension, or turmoil within the team.

Similarly, another area coaches should address with athletes is communication at the competition site (Orlick, 2000). Recognising individual differences in the way athletes prepare and respond in competition, it is suggested that coaches assess ahead of time what their athletes' needs and preferences are.

As for athlete-coach interactions, athletes need feedback as to where they stand and how they are progressing in relation to individual and team goals. Research indicates that *evaluative feedback* is an important part of the goal-setting process and is directly tied to communication. Unfortunately, some coaches are not very good at giving feedback in a positive and supportive manner (Orlick, 2000). This can lead to motivation problems and performance inconsistencies. In contrast, many athletes have difficulty internalising feedback for what it is and, as a consequence, take feedback personally as opposed to constructively.

In addition to providing tangible feedback about performance accomplishments, many athletes will seek out their coach to talk about things outside of sport that may be affecting their lives and self-esteem. Thus, a coach is often asked to take on many mentoring roles (e.g. counsellor, confidant, teacher, friend, role model, and sometimes substitute parent). For these reasons, it is important that lines of communication are open between athlete and coach, and that a trusting relationship is established.

As for breakdowns in coach–athlete communications, many athletes do not feel confident approaching a coach if they do not trust or respect him or her. Although it is common for coaches to have a so-called open-door policy, many athletes find it difficult to walk through the door if they feel the coach is not going to listen to their concerns with genuine interest, or if they perceive a hidden agenda.

Likewise, situations often arise during the course of a season that can cause communication problems between the coach and athlete (e.g. frustration associated with losing, poor performance, lack of playing time, stress and fatigue, personality clashes, and injury, to name just a few). In situations like these, athletes often perceive the coach as being insensitive, unappreciative, unapproachable, or uninterested. As a result, it is not unusual for an athlete to feel apprehensive about approaching the coach. Rather than clam up, athletes need to learn how to express themselves in an assertive manner.

Coaches should create an environment that encourages athletes to initiate communication freely. Athletes must feel that communication lines are truly open and things could be voiced without fear of reprisal. Communication is a two-way street; hence, both the coach and the athlete have a responsibility to make it work!

In terms of coach–athlete communications, Anshel (1997), Janssen and Dale (2002), Lynch (2001), Orlick (2000), Martens (1987, 2004), and Thompson (1993) offer several practical interventions to facilitate improved relations. Some key considerations include: being honest, sincere, direct, positive, genuine, consistent and empathetic. Box 14.2 presents a summary of tips for improving coach–athlete communications.

BOX 14.2: TIPS FOR IMPROVING COACH – ATHLETE COMMUNICATION

- To communicate successfully, you must understand that each person with whom you communicate has had different experiences than you.
- Communicate in a manner that is consistent with your personality and coaching philosophy.

- Recognise individual differences in the way people respond to you. Do not assume that you and the other person(s) will interpret the information in the same manner.
- Degrading or demeaning comments are poor communication techniques and should be discouraged.
- The skillful use of positive reinforcement can increase motivation and strengthen a person's self-esteem.
- When coaches lose control of their emotions, frustration may override the content element of communication and what gets heard.
- Put yourself in the shoes of your athletes (empathy). Show genuine concern for them as people. Listen attentively to their feelings and concerns and work jointly with them to find appropriate solutions.
- Convey rationales as to why athletes should or should not show certain behaviours.
- If you have an open-door policy, show athletes (and your assistants) that you are sincere about using it!
- Evaluate and monitor group process. Set aside time with the team to discuss openly how things are going.

Athlete–athlete communications

As for athlete–athlete communication, it is important that teammates establish and maintain harmonious working relationships with each other. Ideally, they should show genuine support and care for each other both on and off the athletic field. In fact, some of the most cohesive teams I have ever been associated with had a special relationship off the field (i.e. a 'bonding together feeling') that propelled them to be successful as a team during competitions. This was particularly evident during pressure situations within a competitive contest when they needed to trust each other most.

Along these lines, athletes can be a great source of support for one another; they often spend a lot of time together and share common experiences that are unique to their own peer subculture. In order for teams to get to know one another better and develop a sense of team camaraderie, I often employ team-building activities that promote personal disclosure through mutual sharing. For instance, I might have a team go around a circle discussing individual and team assets and strengths, or a life event that significantly influenced them as a person or team (Yukelson, 1997). These team disclosures promote diversity, team cohesion, and lend depth to understanding teammates. Recent qualitative research by Dunn and Holt (2004) as well as anecdotal accounts from coaches (Yukelson, *et al.*, 2003) noting the benefits of using personal disclosure/mutual sharing team-building activities before major competitions, has been documented in the literature (Cannon-Bowers and Salas, 2001; Dunn and Holt, 2004; Yukelson *et al.*, 2003).

Teams are very much like families. Some degree of tension, frustration, and conflict is inevitable.

Learning how to communicate effectively is an important first step in developing satisfying interpersonal team relationships.

Box 14.3 offers some suggestions derived from Orlick (1986, 2000) and from my personal experiences to help you improve interpersonal communication processes within a team.

BOX 14.3: TIPS FOR IMPROVING INTERPERSONAL COMMUNICATION PROCESSES

- Make sure everyone is pulling in the same direction. Recognise that the more open you can be with each other, the better are your chances of getting along and achieving your goals.
- Discuss strategies for improving team harmony, including ways to support and help each other both on and off the athletic field.
- Listen to others; they will listen to you! Put yourself in the shoes of others; try to understand the other person's perspective.
- Learn how to give and receive feedback or criticism constructively.
- Avoid backstabbing and gossiping about teammates. Interpersonal cliques and petty jealousies will destroy team morale quickly.
- Keep confrontations private. Deal with the person directly (e.g. 'Here is how your behaviour influences others and is perceived by others').
- Recognise that not all conflicts can be resolved, but most can be managed more effectively if both parties communicate.

Although it is easier said than done, I am in total agreement with Orlick when he states, 'The most important thing you can do to increase team harmony is to make a commitment to do so' (Orlick, 1986: p. 98).

REFERENCES

Anshel, M. (1997) *Sport Psychology: From Theory to Practice* (3rd ed.). Scottsdale, AZ: Gorsuch Scarisbrick.

Cannon-Bowers, J.A. and Salas, E. (2001) Reflections on shared cognition. *Journal of Organizational Behavior*, 22, 105–202.

Carron, A.V. and Hausenblas, H.A. (1998) *Group Dynamics in Sport* (2nd ed.). Morgantown, WV: Fitness Information Technology.

DePree, M. (1989) *Leadership is An Art*. New York: Doubleday.

Dunn, J.G.H. and Holt, N.L. (2004) A qualitative investigation of a personal-disclosure mutual-sharing team building activity. *The Sport Psychologist*, 18, 363–380.

Harris, D.V. and Harris, B.L. (1984) *Sports Psychology: Mental Skills For Physical People*. Champaign, IL: Leisure Press.

Henschen, K. and Miner, J. (1989) *Team Principles For Coaches*. Ogden, UT: Educational Sport Services.

Janssen, J. (1999) *Championship Team Building*. Tucson, AZ: Winning the Mental Game.

Janssen, J. and Dale, G. (2002) *The Seven Secrets of Successful Coaches: How to Unlock and Unleash Your Team's Full Potential*. Cary, NC: Winning the Mental Game.

Katzenbach, J.R. and Smith, D.K. (1993) *The Wisdom of Teams*. Boston, MA: Harvard Business School Press.

Kouzes, J.J. and Posner, B.Z. (1995) *The Leadership Challenge: How to Keep Getting Extraordinary Things Done in Organizations* (2nd ed.). San Francisco, CA: Jossey-Bass.

Lynch, J. (2001) *Creative Coaching*. Champaign, IL: Human Kinetics Publishers.

Martens, R. (1987) *Coaches Guide to Sport Psychology*. Champaign, IL: Human Kinetics.

Martens, R. (2004) *Successful Coaching* (3rd ed.). Champaign, IL: Human Kinetics.

Orlick, T. (1986) *Psyching For Sport*. Champaign, IL: Human Kinetics.

Orlick, T. (2000) *In Pursuit of Excellence* (3rd ed.). Champaign, IL: Human Kinetics.

Riley, P. (1993) *The Winner Within*. New York: Putnam.

Shaw, M. E. (1981) *Group Dynamics: The Psychology of Small Group Behavior* (3rd ed.). New York: McGraw-Hill.

Thompson, J. (1993) *Positive Coaching: Building Character and Self-esteem Through Sports*. Dubuque, IA: William C. Brown.

Walsh, B. (1998) *Finding the Winning Edge*. Champaign, IL: Sports Publishing Inc.

Yukelson, D. (1984) Group motivation in sport teams. In J. Silva and R. Weinberg (eds), *Psychological Foundations in Sport* (pp. 229–240). Champaign, IL: Human Kinetics.

Yukelson, D. (1997) Principles of effective team building interventions in sport: A direct service approach at Penn State University, *Journal of Applied Sport Psychology*, 9, 73–96.

Yukelson, D., Sullivan, B.A., Morett, C. and Dorenkott, B. (2003) *Coaches' Perspectives on Applying Sport Psychology into Their Coaching*. Invited symposium presented at the annual meeting of the Association for the Advancement of Applied Sport Psychology, Philadelphia, PA.

Zaccaro, S.J., Blair, V., Peterson, C. and Zazanis, M. (1995) Collective efficacy. In J. Maddox (ed.), *Self-efficacy, Adaptation, and Adjustment* (pp. 305–328). New York: Plenum Press.

CHAPTER 15

VALUING DIVERSITY[1]

Neil Thompson

INTRODUCTION

When we interact with other people, we do not start from a neutral standpoint. We bring with us a whole range of values, beliefs and assumptions. These are linked to the person we are, the range of social factors that influence and shape identity. For example, the way I relate to other people will owe much to my gender, my ethnic group, my class background and so on. These factors, in turn, will interact significantly with the equivalent factors for the persons concerned. That is, the gender, class and so on of the other people involved will also be significant in influencing the outcome of the interactions.

This presents a very complex picture in terms of the possible mix of interlinking factors (Figure 15.1). Man/woman, black/white, young/old are just some of the variables that play a part in shaping social interactions. Each individual is a member of a variety of social groups (gender, class, ethnic group and so on), and these have a significant bearing on our experience. It is often on the basis of such social groups that people are subject to discrimination and oppression. There is no end to the ways in which people can be discriminated against or oppressed. You do not have to be a member of a particular social group to experience the negative effects of prejudice and discrimination. However, it would be naïve not to recognise that certain groups in society are exposed to

---

[1] Edited from Thompson, N. (2002) 'Valuing diversity' in *People Skills* (2nd edn), pp. 75–85, Basingstoke: Palgrave Macmillan.

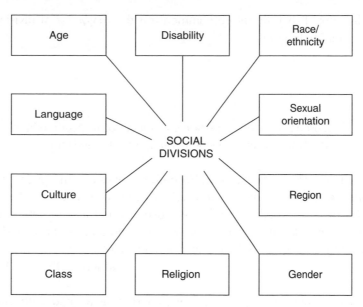

Figure 15.1 Social divisions

Source: Thompson 1994

a disproportionate amount of negative attention, for example women, black, disabled or older people.

In the interactions between individuals and groups, there is therefore an ever-present danger of certain people being disadvantaged in the process. In this way, diversity (the differences between people) is a potential source of discrimination and oppression.

Being different from the mainstream can so easily be equated with being inferior, and so there is a need to respond positively to diversity, to value differences and be sensitive to the dangers of discrimination. This chapter therefore explores some of the key issues in relation to valuing diversity.

ASPECTS OF DIVERSITY

Diversity relates to the fact that we are all unique individuals. However, diversity also relates to the fact that society is made up of various groups to which power, influence and opportunities are unequally allocated. Equality of opportunity (or its absence) owes much to the ways in which society is structured – its social divisions. I shall therefore comment on the major social divisions and some of their implications.

Class

Class is a term used to describe a person's socioeconomic position in society and is therefore closely linked to issues of income, wealth and status.

> The major classes that exist in Western societies are an upper class (the wealthy, employers and industrialists, plus top executives – those who own or directly control productive resources); a middle class (which includes most white-collar workers and professionals); and a working class (those in blue-collar or manual jobs).
>
> (Giddens, 1993: p. 215)

Unfortunately, there is a great deal of prejudice associated with class. For example, working-class people are often assumed to be less capable or intelligent than their middle-class counterparts. In working with people from different class backgrounds, it is important not to make assumptions based on class stereotypes.

A further important issue with regard to class is the need to avoid any class differences between you and your customers being emphasised by mannerisms, style of speech or body language. This does not mean that middle-class workers should pretend to be what they are not, or vice versa. But, it does mean that we need to be aware of those class characteristics that may act as a barrier to positive interpersonal relations.

Race and culture

The UK shares with the majority of Western societies a status as a multicultural society. That is, the overall population is composed of a wide variety of ethnic groups, representing a range of cultures, religions and languages. The common tendency to see the UK as a white homogeneous nation is a gross distortion and oversimplification of the actual situation. It is also a dangerous view in so far as it:

- devalues minority cultures;
- disregards significant aspects of people's lives;

- acts as a platform for racist attitudes and actions;
- stands as a barrier to good practice in people work.

Practice therefore needs to be *ethically sensitive*. That is, it needs to address questions of cultural values, practices and needs.

However, ethnically sensitive practice is not enough on its own. Practice also needs to be *anti-racist*. This is because ethnic differences become confused with assumed biological differences on the grounds of 'race'. In particular, superficial differences such as skin colour are often misinterpreted as indicators of profound biological differences.

People workers have to be very mindful of the existence of racism and the ways in which the celebration of human diversity gets lost in a destructive mythology of racial inferiority.

Gender

The development of the Women's Movement has helped to bring to our attention the unequal distribution of power and life chances between men and women. Interactions between men and women are therefore strongly influenced by the power differences that are brought to bear. An uncritical approach to gender is therefore likely to lead to a number of problems:

- Women's needs are likely to be overlooked.
- Male dominance will be reinforced and legitimated.
- Women's problems will be constructed in men's terms.
- Stereotypical gender expectations will not be challenged.
- Gender-related problems (depression or sexual abuse, for example) may pass unnoticed.

The notion that 'It's a man's world' is a significant and powerful one. And, of course, it will remain 'a man's world' unless the sexism inherent in society is challenged and undermined.

There are also problems for men associated with sexism – problems arising from rigid stereotypes concerning how men are expected to think, feel and act (Thompson, 1995). There is, therefore, a pressing need for the significance of gender to be fully recognised and to be incorporated within the theory base that informs our work.

Sexual orientation

Good practice is premised on a non-judgemental approach. That is, people should be treated with dignity, respect and fairness without any judgement being made as to their social worth. This is particularly important with regard to a person's sexual orientation in view of the widespread prejudice against gay men, lesbians and bisexuals.

It is important that interactions with gay men and lesbians are not beset with problems of discrimination and prejudice. Such discrimination has now come to be known as 'heterosexism' and is closely linked to sexism in so far as it hinges, to a large extent, on stereotypical gender expectations.

In working with people, the issue of sexual orientation can be seen to be a very significant issue. In view of this, it is necessary to avoid falling into the trap of seeing sexuality in narrow biological terms, for the following reasons:

- It legitimates oppression by seeing a *different* sexual orientation as a problem, an illness to be cured. Indeed, for many years homosexuality was mistakenly defined as a psychiatric disorder.
- It creates unnecessary barriers between worker and service user. Prejudice stands in the way of effective interpersonal interactions.
- It reinforces gender stereotypes and thereby contributes to the persistence of sexism as a form of oppression.

Good practice is therefore premised on the need to avoid falling into the pseudobiological trap of heterosexism.

Age

Ageism is a term that is generally applied to discrimination against older people, although it is sometimes used to refer to discrimination against children. For present purposes I shall focus on older people.

Ageism can be seen to be characterised by a number of destructive forces:

- *Marginalisation*   Older people and their needs are rarely seen as a priority or a central concern.
- *Dehumanisation*   Older people are often represented as 'past it', and of little use to society.

▣ *Infantilisation*   Older people tend to be treated like children much of the time.

In working with older people, then, we need to be careful that we are not following the well-worn path of demeaning older people by allowing ageist stereotypes and assumptions to distort our interactions with them. In particular, we need to:

▣ Avoid ageist language and patronising terminology ('old dear').
▣ Avoid seeing old age in unduly negative terms. The extent of illness, disability and related problems is generally greatly exaggerated.
▣ Focus on empowerment, not dependency. It is important to ensure we do not allow the ageist stereotype of dependency to distract us from seeing possibilities for empowerment.
▣ Value the experience of older people and recognise that they have not only needs but also a great deal to offer.

At all times we should seek to ensure that age discrimination does not act as a barrier to positive interaction with people of any age group.

Disability

Disability is traditionally seen as a medical matter, a physical impairment that stands in the way of normal social functioning. However, a number of writers (for example, Oliver, 1990) have shown this to be too narrow a view. In its place, they propose a social model of disability, one that emphasises the destructive effects of social attitudes towards disability.

It can therefore be seen that it is the social attitudes that are disabling, rather than the impairment itself. For example, it is not the use of a wheelchair that denies access to certain buildings, but rather the failure/refusal to provide ramps. Failing to recognise the significant role of society in 'constructing' disability also fails to recognise the discrimination and oppression disabled people experience.

The social model of disability therefore draws our attention to the prevalence of:

▣ the tendency for disabled people to be marginalised, dehumanised and patronised (there is a strong parallel here with ageism);

- a disabling focus on limitations rather than capabilities and potential;
- a lack of awareness of the physical and attitudinal barriers that prevent disabled people from becoming fully integrated in mainstream society;
- a tendency to focus on dependency rather than empowerment (another parallel with ageism).

In working with disabled people, then, it is necessary to recognise the social roots of disability so that we can avoid allowing negative stereotypes to mar interpersonal interactions.

We need to be sensitive to the fact that disability acts as a form of social oppression, and practice therefore needs to be geared towards challenging such oppression, rather than reinforcing it.

These, then, are some of the major aspects of diversity. I have presented them individually, although it needs to be remembered that they do not occur in isolation. They intertwine in various combinations to act as dimensions of each individual's experience. In order to understand, and work with, the individual, we need to understand the aspects of diversity that apply to him or her.

AFFIRMING DIVERSITY

The picture I have sketched out in this chapter is one of considerable human diversity in which dignity and social worth are threatened by the dominance of mainstream ideas and attitudes that leave little room for variation from an assumed norm.

It is essential, then, that we are sensitive to the significance of diversity, and the inequalities that arise due to a failure to respect that diversity. This sensitivity does not arise overnight and needs to be carefully nurtured over an extended period of time. Each individual worker must take responsibility for developing his or her awareness of these issues, but the following pointers can at least play a part in the process:

- *Be wary of stereotypes*   We need to respond to the unique individual, not the oversimplified stereotype.
- *Take steps to learn about other perspectives, other life experiences*   This will help you to appreciate, for example, the values, beliefs and practices of cultures other than your own.

neil thompson

- *Focus on dignity*   This is an important concept that helps to ensure that people's rights, values and beliefs are respected and the individual is valued in his or her own right.
- *Consider your own power*   In dealing with people from less powerful groups, it is important to understand the extent of your own power and influence.
- *Review your practice*   If we are not careful, practice can became routine and uncritical, and thereby lose its sensitivity. By reviewing practice from time to time, we can help to maintain a critical and sensitive edge.
- *Ask for feedback*   By asking for feedback (from service users and colleagues, for example), we can monitor the effectiveness of our practice by matching the perceptions of others against our own. This helps to sharpen our awareness of other people's perspectives.
- *Seek training*   The issues outlined in this chapter are complex and far-reaching and so it would be unrealistic to expect to address them fully simply by reading about them. Opportunities for discussing issues and applying them to practice situations can prove invaluable.
- *Work together*   These issues affect all people workers, and so there is excellent scope for collaborating with colleagues in taking your learning forward. A supportive collective approach can achieve far more than an individual one.

These are not the only steps that can be taken but they do provide a firm foundation for building a practice that respects, affirms and indeed celebrates, diversity.

CONCLUSION

Working with people involves empathy, the ability to appreciate the feelings and circumstances of others even though we do not share those feelings or circumstances. In order to develop and maintain empathy, we need to be able to understand, and respond appropriately to, the different cultural, linguistic and other aspects of a person's background. That is, we need to be sensitive to the role of diversity in shaping the situations we encounter in our work. In particular, we need to be aware of the ways in which difference comes to be seen in negative terms – we need to understand the discrimination and oppression that many people encounter in their lives.

REFERENCES

Giddens, A. (1993) *Sociology*. 2nd edition. Cambridge: Polity.

Oliver, M. (1990) *The Politics of Disablement*. London: Macmillan Press – now Palgrave Macmillan.

Thompson, N. (1994) *The Value Base of Social and Health Care*. Wrexham: Prospectors Publications.

Thompson, N. (1995) Men and anti-sexism. *British Journal of Social Work*, 25(4).

SECTION 4

LEADING PEOPLE AND TEAMS

INTRODUCTION

This section introduces you to some key ideas about leadership and management in sport and fitness settings. We take the position that an understanding of leadership is important in your development as an effective practitioner, whether you have a specific leadership or management post. Indeed, many of the ideas that we will be exploring here are relevant to all those leading sport and fitness activities as coaches and instructors, as well as their managers.

Section 4 starts by looking at the historical development of our understanding of leadership, from earlier ideas focused on completing tasks to more recent notions which place more emphasis on people and motivation. We then look at some key themes in leading individuals and teams in the workplace, and move on to consider some major aspects of organisational culture and leading and managing change in organisations.

Chapter 16, by Michele Doyle and Mark Smith, both from YMCA George Williams College, London, traces the development of ideas about what constitutes 'leadership'. They look at classical approaches to leadership, where leaders are seen as part of a hierarchical structure, and have special qualities and attributes which set them apart from followers. The authors then move on to explore more recent ideas about shared leadership which arises from social situations and people acting together.

Lesley Anderson of the Open University develops this theme further in Chapter 17, exploring a leadership approach to managing people. Anderson argues that people are the key resource in all organisations, and contrasts instrumental and humanistic approaches to leadership. She points out that effective leadership depends on understanding people in organisations – how and why they behave and react as they do, and how they are motivated to perform successfully.

Chapter 18, by Lesley Anderson and Maggie Preedy of the Open University, moves on to look at some key aspects of successful team leadership. They examine the differences between groups and teams and the process of team building and team roles and behaviours. Later sections of the chapter consider the characteristics of effective teams, the barriers to successful teamwork and some strategies for resolving conflict among team members.

Chapter 19 is written by Russell Hoye, Aaron Smith and Hans Westerbeek of La Trobe University, Melbourne, and Bob Stewart and Matthew Nicholson of Victoria University, Melbourne. The chapter considers organisational culture, often described as 'the way we do things round here'; it is a key dimension of life in the workplace, influencing how people behave and interpret events. The chapter examines why culture is so important in sport organisations and how different contexts affect this culture. The authors go on to explore the main visible and underlying aspects of organisational culture and the issues involved in cultural change.

The final chapter in this section, Chapter 20, by Maggie Preedy, explores how successful leaders manage change and strategic planning for the future. The author argues that change is the only constant factor in our personal lives and in the workplace, and it is therefore vital for sport and fitness practitioners to handle change successfully. The chapter looks at various types of organisational change and some useful approaches to the effective leadership of change. Later sections of the chapter explore strategic planning, a key aspect of managing change.

CHAPTER 16

WHAT IS LEADERSHIP?[1]

Michele Erina Doyle and Mark K. Smith

CLASSICAL LEADERSHIP

Leadership is one of those qualities that you can recognise when you see it, but is nonetheless difficult to describe. There are almost as many definitions as there are commentators, however many associate leadership with one person leading. Four things stand out in this respect: (i) to lead involves influencing others; (ii) where there are leaders there are followers; (iii) leaders seem to come to the fore when there is a crisis or special problem, in other words, they often become visible when an innovative response is needed; and (iv) leaders are people who have a clear idea of what they want to achieve and why. Thus, leaders are people who are able to think and act creatively in non-routine situations – and who set out to influence the actions, beliefs and feelings of others. In this sense being a leader is personal, it flows from an individual's qualities and actions, however, it is also often linked to some other role such as manager or expert. Here there can be a lot of confusion, for example, not all managers are leaders and not all leaders are managers.

In the recent literature of leadership (that is over the last 80 years or so) there have been four main 'generations' of theory:

1   Trait theories
2   Behavioural theories
3   Contingency theories
4   Transformational theories

[1]   Edited from Doyle, M.E. and Smith, M.J. 'What is leadership' in *Leading Work with Young People*, Harrison, R., *et al*. (eds), pp. 7–24, London: SAGE Publications. Originally published in (1999) *Born and Bred? Leadership, Heart and Informal Education*, London: YMCA George Williams College/The Rank Foundation.

TRAITS

Leaders are people who are able to express themselves fully, says Warren Bennis. 'They also know what they want', he continues, 'why they want it, and how to communicate what they want to others, in order to gain their co-operation and support'. Lastly, 'they know how to achieve their goals' (Bennis, 1998: p. 3). But what is it that makes someone exceptional in this respect? As soon as we study the lives of people who have been labelled as great or effective leaders, it becomes clear that they have very different qualities. We only have to think of political figures like Nelson Mandela, Margaret Thatcher and Mao Zedong to confirm this.

Instead of starting with exceptional individuals many turned to setting out the general qualities or *traits* they believed should be present. Surveys of early trait research by Stogdill (1948) and Mann (1959) reported that many studies identified personality characteristics that appear to differentiate leaders from followers. However, as Peter Wright (1996: p. 34) has commented, 'others found no differences between leaders and followers with respect to these characteristics, or even found people who possessed them were less likely to become leaders'. Yet pick up almost any of the popular books on the subject today and you will still find a list of traits that are thought to be central to effective leadership. The basic idea remains that if a person possesses these she or he will be able to take the lead in very different situations. At first glance, the lists seem to be helpful (see, for example, Figure 16.1). But spend any time around them and they can leave a lot to be desired.

John Gardner studied a large number of North American organizations and leaders and came to the conclusion that there were some qualities or attributes that did appear to mean that a leader in one situation could lead in another. These included:

• Physical vitality and stamina
• Intelligence and action-oriented judgement
• Eagerness to accept responsibility
• Task competence
• Understanding of followers and their needs
• Skill in dealing with people
• Need for achievement
• Capacity to motivate people
• Courage and resolution
• Trustworthiness
• Decisiveness
• Self-confidence
• Assertiveness
• Adaptability/flexibility

Figure 16.1 Gardner's (1989) leadership attributes

The first problem is that the early reseachers of traits often assumed that there was a definite set of characteristics that made a leader – whatever the situation. In other words, they thought the same traits would work on a battlefield and in the staff room of a school. They, and later writers, also tended to mix some very different qualities. Some of Gardner's qualities, for example, are aspects of a person's behaviour, some are skills, and others are to do with temperament and intellectual ability. Like other lists of this nature it is quite long – so what happens when someone has some but not all of the qualities? On the other hand, the list is not exhaustive and it is possible that someone might have other 'leadership qualities'. What of these?

Behaviours

As the early researchers ran out of steam in their search for traits, they turned to what leaders did – how they behaved (especially towards followers). They moved from leaders to leadership and this became the dominant way of approaching leadership within organisations in the 1950s and early 1960s. Different patterns of behaviour were grouped together and labelled as styles. Various schemes appeared, designed to diagnose and develop people's style of working. Despite different names, the basic ideas were very similar. The four main styles that appeared as described by Wright (1996: pp. 36–7) are:

- **Concern for task**. Here leaders emphasise the achievement of concrete objectives. They look for high levels of productivity and ways to organise people and activities in order to meet those objectives.
- **Concern for people**. In this style, leaders look upon their followers as people – their needs, interests, problems, development, and so on. They are not simply units of production or means to an end.
- **Directive leadership**. This style is characterised by leaders taking decisions for others and expecting followers or subordinates to follow instructions.
- **Participative leadership**. Here leaders try to share decision-making with others.

Often, we find two of these styles present in books and training materials. For example, concern for task is set against concern for people (after Blake and Mouton, 1964) and directive is contrasted with participative leadership (for example, McGregor's [1960] portrayal of managers as 'Theory X' or 'Theory Y'). If you have been on a teamwork or leadership development course then it is likely you will have come across some variant of this in an exercise or discussion.

Many of the early writers that looked to participative and people-centred leadership, argued that it brought about greater satisfaction among followers (subordinates). However, as Sadler (1997) reports, when researchers really got to work on this it didn't seem to stand up. There were lots of differences and inconsistencies between studies. It was difficult to say style of leadership was significant in enabling one group to work better than another. Perhaps the main problem, though, was one shared with those who looked for traits (Wright, 1996: p. 47). The researchers did not look properly at the context or setting in which the style was used. Is it possible that the same style would work as well in a gang or group of friends, and in a hospital emergency room? The styles that leaders can adopt are far more affected by those they are working with and the environment they are operating within, than had been thought originally.

SITUATIONS

Researchers began to turn to the contexts in which leadership is exercised and the idea that what is needed changes from situation to situation. Some looked to the processes by which leaders emerge in different circumstances, for example, at moments of great crisis or where there is a vacuum. Others turned to the ways in which leaders and followers viewed each other in various contexts, for example, in the army, political parties and in companies. The most extreme view was that just about everything was determined by the context. But most writers did not take this route. They brought the idea of style with them, believing that the style needed would change with the situation. Another way of putting this is that particular contexts would demand particular forms of leadership. This placed a premium on people who were able to develop an ability to work in different ways, and could change their style to suit the situation.

What began to develop was a *contingency* approach. The central idea was that effective leadership was dependent on a mix of factors. For example, Fred E. Fiedler argued that effectiveness depends on two interacting factors: leadership style and the degree to which the situation gives the leader control and influence. Three things are important here:

- **The relationship between the leaders and followers**. If leaders are liked and respected they are more likely to have the support of others.
- **The structure of the task**. If the task is clearly spelled out as to goals, methods and standards of performance then it is more likely that leaders will be able to exert influence.

■ **Position power**. If an organisation or group confers powers on the leader for the purpose of getting the job done, then this may well increase the influence of the leader (Fiedler and Garcia, 1987: pp. 51–67; see also Fiedler, 1997).

Models like this can help us to think about what we are doing in different situations. For example, we may be more directive where a quick response is needed, and where people are used to being told what to do, rather than having to work at it themselves. The models have found their way into various management training aids, such as Hersey and Blanchard's (1977) very influential discussion of choosing the appropriate style for the particular situation, as shown in Figure 16.2.

Aside from their very general nature, there are some issues with such models. First, much that has been written has a North American bias. There is considerable evidence to suggest cultural factors influence the way that people carry out, and respond to, different leadership styles. For example, some cultures are more individualistic, or value family as against bureaucratic models, or have very different expectations about how people address and talk with each other. All this impacts on the choice of style and approach.

Hersey and Blanchard identified four different leadership styles that could be drawn upon to deal with contrasting situations:

Telling (high task/low relationship behaviour). This style or approach is characterized by giving a great deal of direction to subordinates and by giving considerable attention to defining roles and goals. The style was recommended for dealing with new staff, or where the work was menial or repetitive, or where things had to be completed within a short time span. Subordinates are viewed as being unable and unwilling to 'do a good job'.

Selling (high task/high relationship behaviour). Here, while most of the direction is given by the leader, there is an attempt at encouraging people to 'buy into' the task. Sometimes characterized as a 'coaching' approach, it is to be used when people are willing and motivated but lack the required 'maturity' or 'ability'.

Participating (high relationship/low task behaviour). Here decision making is shared between leaders and followers – the main role of the leader being to facilitate and communicate. It entails high support and low direction and is used when people are able, but are perhaps unwilling or insecure (they are of 'moderate to high maturity' (Hersey, 1984).

Delegating (low relationship/low task behaviour). The leader still identifies the problem or issue but the responsibility for carrying out the response is given to followers. It entails having a high degree of competence and maturity (people know what to do and are motivated to do it).

Figure 16.2 Hersey and Blanchard (1977) on leadership style and situation

Second, there may be different patterns of leadership linked with men and women. Some have argued that women may have leadership styles that are more nurturing, caring and sensitive. They look more to relationships. Men are said to look to task. However, there is a lot of debate about this. We can find plenty of examples of nurturing men and task-oriented women. Any contrasts between the style of men and women may be down to the situation. In management, for example, women are more likely to be in positions of authority in people-oriented sectors, so this aspect of style is likely to be emphasised.

TRANSFORMATIONS

Burns (1978) argued that it was possible to distinguish between transactional and transforming leaders (Figure 16.3). The former 'approach their followers with an eye to trading one thing for another' (1978: p. 4), while the latter are visionary leaders who seek to appeal to their followers' 'better nature and move them toward higher and more universal needs and purposes' (Bolman and Deal, 1997: p. 314). In other words, the leader is seen as a change agent.

There is strong emphasis in the contemporary literature of management leadership on charismatic and related forms of leadership. However, whether there is a solid body of evidence to support its effectiveness is an open question. Indeed, Wright (1996: p. 221) concludes 'it is impossible to say how effective transformational leadership is with any degree of certainty'. We will return to some questions around charisma later, but first we need to briefly examine the nature of authority in organisations (and the relationship to leadership).

Transactional	**Transformational**
The transactional leader	The transformational leader
Recognizes what it is that we want to get from work and tries to ensure that we get it if our performance merits it	Raises our level of awareness, our level of consciousness about the significance and value of designated outcomes, and ways of reaching them
Exchanges rewards and promises for our effort	Gets us to transcend our own self-interest for the sake of the team, organization or larger polity
Is responsive to our immediate self-interests if they can be met by getting the work done	Alters our need level (after Maslow) and expands our range of wants and needs

Figure 16.3 Transactional and transformational leadership (Bass, 1985; Wright, 1996: p. 213)

AUTHORITY

Frequently we confuse leadership with authority. To explore this we can turn to Heifetz's (1994) important discussion of the matter. Authority is often seen as the possession of powers based on formal role. In organisations, for example, we tend to focus on the manager or officer. They are seen as people who have the right to direct us. We obey them because we see their exercise of power as legitimate. It may also be that we fear the consequences of not following their orders or 'requests'. The possibility of them sacking, demoting or disadvantaging us may well secure our compliance. We may also follow them because they show leadership. As we have seen, the latter is generally something more informal – the ability to make sense of, and act in, situations that are out of the ordinary. In this way leaders don't simply influence, they have to show that crises or unexpected events and experiences do not faze them. Leaders may have formal authority, but they rely in large part on informal authority. This flows from their personal qualities and actions. They may be trusted, respected for their expertise, or followed because of their ability to persuade.

Leaders have authority as part of an exchange: if they fail to deliver the goods, to meet people's expectations, they run the risk of authority being removed and given to another. Those who have formal authority over them may take this action. However, we also need to consider the other side. Followers, knowingly or unknowingly, accept the right of the person to lead – and he or she is dependent on this. The leader also relies on 'followers' for feedback and contributions. Without these they will not have the information and resources to do their job. Leaders and followers are interdependent.

People who do not have formal positions of power can also enjoy informal authority. In a football team, for example, the manager may not be the most influential person. It could be an established player who can read the game and energise that colleagues turn to. In politics a classic example is Gandhi, who for much of the time held no relevant formal position but through his example and his thinking became an inspiration for others.

Having formal authority is both a resource and a constraint. On the one hand it can bring access to systems and resources. Handled well it can help people feel safe. On the other hand, formal authority carries a set of expectations and these can be quite unrealistic in times of crisis. Being outside the formal power structure, but within an organisation, can be an advantage. You can have more freedom of movement, the chance of focusing on what you see as the issue (rather than the organisation's focus), and there is a stronger chance of being in touch with what people are feeling 'at the frontline'.

CHARISMA

Before moving on it is important to look at the question of charisma. It is so much a part of how we look at leadership but it is a difficult quality to tie down. Charisma is, literally, a gift of grace or of God (Wright, 1996: p. 194). Max Weber, more than anyone, brought this idea into the realm of leadership. He used 'charisma' to talk about self-appointed leaders who are followed by those in distress. Such leaders gain influence because they are seen as having special talents or gifts that can help people escape the pain they are in (Gerth and Wright Mills, 1991: pp. 51–55).

When thinking about charisma we often look to the qualities of particular individuals – their skills, personality and presence. But this is only one side of things. We need to explore the situations in which charisma arises. When strong feelings of distress are around there does seem to be a tendency to turn to figures who seem to have answers. To make our lives easier we may want to put the burden of finding and making solutions on someone else. In this way we help to make the role for 'charismatic leaders' to step into. They in turn will seek to convince us of their special gifts and of their solution to the crisis or problem. When these things come together something very powerful can happen. It doesn't necessarily mean that the problem is dealt with, but we can come to believe it is. Regarding such leaders with awe, perhaps being inspired in different ways by them, we can begin to feel safer and directed. This can be a great resource. Someone like Martin Luther King used the belief that people had in him to take forward civil rights in the United States. He was able to contain a lot of the stress his supporters felt and give hope of renewal. He articulated a vision of what was possible and worked with people to develop strategies. But there are also considerable dangers.

Charisma involves dependency. It can mean giving up our responsibilities. Sadly, it is all too easy to let others who seem to know what they are doing get on with difficult matters. By placing people on a pedestal the distance between 'us' and 'them' widens. They seem so much more able or in control. Rather than facing up to situations and making our own solutions, we remain followers (and are often encouraged to do so). There may well come a point when the lie implicit in this confronts us. Just as we turned to charismatic leaders, we can turn against them.

It could be we recognise that the 'solution' we signed up to has not made things better. It might be that some scandal or incident reveals the leader in what we see as a bad light. Whatever, we can end up blaming, and even destroying, the leader. Unfortunately, we may simply turn to another rather than looking to our own capacities.

In this part of the chapter, we have tried to set out some of the elements of a 'classical' view of leadership. We have seen how commentators have searched for special traits and behaviours and looked at the different situations where leaders work and emerge. Running through much of this is a set of beliefs that we can describe as a classical view of leadership where leaders:

- Tend to be identified by position; they are part of the hierarchy.
- Become the focus for answers and solutions. We look to them when we don't know what to do or when we can't be bothered to work things out for ourselves.
- Give direction and have vision.
- Have special qualities setting them apart. These help to create the gap between leaders and followers.

This view of leadership sits quite comfortably with the forms of organisation that are common in business, the armed forces and government. Where the desire is to get something done, to achieve a narrow range of objectives in a short period of time, then it may make sense to think in this way. However, this has its dangers. While some 'classical' leaders may have a more participative style, it is still just a style. A great deal of power remains in their hands and the opportunity for all to take responsibility and face larger questions is curtailed. It can also feed into a 'great-man' model of leadership and minimise our readiness to question those who present us with easy answers. As our awareness of our own place in the making of leadership grows, we may be less ready to hand our responsibilities to others. We may also come to realise our own power:

> I don't think it's actually possible to lead somebody. I think you can allow yourself to be led. It's a bit like other things – you can't teach, you can only learn – because you can only control yourself.

More inclusive and informal understandings of leadership offer some interesting possibilities, as we can see in our discussion of shared leadership in the second part of this chapter.

SHARED LEADERSHIP

Leadership can be explored as a social process – something that happens between two people. It is not much what leaders do, as something that arises out of social relationships. As such, it does not depend on one person, but on how people act together to make sense of the situations that face them, as the following comments suggest.

> The group took over. There was a whole group leadership thing, I don't think leadership's necessarily about one person sometimes – everyone has the qualities of being a leader or taking some form of responsibility in their lives, and sometimes that's a whole group ethos.
> I want to work in a situation where people can take on roles and responsibilities, tasks, whatever they want to do. As long as I can assist in this, rather than being the forerunning force taking it over, then that's what I'm aiming for.

EVERYDAY LEADERSHIP

If we look at everyday life – the situations and groups we are involved in – then we soon find leadership. Friends deciding how they are going to spend an evening, families negotiating over housework – each involve influence and decision. However, such leadership often does not reside in a person. It may be shared and can move. In one situation an individual may be influential because of their expertise or position; in another it can be someone completely different. What these people may be able to do is to offer an idea or an action that helps to focus or restructure the situation and the way in which others see things.

Sometimes there may not even be one person we can readily label as leader – just a group working together to achieve what is wanted. Rather than people leading, it is ideals and ideas. We don't follow an individual; we follow the conversation. Through listening and contributing, thoughts and feelings emerge and develop. It is not the force of personality that leads us on but the rightness of what is said.

From this we can see that it is not our position that is necessarily important, but our behaviour. The question is whether our actions help groups and relationships to work and achieve. Actions that do this could be called leadership, and can come from any group member. Many writers – especially those looking at management – tend to talk about leadership as a person having a clear vision and the ability to make it real. However, as we have begun to discover, leadership lies not so much in one person having a clear vision as in our capacity to work with others in creating one.

We may also recognise the power of self-leadership, as one worker put it: 'me trying to get the most out of my own resources'. Some people have talked of this as the influence we exert on ourselves 'to achieve the self-motivation and self-direction we need to perform' (Manz and Sims, 1989). Such self-motivation and self-direction can impact on others. The worker continued:

> [It] then moves onto staff, for them to discover the self-resources that they have within themselves and then look for anything that needs developing.

The leadership process is part of our daily experience. We may lead others, ourselves, or be led. We play our part in relationships and groups where it is always around. Sometimes there is an obvious 'leader', often there isn't. Nor are there always obvious followers. The world is not neatly divided in this respect. Part of our responsibility as partners in the process is to work so that those who may label themselves as followers come to see that they, too, are leaders.

> What I understand of leadership is encouraging, or getting, people to realise their own resources, what they've got within them.

ETHICS

We also want to take things a stage further. For something to qualify as 'leadership' we must also make judgements about the quality of what happens. It should enrich the lives we all lead. Here we want to highlight two aspects. Leadership must be:

- **Inclusive** – we all share in the process.
- **Elevating** – we become wiser and better people by being involved (Heifetz, 1994).

We want to include these ethical qualities so that we can make proper judgements about leadership. For example, if we stay with a simple technical definition such as that offered by Bass (1990) (leadership as the exercise of influence in a group context) then we can look at a figure like Hitler and say he was, in many respects, a great leader. He had a vision, was able to energise a large number of people around it, and develop the effectiveness of the organisations he was responsible for. However, as soon as we ask whether his actions were inclusive and elevating we come to a very different judgement. He was partly responsible for the death and exclusion of millions of people. He focused people's attention on the actions of external enemies, internal scapegoats and false images of community while avoiding facing a deeper analysis of the country's ills.

Hopefully, the point is made. Leadership involves making ethical as well as technical judgements.

Craig Johnson (2001: pp. 9–23) has usefully employed the metaphor of shadow and light in this respect. He argues that leaders 'have the power to illuminate the lives of followers or to cover them in darkness' (2001: p. 9) and they cast shadows when they:

- *Abuse power*. Power can have a corrosive effect on those who possess it. Large differentials in the relative power of leaders and followers can also contribute towards abuse. Power deprivation exerts its own corruptive influence. Followers can become fixated on what minimal influence they have, becoming cautious, defensive and critical of others and new ideas. They may even engage in sabotage (2001: pp. 10–14).
- *Hoard privileges*. Leaders nearly always enjoy greater privileges (in the form of perks, pay and access). Leaders that hoard power are also likely to hoard wealth and status as well, and in so doing contribute to a growing gap between the haves and the have-nots (2001: pp. 14–15).
- *Encourage deceit*. Leaders have more access to information than others in an organisation. They are more likely to participate in the decision-making processes, network with those with power, have access to different information sources such as personnel files. Patterns of deception, whether they take the form of outright lies or hiding or distorting information, destroy the trust that binds leaders and followers together (2001: pp. 15–18).
- *Act inconsistently*. Diverse followers, varying levels of relationships and elements of situations make consistency an ethical burden of leadership. Shadows arise when leaders appear to act arbitrarily and unfairly (2001: pp. 18–19).
- *Misplace or betray loyalties*. Leaders have to weigh a range of loyalties or duties when making choices. Leaders cast shadows when they violate the loyalty of followers and the community (2001: pp. 19–20).

- *Fail to assume responsibilities*. Leaders act irresponsibly when they fail to make reasonable efforts to prevent followers' misdeeds; ignore or deny ethical problems; don't shoulder responsibility for the consequences of their directives; deny their duties to their followers; and hold followers to higher standards than themselves (2001: pp. 21–22).

DEMOCRATIC LEADERSHIP AND SHARED LEADERSHIP

Aspects of the approach we are exploring here are sometimes called democratic leadership. It involves people, and can foster a belief in democratic principles and processes such as self-determination and participation. These are concerns that we share. However, we want to widen things out. We want to include everyday behaviour that is inclusive and looks to enriching all our lives, but that does not have an explicit democratic focus. We call this 'shared leadership'.

For such leadership to develop we need to pay special attention to three things. We need to encourage (after Gastil, 1997):

- **Ownership**. Problems and issues need to become a responsibility of all with proper chances for people to share and participate.
- **Learning**. An emphasis on learning and development is necessary so that people can share, understand and contribute to what's going on.
- **Sharing**. Open, respectful and informed conversation is central.

We want to look at each of these in turn.

Ownership

> Leadership to me is around taking some form of responsibility in any given situation.

There are some very practical reasons for encouraging people to own the problems facing them. For example, where the problem is non-routine and needs an unusual response, it is important to have the right information. Involving those with a stake in the situation – especially those at the sharp end – gives a chance for insights to emerge. Further, the more people take on an issue or problem as theirs and involve themselves in thinking through responses, the more likely they are to act and to carry things through. They have an investment in making things happen. It is their solution, not somebody else's. When we own a problem it becomes our responsibility. If things go wrong when trying to find a solution, we cannot blame others. For these reasons alone we may be very resistant to shouldering responsibility.

We may also be frightened and lost. Sometimes the issue facing us is so complex or of such a scale that we don't know where to start. We may be worried about getting things wrong, of not understanding what the issues are, or adding to conflict. Faced by a crisis or an apparently insoluble problem, we may look for strong leadership. It may be through anxiety, hostility or helplessness (to name just a few emotions) that we are ready to turn to those who seem to have an answer.

We may also try to avoid taking responsibility for things because we are lazy or want others to do things for us. After all, if we own a problem then we will have to act at some point. Why bother exerting ourselves if we can sit back and let someone else take the strain? This takes us straight into the realm of ethical questions. Is it fair that someone should take a ride on the back of others? Is it right to benefit from belonging to a group, team or organisation without making the fullest contribution we can?

Learning

> I don't think leadership is about being a manager and cracking the whip and getting people to do the job, but do I think it is about just keeping the learning on track, so there is some sort of agreed … way forward.

To act for the best we need to be informed. Our actions have to be shaped by a good understanding of the situation and of the possibilities open to us. We also need to develop some very practical skills and to attend to our feelings. In short we need to deepen our understanding and develop and share in this with others. Leadership entails learning; it means becoming wiser and more knowledgeable.

Wisdom is not something that we possess like a book or computer. It is a quality that appears in action. The people we describe as wise do not necessarily know a lot of things. They are not encyclopedias. Rather, they are able to reflect on a situation and, as likely or not, encourage others to join with them. Crucially they are also able to relate this to the sorts of practical actions that are right for the situation (Kekes, 1995).

Yet there is something more at work here. Wisdom is wrapped up with morality. To be wise, we would argue, is also to have a care for people (including ourselves)

michele erina doyle and mark k. smith

and for how we may all live more fulfilling lives. If we are to think and to evaluate we must have standards by which to judge what we find. This means looking to what philosophers like Aristotle talked about as the good life. This involves having an understanding of the different things that need to come together if people are to flourish. Wisdom lies in not having fixed ideas, but in taking a position and modifying it in the light of experience. We must have some humility – to be open to others, to experiences and to criticism.

This is a theme picked up by writers like Ronald Heifetz. He argues that true leaders are educators. Their task is to work with communities to face problems and lead themselves rather than to influence people to agree to a particular position. They help to build environments in which people can reflect upon how they can help with solving problems and with achieving goals. Furthermore, there is a need to develop people's ability to make decisions, work together and think in ways that respect others.

Sharing

> I feel if there's openness and honest sharing, I think you can deal with things. If the climate is not set, people won't share and things are harder to deal with.

Alongside spreading ownership and cultivating learning we need to develop open and productive ways of sharing our thoughts and feelings. This isn't just so that we can make better decisions, but also so we can talk with others. In short this means developing conversations that involve people, deepen understanding and help us make sound judgements and decisions.

Good conversation involves us in cooperating, thinking of each other's feelings and experiences, and giving each room to talk. It is for this reason that Peter Senge (1990) accords dialogue a central role in the learning organisation. The virtues it involves are central to building stronger and healthier communities and organisations:

- **Concern**. To be with people, engaging them in conversation involves commitment to each other. We feel something for the other person as well as the topic.
- **Trust**. We have to take what others are saying in good faith. This is not the same as being gullible. While we may take things on trust, we will be looking to check whether our trust is being abused.

- **Respect**. While there may be considerable differences between partners in conversation, the process can only continue if there is mutual regard.
- **Appreciation**. Linked to respect, this involves valuing the unique qualities that others bring.
- **Affection**. Conversation involves a feeling with, and for, those taking part.
- **Hope**. We engage in conversation in the belief that it holds possibility. Often it is not clear what we will gain or learn, but faith in the process carries us forward (Burbules, 1993).

In good conversation the topic takes over; it leads us, rather than us leading it. Where conversation has taken over, people run with the exchanges and gain learning from that. It turns into a journey of discovery rather than a route with a fixed destination. For leadership this can be liberating. It means that as individuals we don't have to know the answers. What we need is to develop ways of being in conversation (including silence) that allow those answers to surface.

CONCLUSION

We have seen some deeply contrasting views of leadership, and we can see how easy it is for people to misunderstand each other. When we talk of leadership are we looking to position or process, individual activity or social interaction, orders or conversation? What one person means can be very different to another.

Both classical and shared leadership approaches have their pitfalls. We have already discussed some of the problems with classical approaches. Here we highlight four associated with shared leadership. First, the emphasis on process can lead to a lack of attention to product or outcome. It can provide an alibi for laziness and incompetence when little is achieved. Care needs to be taken not to lose sight of the question or problem that is the subject of decision-making.

Second, the emphasis on group life within shared leadership approaches may mean that the excellence or flair of the individual is not rewarded. The person concerned can experience this as unfair and demotivating – and the group may lose out as a result. Resentment might grow, and innovative solutions to problems may not be forthcoming. There will be times when it makes sense to follow the lead of a gifted individual.

Third, the commitments, understandings and practices of shared leadership are sophisticated and it is easy to see why, at this level alone, people may shy away from it. It is an 'ideal model' and as such can easily mutate.

Fourth, all models of leadership are culturally specific. What may be viewed as appropriate in one society or group may not be so in another.

This said, thinking about leadership in these ways allows us to begin to get to the heart of what it may involve and how we may respond.

REFERENCES

Bass, B.M. (1985) *Leadership and Performance Beyond Expectation*. New York: Free Press.

Bass, B.M. (1990) *Bass and Stogdill's Handbook of Leadership* (3rd edn). New York: Free Press.

Bennis, W. (1998) *On Becoming a Leader*. London: Arrow.

Blake, R.R. and Mouton, J.S. (1964) *The Managerial Grid*. Houston. TX: Gulf.

Bolman, L.G. and Deal, T.E. (1997) *Reframing Organizations. Artistry, Choice and Leadership* (2nd edn). San Francisco: Jossey-Bass.

Burbules, N.C. (1993) *Dialogue in Teaching*. New York: Teachers College Press.

Burns, J.M. (1978) *Leadership*. New York: Harper Collins.

Fiedler, F.E. (1997) Situational control and a dynamic theory of leadership. In K. Grint (ed.), *Leadership: Classical, Contemporary and Critical Approaches*. Oxford: Oxford University Press.

Fiedler, F.E. and Garcia, J.E. (1987) *New Approaches to Effective Leadership*. New York: John Wiley.

Gardner, J. (1989) *On Leadership*. New York: Free Press.

Gastil, J. (1997) A definition and illustration of democratic leadership. In K. Grint (ed.), *Leadership*. Oxford: Oxford University Press.

Gerth, H. and Wright Mills, C. (eds) (1991) *From Max Weber. Essays in Sociology*. London: Routledge.

Heifetz, R.A. (1994) *Leadership Without Easy Answers*. Cambridge, MA: Belknap Press.

Hersey, P. and Blanchard, K.H. (1977) *The Management of Organizational Behaviour* (3rd edn). Upper Saddle River, NJ: Prentice Hall.

Johnson, C.E. (2001) *Meeting the Ethical Challenges of Leadership. Casting Light or Shadow*. Thousand Oaks, CA.: Sage.

Kekes, J. (1995) *Moral Wisdom and Good Lives*. Ithaca, NY: Cornell University Press.

McGregor, D. (1960) *The Human Side of Enterprise*. New York: McGraw Hill.

Mann, R.D. (1959) A review of the relationship between personality and performance in small groups. *Psychological Bulletin*, 66(4): 241–270.

Manz, C.C. and Sims, H.P. (1989) *Superleadership: Leading Others to Lead Themselves*. New York: Prentice Hall.

Sadler, P. (1997) *Leadership*. London: Kogan Page.

Senge, P.M. (1990) *The Fifth Discipline. The Art and Practice of the Learning Organization*. London: Random House.

Stogdill, R.M. (1948) Personal factors associated with leadership: a survey of the literature. *Journal of Psychology*, 25: 35–71.

Wright, P. (1996) *Managerial Leadership*. London: Routledge.

michele erina doyle and mark k. smith

CHAPTER 17

A LEADERSHIP APPROACH TO MANAGING PEOPLE

Lesley Anderson

PEOPLE AND ORGANISATIONS

Without people, organisations would not exist and, without them, there would be no need for leaders or for leadership. It is people themselves who create the need for leadership and management, both of people and of other resources used by organisations such as finance, time and premises. This need for people to be led and managed arises because, as individuals, we each have values, beliefs and needs: all of which influence the way we behave and respond to one another and use the other resources. People's performance may also vary and any one of us may not be fulfilling his/her full potential without leadership and management. This situation is not only detrimental for the organisation as a whole but affects each person. Thus, people are integral to both leadership and management. Furthermore, it follows that, in order to understand the nuances of effectively leading and managing, it is necessary to understand people in organisations – how and why we behave and react as we do, both as leaders and managers, and as those being led and managed.

In this chapter we draw on generic theories of organisations, leadership and management of people to help us understand and explain organisations and groups concerned with sport and fitness.

UNDERSTANDING THE TERMINOLOGY

As with any communication, it is important that we share an understanding about the meaning of the words used. For this reason we start by considering five key words that are used in this chapter.

The word 'people' includes the various categories in the context of sport and fitness. Some of the people are employees – of gyms and sports centres, some are their customers, some are volunteers playing sport or working with the participants and some may be professional sports people.

The next word we use is 'teams'. What makes a group of people into a team is considered in detail elsewhere in this book. It is, therefore, sufficient to say here that the purpose of a team is to work together to achieve shared outcomes and that, in a commercial sense at least, it is usual to expect that it is done as effectively as possible. We all know about sports teams. However, a group of people working together supporting a sporting or fitness activity indirectly, for example, looking after the customers, may also work together as a team.

We are also concerned with 'leading' (and 'leadership'). These are complex activities that research suggests are key factors for effective organisation (Sammons et al., 1997). Three definitions of leadership are highlighted here. The first describes leadership as 'path-finding' (Hodgson, 1987) and implies there is movement towards an endpoint or goal. The next one – 'doing the right things' (Bennis and Nanus, 1985) – is, in many ways, similar because the implication is that in 'doing the right things' the 'unit' being led is moving towards the desired endpoint. The third definition, Bryman's (1986) 'focus on the creation of a vision about a desired future state', differs in that it does not suggest movement towards the required situation. However, like the others, it looks forward to a changed condition which, it is assumed, is better than the present. Thus, together, these definitions convey the idea of identifying a future state that is desired for the organisation or team as well as ways in which it can move forward to this position.

The next word, 'managing', is about the actual process of moving the organisation along the path towards the identified vision. It involves putting plans, structures and procedures in place and enacting them through the people within the organisation to achieve improvement. The definitions of management offered by the same three sets of writers as mentioned above are:

- Path-following (Hodgson, 1987).
- Doing things right (Bennis and Nanus, 1985).
- A preoccupation with the here-and-now of goal attainment (Bryman, 1986).

Hence, from a theoretical perspective, we begin to unravel the relationship between leadership and management. However, in practice the terms tend to be used interchangeably and leading is frequently seen as an aspect of management. Thus, here the two functions are considered side by side.

The final word that needs explaining in the context of this book is 'organisation'. We are using the word in its broadest sense to include a group of people who are working together to achieve an agreed outcome. So, whilst we often associate the word with a commercial enterprise, in this chapter it also includes non-commercial activity.

It is reasonable to assume that all organisations exist to succeed whatever criteria are used to assess that success. In most commercial organisations, the overall success criterion is likely to be linked to profit. In the field of sport, success is usually in terms of winning. For this discussion an effective organisation is taken as one that 'produces' the highest-quality service (or result) and the purpose of leadership and management within the organisation is to achieve such outcomes.

LEADING AND MANAGING PEOPLE FOR A PURPOSE

We have already identified that organisations need people 'in place' to be led and managed and it follows that these people have to be recruited and selected. Furthermore, in order to be 'suitable', they require relevant knowledge, understanding, skills and abilities to carry out the 'work'. Of course, appointing 'suitable' people is an important aspect of the manager's role in relation to staff, although expecting to find a person who 'fits perfectly' on every occasion is unrealistic. It is, therefore, anticipated that people new to a post will often require training and/or support initially in terms of the details of their actual role and responsibilities and in understanding the organisation. Helping appointees become familiar with and understand the culture of the organisation, alongside the ongoing development of employees and team members, are other parts of a manager's job.

Thus, there are a range of activities that can be described as the 'functional' management of people in organisations. The key areas are summarised below:

- Recruitment and selection
- Induction and mentoring
- Performance review and appraisal
- Staff development

In addition, effective leaders and managers are sensitive to a range of other issues that affect the way people perform at work. Therefore, the focus of the rest of this chapter is on these matters.

171

APPROACHES TO LEADING AND MANAGING PEOPLE

People are marked out from other living beings by their feelings, emotions, values, beliefs and attitudes. These attributes are acquired throughout a lifetime and are unique to each person. They influence the individual's personality, what he or she strives to do in his or her life and how he or she goes about it. Riches (1997: p. 26) describes individuals as having a 'unique pattern of motivations … [which they] are striving to satisfy', while, according to Whitaker (1993: pp. 8–9), 'in the end our behaviour will depend on the ways in which our intentions … are empowered into action'. It follows that behaviour depends on the way in which people believe they, as an individual, are treated as a worker, as a member of a team and as part of an organisation.

Goss (1994) defines two approaches to managing people: 'instrumental' or 'humanistic'. He describes the first as being concerned only with outcomes at any cost. The second model also emphasises the need to achieve the competitive advantage but not necessarily at the expense of the people involved. It attempts to balance the overall strategic management of the organisation with the management of its 'workers'. A similar approach is described by Storey (1987) in his use of 'hard' and 'soft' models for managing people. Hall has suggested some differences in approaches to managing people arising from Storey's hard and soft models (see Table 17.1). The former is concerned with the 'ends' rather than the 'means' while both are important in the latter. Riches (1997: p. 20) also supports the 'soft' model and asserts that 'people are employees and performers with legal and moral rights: they are to be treated as ends and not only means to an organisational end'. Commenting on Storey's model, Hall's (1997) point is that although it is an oversimplification, particularly in the assumption that 'soft' approaches are less controlling than hard ones, it is useful in that it highlights the fact that leading and managing people is always values driven.

LINKING LEADING AND MANAGING PEOPLE TO THE ORGANISATION'S CULTURE

The approach to leading and managing people in an organisation connects directly with its culture. Indeed, for most people, it is the culture that plays a significant part in influencing the way they each develop and enact their individual approach to leading and managing and/or how they expect to be led and managed (Bennett, 2001: pp. 98–122). In the case of the overall leader, the situation is likely to be reversed in that the culture that predominates is

172

Table 17.1 Hard and soft models of managing people

Hard	Soft
Systems led/market led	People led
Cost effectiveness	Effective learning
Improbable goals	Diverse goals, 'visions'
Periphery workers = variable costs	All workers important
Selection to 'fit'	Something to offer
Targeted development	Development for all
'Accountable' appraisal	'Development' appraisal
Human resources	Resourceful humans
People – means to an end	People – ends in themselves
Control, compliance, 'fit'	Consensualism, mutuality, commitment
Training for now	Development for the future
Strategic concern	Excellence ethos
Mechanistic	'Organic'
Uniformity	Flexibility

Source: Hall (1997), p. 145

usually attributable to that person as an expression of his or her personal values. Therefore, in seeking to understand how and why people behave in organisations it is relevant to include a study of organisational culture.

Prosser (1999: p. xii) explains it, in its broadest sense, as a totality, as a way of constructing reality. He suggests that, in practice, culture is usually defined as a system of related subsystems, for example, organisational communication, resource allocation and control systems, combined together with factors such as values and beliefs, norms of behaviour, roles and status, rituals and traditions.

Hall (1997: p. 154) considers whether culture can be managed. She bases her discussion on what she calls her eight 'Cs' of workplace culture: commitment, conditions of service, communication, consultation, creativity, collaboration, conflict, control. Consideration of each 'C' suggests there are ways in which these areas can be developed and culture changed over time. In particular, Hall (1997: p. 158) points to communication, consultation, conflict and control and suggests that these provide 'some clues as to how … boundaries can be made more permeable and obstacles to achieving this'. Her point is that, although these processes provide opportunities to influence the culture of the organisation through choice, they are also demanding and can constrain. For example, consultation may enhance employee commitment but it is also time-consuming and can also raise issues of conflict and control.

LEADING, MANAGING AND PERFORMANCE

The performance of individuals and teams within the organisation is a key issue for both leaders and managers. Whatever their values, beliefs and ways of doing things, leaders' and managers' raison d'être is to enhance the performance of the people within their organisation and make it more effective in whatever way effectiveness is judged. Thus, understanding performance and how it can be managed are important aspects of leading and managing people.

Performance – the way in which people carry out their 'work' – is influenced by many factors and it may change over time, in both the short- and long term. A starting point for performance is the individual's or team's competency in the required tasks. If the appropriate knowledge, understanding or skills are not available, adequate performance is not possible. A lack of information, resources, authority or power can influence performance adversely. Situational variables such as organisational characteristics or leadership affect performance as can external, 'out of work' matters that may, or may not, be in the control of the individual. Other factors, like relationships between colleagues, can also be influential: uncomfortable relationships often result in anxiety and tensions. These can hinder effective performance because emotions are involved which can affect people's performance, both positively and negatively. Unlike other resources, people, as a human resource, have feelings about themselves and their role in the workplace and these influence their motivation to work.

Inevitably, if the purpose of leading and managing is to achieve success and that depends on effectiveness, objective information about actual performance is important for leaders and managers. However, Riches (1997: p. 17) points out that evaluation of performance is fraught with subjectivity. People are inconsistent in their performance or conditions in which performance takes place may vary (Cascio, 1991). Different methods of observing job performance may result in different conclusions about it and, although a variety of predictors can be used, in practice this does not happen and results tend to be unreliable (Ronan and Prien, 1971). Withstanding these reservations, management approaches include evaluation and operate in an attempt to effect performance. Two overall approaches are acknowledged here: those that are performance centred and those that focus on people and factors such as motivation. Performance-centred approaches are distinguishable by their use of frameworks for 'measuring' performance, for example, management by objectives, management competences, inspection frameworks and value-added measures. It is important to acknowledge that performance-centred approaches differ in the extent to which the performance standards in each are internally generated, customised, developmentally orientated or confidential (Middlewood and Lumby, 1998: p. 18). Performance, then, can be managed in a variety of ways and there are obvious similarities with Storey's 'hard' and 'soft' management models.

LEADING AND MANAGING TO MOTIVATE

It goes without saying that a 'workforce' with low morale and self-esteem, and few rewards, will lack motivation. Thus, the management of motivation is a key factor in the successful leadership and management of people within an organisation whether a people- or performance-centred approach is adopted. By understanding what motivates and managing to achieve it, leaders and managers can enhance the performance of the people and teams. Various theories of motivation have been put forward, although Maslow's (1943) hierarchy of needs is probably the best known. Maslow argues that motivation relates to meeting a hierarchy of needs represented within an isosceles triangle. Motivation is directly influenced by the satisfaction of a sequence of needs that move from survival at the lowest level through security, belonging, prestige to self-fulfilment at the apex of the triangle. Maslow's key finding is that people display no motivation to pursue higher-level needs until lower ones are satisfied.

Turning to what we know about human nature generally, it is evident that motivation is aligned with rewards. However, this then raises the issue as to what counts as a reward. Like people, rewards come in various shapes and sizes and are, to a large extent, personal to the individual in as far as he or she values a 'reward' and feels it is appropriate. Pay is the obvious reward although its role in this context is not only about the material welfare it provides. As well as its basic monetary value, Thierry (1992) suggests that pay is meaningful to the employee because it conveys information about important aspects of employment. In other words, pay is an indicator of the level of recognition of the contributions made.

Individuals also seek and, hopefully, achieve rewards from their 'work' in other ways, such as through a sense of 'fit', job satisfaction and self-fulfilment. These are intrinsic rewards and are influenced by a range of factors operating at various levels. They include people's individual attitudes, interests and specific needs, factors that relate to the nature of the job such as level of responsibility and control and, at the organisation level, variables like culture, relationships, leadership and systems-wide rewards (Vandevelde, 1988: p. 12). Some people have what has been described as a 'vocational calling' to a particular professional role while others thrive on responsibility and it is in these types of ways that the rewards of job satisfaction and self-fulfilment can be actualised. It is also evident that pay is not the motivator for those working as volunteers and that intrinsic approaches outweigh anything else here.

Using a typology adapted from Steers and Porter (1991), Goss (1994: p. 87) categorises rewards using a two-dimensional model. Rewards are either extrinsic or intrinsic and are offered to an individual or to a group of people collectively. An adaptation is shown in Figure 17.1. According to Goss, it is useful to think of the quadrants not as mutually exclusive categories but as aspects of a particular reward policy that may be present (in combination to a greater or lesser extent).

Extrinsic

Physical working conditions Administrative support Positive public recognition of profession and/or institution Collective CPD Security (pension, life assurance) Flexible working arrangements (out-of-term time)	Performance-related pay Promotion prospects Career enhancement CPD
Collegiality Relationships with colleagues Feelings of being valued by significant others	Trust Doing a worthwhile job Using personal/professional expertise and experience Autonomy Feeling of personal worth and value

Collectively offered ← → *Individually offered*

Intrinsic

Figure 17.1 Examples of types of reward. CPD, continuing professional development

Source: Adapted from Steers and Porter (1991)

The ways in which leaders and managers enable these rewards to be attained are linked to the themes of this chapter. Here, again, the organisational culture and style of leadership are significant, as are the effective management of the functional aspects of managing people. In respect of the latter, investment in the induction process and knowledge of the individual alongside a strategic approach to staff development are examples of ways in which managers can address the motivation and, hence, the performance of their colleagues.

A LEADERSHIP APPROACH TO MANAGING PEOPLE

This chapter has highlighted a number of themes and issues for leading and managing people and teams. Among them is the relationship between these two functions and its importance, at both a theoretical and practical level, in the effectiveness of organisations. Moreover, it is relevant for those people involved in a leadership capacity at any level within an organisation to understand the concept of a leadership approach, alongside the overall management of people within their organisation. This includes knowing about the people being led and managed, communicating values and priorities and modelling good practice. Effective leaders adopt a strategic approach and lead by example; the key point here being that leaders and managers are themselves subject to the same practices and, therefore, they have a vested interest at a personal level as well as in terms of the effectiveness of their organisation. Perhaps, most importantly, they know that people are their key resources and, without them, there would be no organisation to lead and manage.

REFERENCES

Bennett, N. (2001) Power, structure and culture: an organisational view of school effectiveness and school improvement. In A. Harris and N. Bennett (eds), *School Effectiveness and School Improvement: Alternative Perspectives*. London: Continuum.

Bennis, W. and Nanus, B. (1985) *Leaders*. New York: Harper & Row.

Bryman, A. (1986) *Leadership and Organizations*. London: Routledge & Kogan Page.

Cascio, W.F. (1991) *Applied Psychology in Personnel Management* (4th edn). Englewood Cliffs, NJ: Prentice-Hall.

Goss, D. (1994) *Principles of Human Resource Management*. London: Routledge.

Hall, V. (1997) Managing staff. In B. Fidler, S. Russell and T. Simkins (eds), *Choices for Self-Managing Schools.* London: Paul Chapman Publishing.

Hodgson, P. (1987) Managers can be taught, but leaders have to learn. *ICT*, 19(6): pp. 13–15.

Maslow, A. (1943) A theory of human motivation. *Psychological Review*, 50: 37–96.

Middlewood, D. and Lumby, J. (eds) (1998) *Strategic Management in Schools and Colleges.* London: Paul Chapman Publishing.

Prosser, J. (ed) (1999) *School Culture.* London: Paul Chapman Publishing.

Riches, C. (1997) Managing for people and performance. In T. Bush and D. Middlewood (eds), *Managing People in Education.* London: Paul Chapman Publishing.

Ronan, W.W. and Prien, E.P. (1971) *Perspectives on the Measurement of Human Performance.* New York: Appleton-Century-Crofts.

Sammons, P., Hillman, J. and Mortimore, P. (1997) Key characteristics of effective schools: a review of school effectiveness research. In J. White and M. Barber (eds), *Perspectives on School Effectiveness and School Improvement.* London: Institute of Education, University of London, Bedford Way Papers.

Steers, R. and Porter, L. (eds) (1991) *Motivation and Work Behaviour.* New York: McGraw-Hill.

Storey, J. (1987) Developments in the management of human resources: an interim report. Warwick papers: In industrial Relations, 17. IRRU School of Industrial and Business Studies. University of Warwick.

Thierry, H. (1992) Pay and payment systems. In J. Hartley and G. Stephenson (eds), *Employment Relations.* Oxford: Blackwell.

Vandevelde, B.R. (1988) *Implications of Motivation Theories and Work Motivation Studies for the Redeployment of Teachers.* Sheffield: Sheffield City Polytechnic for Educational Management and Administration.

Whitaker, P. (1993) *Practical Communication in Schools.* Harlow: Longman.

CHAPTER 18

LEADING TEAMS FOR SUCCESS

Lesley Anderson and Maggie Preedy

Successful teamwork is essential in sports teams and workplace settings. This chapter looks at some of the main factors in developing and sustaining effective teams. The main emphasis is on teams in the workplace, but many of the principles also apply to the leadership and coaching of sports teams. Indeed, the experiences of sports teams are often used in the teamwork literature to illustrate wider leadership principles.

GROUPS AND TEAMS

We start by considering how we use the word 'team' in a sport and fitness context. Often we mean a number of people playing a sport together as one side in a game involving two teams, for example, a football or hockey team. Sometimes we may mean individuals (usually) performing the same sport separately and pooling the outcomes to achieve a 'team' result, for example, in swimming and skiing competitions. In all these situations, the people involved are working – or playing – *together* to achieve the same desired outcome: winning the match or event. Each individual has a role to play in the team and the outcome is enhanced when people work together rather than competing on their own. Team members rely on each other to contribute effectively and to the best of their ability.

Turning to the idea of a group, as opposed to a team, the users of a sports centre may be described as a group who want to improve or maintain their fitness although, unless they work actively together to achieve a pre-agreed level in activity sessions, they cannot be described as a team. In the same way, we talk about slimming or book groups rather than teams because individual members experience different outcomes which, in themselves, are not dependent on the efforts of all the other people who make up the group. So a group is a looser notion than a team.

Everard *et al.* (2004: p. 163) provide a useful definition of a team:

> A team is a group of people with common objectives that can effectively tackle any task which it has been set up to do ... The contribution drawn from each member is of the highest possible quality, and is one which could not have been called into play other than in the context of a supportive team.

In workplace settings, teams provide a powerful management approach in many situations when there is a 'job' to be done. They may be used as a formal way to manage activities, for example, the marketing or coaching team. On occasions, an informal team may be created (sometimes called a working party) to investigate a specific situation, for example, a leisure centre's compliance with health and safety legislation.

In a voluntary club there may be a team of people working together to enable a group of young people to participate in a sporting activity such as rugby league or athletics. The 'team' may include a coach, the people who provide equipment and facilities for practice as well as parents and others who transport the young people to the events, wash the kit and provide refreshments.

TEAM BUILDING

Anyone who has coached or worked with a 'team' of any sort will know that teams need to be nurtured and developed if they are going to function well and be successful. By labelling a group 'a team' it does not guarantee that teamwork will follow and team building may be necessary to achieve the desired practice and outcomes.

Tuckman and Jensen (1977) identified various stages that teams may move through as they develop towards effective performance (see Table 18.1).

According to Tuckman and Jensen (1977), the initial forming stage is often accompanied by anxiety as team members seek to establish the purpose of the team and their own role within it. The subsequent 'storming' stage is characterised by conflict as different views are expressed. During the 'norming' stage, working procedures are established and the team builds its own identity.

Table 18.1 Stages of team development

Forming
In the early stages of the team coming together, the role of the team leader is crucial in determining who is in the group, helping members get to know one another, putting members at ease, clarifying goals, roles, responsibilities and procedures. The leader should allow any uncertainties, fears or confusions to be expressed and dealt with at this stage.

Storming
In this phase, members begin to explore their relationships and to test the boundaries. Tensions frequently emerge in the early stages of settling in. There may be some challenges to the leadership, including resistance to all or part of the task, attempts to re-define the task and subgroups may emerge. The leader needs to listen, provide feedback that acknowledges differing views and encourage members to work towards shared goals. If managed carefully, clearing the air should help the team gel and become more cohesive. If the leader is autocratic and tries to suppress conflict then that suppressed conflict may eventually re-emerge as a disruptive influence.

Norming
This phase is characterised by a period of developing constructive relationships and ways of working together. The team leader's role is to ensure that the team establishes an agreed set of operating procedures, rules and working practices. Team-building skills are concerned with facilitating cohesion and ensuring that each member continues to identify with the team's purpose and values. The team may offer mutual support and increased focus on the task.

Performing
This is the stage at which the team is cooperating and working efficiently to achieve its goals. Members work as a unit, and differences of opinion can safely be expressed, acknowledged and resolved through compromise. The role of the team leader is to evaluate team effectiveness, look at efforts, satisfactions and successes of individual members and the team as a whole, and to reward the team through positive feedback and de-briefings. Picking out individual members can foster competitiveness and may be destructive to team spirit.

Adjourning (mourning)
Increasingly in organisations, groups are created for a purpose and then disbanded. This may leave people feeling a sense of loss or uncertainty because belonging to a group and performing effectively within it takes up emotional as well as physical and cognitive energy. As the team disbands, leaders need to give members feedback individually and as a team on how they have done and what has been learned. In extreme situations, such as an institution being radically reorganised, merged or closed, members may be reluctant to let the team finally disband. They may show some bereavement behaviours such as denial and anger before they are able to move on.

(continued)

Table 18.1 (continued)

Dorming
Sometimes groups keep going beyond their 'sell by' date. The project or task is completed but the group is never adjourned or disbanded. Leaders need to be able to grasp the nettle of disbanding such teams and instilling a new sense of role and purpose in their members through encouraging them to move to new activities.

Reforming
This may be necessary if, for example, a project or task has not been satisfactorily completed, or if critical characteristics of the external environment change, or if the initial phase was focused on evaluating a pilot activity then a new phase may need a different team to operationalise the innovation.

Source: Adapted from Tuckman and Jensen (1977)

By the time the team reaches the 'performing' stage high levels of trust and support should be evident.

Bell (1992: p. 53) suggests that there are also four central factors in the development of successful teams. These are the team objectives, procedures, processes and review – all team members need to understand and participate in each of them. Procedures include decision-making and planning, while processes are concerned with what has to be done by whom, by when and with what resources. Bell argues that the team should review its work regularly as part of its ongoing development.

TEAM ROLES AND BEHAVIOURS

As indicated above, each member has a role to play in the activities of a team. In the case of a netball team, the goal shooter and goal defence have different roles; similarly in a football team, the centre forward has different responsibilities from those in midfield. Alongside these roles and responsibilities that are prescribed by the situation, research has shown that individuals working as team members tend to behave, contribute and interrelate with others in certain ways. Belbin (1981) observed how team members interact and the resulting impact on team performance during training in business settings and, from this work, developed theory relating to the optimum combination of team roles. Subsequently, it has been found that this theory applies to a wide range of teams, not just those in a business setting. Belbin's roles, their characteristics and other qualities are summarised in Table 18.2.

lesley anderson and maggie preedy

Table 18.2 Belbin's team roles

Type	Characteristics	Positive qualities	Allowable weaknesses
Implementer	Translates ideas into practice. Gets on with the job. Works with care and thoroughness.	Organising ability. Common sense. Integrity. Hard working. Self-disciplined. Loyal.	Lack of flexibility and adaptability.
Coordinator	Controls and co-ordinates. Driven by objectives. Utilises team resources.	Enthusiastic. Assertive. Flexible. Strong sense of duty.	Not really creative or inspirational.
Shaper	Pushes to get the job done. Inspires. Makes things happen.	Drive. Enthusiasm. Challenges roles. Commands respect. Intolerant of vagueness.	Needs to be in charge. Impulsive. Impatient. Unduly sensitive to criticism.
Innovator	Advances new ideas. Synthesises knowledge.	Intelligence. Imagination. Creativity. Unorthodox.	Prefers ideas to people. Ignores practical issues.
Resource investigator	Identifies ideas and resources from outside the team. Questions and explores.	Very good at networking. Positive. Cheerful. Sustains the team.	Lacks self-discipline. Impulsive. Quick to loose interest.
Monitor evaluator	Critical thinker. Analyses ideas. Constantly reviews the team.	Interprets complex data. Judgement, hard-headed, objective.	Over-critical. Negative. Intellectually competitive, sceptical and cynical.
Team worker	Socially orientated. Loyal to the team. Promotes harmony. Perceptive of feelings, needs and concerns.	Stable, extrovert, good listener. Promotes strengths. Underpins weaknesses.	Indecisive, can forget a task.
Completer finisher	Drives for task completion – on time and according to specification.	Obsessed with detail. Strong sense of purpose. Driven by targets.	Anxious, compulsive, can lower morale.
Specialist	Having pre-existing specialist skills and knowledge.	Contributes specialist skills and expertise.	Narrow and specific vision.

Source: Adapted from West-Burnham (1992), p. 128

Table 18.3 Personality preferences

Extraversion (E)	Introversion (I)
Sensing (S)	Intuition (N)
Thinking (T)	Feeling (F)
Judging (J)	Perceiving (P)

Belbin found that teams with most, or all, of their members in the 'high achieving' categories did not automatically succeed as might have been expected nor did they always 'gel' as a team. The most successful teams comprise members who are complementary in their range of team roles. For example, a team with several shapers and/or coordinators is likely to experience internal leadership problems that may lead to it not being able to operate effectively. Similarly, a team with many team workers may lack drive and direction.

Belbin and his team used these findings to develop a series of psychometric tests based on personality, mental ability, values and motivations, as these are the key predictors of the team roles that individuals are likely to play. The tests can be used when recruiting to a new team. The information provided by the tests is also very useful for the individual in developing their self-awareness as team members. It is also important to acknowledge that team behaviour may be modified by life experience, by particular constraints such as the presence of someone the team members wish to impress, and by the process of training in team work.

Other instruments have been developed to assess personality type which can then be used to inform the creation of teams and team work. We mention one other here briefly, the Myers-Briggs Type Indicator (MBTI), which is designed to make the theory of psychological types, described by the psychologist Carl Jung, understandable and useful in people's lives. It identifies a number of different personality 'preferences' or characteristics, which can be grouped in pairs or dichotomies, as shown in Table 18.3. The MBTI describes 16 distinctive personality types that result from the interactions among the preferences (see examples in Table 18.4). All types are of equal worth; there is no 'best' type.

CHARACTERISTICS OF EFFECTIVE TEAMS

Teams have both a task dimension – focused on achieving their designated objectives – and a social dimension – oriented towards providing a supportive social setting where members feel that they can work on group objectives

Table 18.4 Examples of personality types

INFJ	ESFP
Seek meaning and connection in ideas, relationships, and material possessions. Want to understand what motivates people, and are insightful about others. Conscientious and committed to their firm values. Develop a clear vision about how best to serve the common good. Organised and decisive in implementing their vision.	Outgoing, friendly, and accepting. Exuberant lovers of life, people, and material comforts. Enjoy working with others to make things happen. Bring common sense and a realistic approach to their work, and make work fun. Flexible and spontaneous, adapt readily to new people and environments. Learn best by trying a new skill with other people.

successfully and develop their own skills. Recognising these two dimensions, we can identify three main criteria for assessing team effectiveness (Hackman, 2002):

Serving customers needs: The team's outputs, products or services meet or exceed customers' expectation in terms of quality and timeliness. Sports organisations and their work teams are service providers, so customers' standards and assessments of the quality of their service are key factors in judging team success. In the voluntary sector, users' standards are similarly important.

Developing as a team: The social processes and dynamics of the team foster members' capabilities to work together interdependently. Over time, team members become highly skilled in coordinating their activities to build commitment and develop team expertise.

Individuals' learning and self-esteem: Experience of working in the group contributes positively to the learning and sense of well-being of team members. Teamwork provides a very helpful setting for expanding individuals' knowledge and skills, and exploring alternative perspectives. It can also give the scope for developing productive professional relationships as the basis for a sense of belonging to a community of practice.

Other criteria for evaluating team effectiveness are suggested by Katzenbach and Smith (1993), focused around team *performance*. Based on extensive research on team work in private and public sector contexts, their study found that major and meaningful performance challenges to the team – for example, being entrusted with achieving one of the organisation's key current priorities – galvanise and energise the team to do its best – team members rise to the challenge. Leaders can promote effective teams best by building a strong performance ethic, aiming at continuous improvement, rather than by building a strong team esprit de corps alone. These authors argue that discipline and clear expectations about performance – both within the team and across the organisation – create the necessary demands and pressures for effective team performance. High expectations provide the incentive for motivation and effort in the collective work of the team. The performance of individuals is important but need not compete or conflict with valuing team performance. In elite sport, the performance of star individuals is often celebrated in the press, but the results of the team are dependent on their collective efforts and achievements as a whole.

You may feel that for both sport and work teams the final point above may be problematic. There are often tensions between recognising and rewarding star performers and maintaining the motivation and morale of the other team members. Contextual factors within the team and the organisation are important here. Hackman (2002) argues that there are several conditions that organisations and team leaders can put into place to encourage and increase the chances that teams will perform strongly on each of the three effectiveness criteria outlined above. These conditions are that the team:

- Is a *real* team – geared towards the performance stage in Tuckman's terms.

  Real teams have the following components: a clear task, defined boundaries, clearly specified authority to manage their own work processes, and membership stability over a reasonable period of time.
- Has a compelling purpose and direction for its work.

  Good direction involves clear but challenging aspirations, and setting end points rather than specific means for reaching them – these features serve to energise, orient and engage team effort.
- Has an enabling structure that facilitates teamwork.

  Good enabling structures include clearly designated responsibilities for each member, group norms of conduct, and the scope for members to practise and develop their skills, and feel a sense of achievement in meeting team goals.
- Has a supportive organisational context.

  This includes processes for recognising and rewarding team performance, provision of information, and technical and other forms of support, and pressure to team achievement in terms of the organisation valuing the team's work.

- Has available expert coaching in teamwork.

  Expert coaching focuses on developing and building key team processes: effort, performance strategy and knowledge and skills.

BARRIERS TO SUCCESSFUL TEAMWORK

So far we have looked at some of the main characteristics of teams and what makes them effective. However, many workplace teams do not perform very successfully, and this can be a source of considerable frustration and stress for their members. Major barriers to teamwork arise from neglect of the factors considered above: lack of teambuilding, allowing for the various stages identified by Tuckman; failure to include members who, between them can cover the main team roles, so that some team functions identified by Belbin and others are neglected; lack of focus on the three criteria of customer needs, team development and personal learning, and the conditions required for teams to meet these criteria.

Another barrier to effective teamwork that sometimes occurs in well-established teams is known as 'groupthink' (Janis, 1982). This takes place where group members come to value consensus and conformity to group norms above all other priorities, and thus avoid any disagreement or conflict. They place undue emphasis on maintaining cohesion in the social dimension of teamwork, neglecting the task aspect, and feel strong pressure to agree with the ideas and suggestions of other members, particularly the team leader and other influential members of the group. This leads to a decline in creativity and innovative thinking and quality of decision-making, and an increase in conservatism, parochialism, failure to challenge and debate views and explore alternatives. While group consensus and harmony are often portrayed as features of successful teams, these need to be balanced by a clear focus on team objectives and tasks, willingness to challenge views and propose alternatives, and to express dissent clearly and overtly.

Constructive debate and disagreement about team goals and means for reaching them are an important part of effective decision-making, ensuring that the range of alternatives is considered. However, many teams experience some degree of *relationship* conflict and disharmony between individuals or groups within the team. Features that are damaging to the team are interpersonal conflict and dysfunctional relationships, leading to a range of undesirable outcomes, such as lack of commitment, opting out, and covert and overt hostility.

MANAGING CONFLICT IN THE TEAM

We can identify three basic approaches to managing conflict, drawing on Walton (1987):

1. Bargaining over a fixed issue, where one party gains and the other loses.
2. Problem-solving to resolve a variable issue, where it is possible to identify underlying shared interests and create a win/win outcome.
3. Relationship structuring, where the parties review and redefine their mutual perceptions and attitudes, how they interpret each others' roles, as a basis for building a reformed relationship based on better mutual understanding.

Clearly approaches 2) and 3) are more desirable than 1) if team harmony is to be re-established and maintained.

In each case, a neutral third party acting as mediator and negotiator may speed the conflict resolution process. This is because conflict resolution is an interactive and reciprocal activity – the stance taken by each party will affect the approach of the other. Pedler *et al.* (2007) argue that the appropriate strategy for conflict resolution depends on two dimensions: the assertiveness/unassertiveness of each party in pursuing her/his own goals; and the degree of cooperativeness/uncooperativeness of each in acknowledging the goals of the other party. This gives rise to five approaches to conflict resolution shown in Figure 18.1. Clearly the parties or their negotiator need to move away from the competing and avoiding positions and towards one of the other three positions in order to reach an agreed solution.

Other strategies for managing team conflict and achieving a win/win outcome or altered relationship between the parties are outlined below (Thompson, 2002).

- Avoiding the tendency of people in conflict to assume that their interests are 100% opposed to those of the other party – often there are considerable areas of shared interest that can be built on. A key factor here is the exchange of information by the parties or their mediator.
- Building trust and rapport based on common interests and views.
- Focusing on objective, rather than subjective arguments, and attending to issues of fairness, equity and need, avoiding emotive issues, and depersonalising the matters subject to negotiation.
- Establishing procedures and norms for negotiating based on simplicity, clarity, justifiability and consensus.

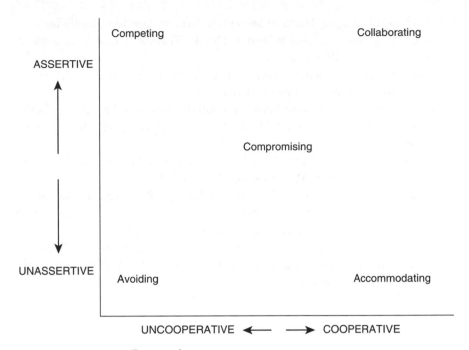

Figure 18.1 Conflict resolution

CONCLUSION

In summary, we can describe leading the effective team as a complex balancing act – between individual, social and task dimensions, between stability and change, and between process and outcomes. The balance between the team and the organisational setting is also important – the success of the team is in large part dependent on establishing supportive conditions for its work, both within the team and in the organisation more broadly. Finally, this chapter has emphasised a collaborative approach to team leadership, where the leader is an enabler and coordinator of equals, recognising that teams comprise talented individuals, and that teams perform most effectively, both in a sporting and a work context, where members are all equally valued and supported in striving to achieve their best.

REFERENCES

Belbin, M. (1981) *Management Teams: Why They Succeed or Fall*. London: Heinemann.

Bell, L. (1992) *Managing Teams in Secondary Schools*. London: Routledge.

Everard, K.B., Morris, G. and Wilson, I. (2004) *Effective School Management*. 4th edn. London: Paul Chapman.

Hackman, R. (2002) *Leading Teams: Setting the Stage For Great Performance*. Boston, MA: Harvard Business School Press.

Janis, I. (1982) *Victims of Groupthink*. 2nd edn. Boston, MA: Houghton-Mifflin.

Katzenbach, J. and Smith, D. (1993) *The Wisdom of Teams*. New York: Harper Business.

Pedler, M., Burgoyne, J. and Boydell, T. (2007) *A Managers Guide to Self Development*. 5th edn. Maidenhead: McGraw-Hill.

Thompson, N. (2002) *People Skills*, 2nd edn. Basingstoke: Palgrave Macmillan.

Tuckman, B.W. and Jensen, M. (1977) Stages of small group development revisited. *Groups and Organisational Studies*, 2: 419–427.

Walton, R. (1987) *Managing Conflict*. 2nd edn. New York: Addison Wesley.

West-Burnham, J. (1992) *Managing Quality in Schools: A TQM Approach*. Harlow: Longman Group.

CHAPTER 19

UNDERSTANDING ORGANISATIONAL CULTURE IN SPORT[1]

Russell Hoye, Aaron Smith, Hans Westerbeek, Bob Stewart and Matthew Nicholson

WHAT IS ORGANISATIONAL CULTURE?

Culture was originally defined by anthropologists as the values and beliefs common to a group of people. These researchers set themselves the task of investigating, interpreting and translating the behavioural and social patterns of groups of individuals by trying to understand the manner in which they relate to their environment. From an organisational perspective, researchers like Miles (1975) and Pettigrew (1979) observed that while people in organisations run the technology and invent the processes, they in turn, as part of the process, have much of their behaviour determined by the system they operate. In other words, there are underlying forces that impact upon behaviour. The concept of culture is a way of putting a name to these forces.

There is no single accepted definition of organisational culture. For example, organisational culture is viewed by some as the 'personality' of an organisation, while for others it represents the things which make an organisation unique. Several assumptions about organisational culture are well accepted though. These are:

1 Culture tends to be inflexible and resistant to easy or rapid change.
2 Culture is shaped by an organisation's circumstances, its history and its members.
3 Culture is learned and shared by members of an organisation and is reflected in common understandings and beliefs.

[1] Edited from Hoye, R., Westerbeek, H., Stewart, B. and Nicholson, M. (2006) 'Organizational cultures' in *Sport Management: Principles and Applications*, pp. 145–161, Oxford: Butterworth-Heinmann.

4   Culture is often covert; the deep values and beliefs causing behaviour can be hidden from organisational members, making them difficult to identify.
5   Culture is manifested in a variety of ways that affect the performance of an organisation and its members.

Although elements of commonality exist in the way in which researchers conceive and define culture in organisations, much inconsistency and controversy can still be found. However, for the purposes of this chapter, we shall discuss organisational culture in a way consistent with the view of Schein (1984, 1997), who invokes a more psycho-dynamic view. This means that he believes culture is, in part, an unconscious phenomenon, driven by deep-level assumptions and beliefs, and where conscious views are merely artefacts and symbolic representations. For example, most sport clubs members would report that on-field winning is important. Schein's interpretation of organisational culture would lead to questions about *why* winning is important. Does it have to do with a need to belong to a successful group, the pressure of peers, or some other more mysterious explanation? While many people involved in sport and fitness would think this question easy to answer, it is less easy to specify the underpinning values that drive unusual rituals, ceremonies, myths, legends, stories, beliefs, memorabilia and attitudes.

In current and former nations of the British Commonwealth, cricket is played with enormous enthusiasm, but can take up to five, six-hour days to complete a single match, which often ends in a draw. Similarly, to the uninitiated, American football seems quite strange with each team comprising separate players for offensive and defensive manoeuvres. Off the field can be just as odd. In Australia, many (Australian Rules) football clubs have 'sausage-sizzles' (BBQs), 'pie-nights' (involving the traditional meal of a meat pie) and a host of rituals associated with drinking beer. In addition, many sport organisations are packed with memorabilia and expect their employees to work during evening training sessions and weekend games. Sport organisations are rich with strong, meaningful cultural symbols, which on the surface seem easy to interpret, but sometimes are only superficial symptoms of deeper issues.

What Schein searches for is not the superficial, but rather the unconsciously held fundamental concepts of right or wrong; what an organisation might perceive as correct or incorrect values. These values, which are the foundation of an organisation's culture, do not simply exist or come into being by their own volition. Instead, they are painstakingly built up by members of the organisation as they gradually learn to interact and achieve their collective and individual aims (Schein, 1984). The originators of the organisation, together with the more powerful of the organisation's past and present members, are usually the most influential in determining the culture. Thus, Schein prefers to examine the long-held assumptions and beliefs in an organisation, believing that they will more likely explain the organisation's culture.

For the purposes of this chapter, we shall define sport and fitness organisational culture as follows:

Sport organisational culture is a collection of fundamental values, beliefs and attitudes that are common to members of a sport organisation, and which subsequently set the behavioural standards or norms for all members (Ogbonna and Harris, 2002; Pettigrew, 1979; Schein, 1985). This definition reflects the view that sport organisations have ways of approaching things that have evolved over time. In many ways, organisational culture therefore holds answers to questions about solving problems. Culture is how 'things are done around here' and how we 'think about things here'. Culture therefore can be seen as a subtle form of 'brainwashing'.

THE IMPORTANCE OF CULTURE TO SPORT ORGANISATIONS

In many countries sport has for some time been regarded as a particularly important social institution. Sporting heroes are often national heroes as well. Examples include Michael Jordan and Vince Lombardi in the United States, Roger Bannister and David Beckham in the United Kingdom, Shigeo Nagashima and Hanada Katsuji (sumo name, Wakanohana) in Japan, and Sir Donald Bradman and Ian Thorpe in Australia. Although these names are not the definitive sporting heroes of the nations identified, their sports and personal profiles are illustrative of the national cultural pressures that influence the sport organisations they host. This quick list, for example, excludes women; a trait common to many sport organisational cultures, and one that many are seeking to change. However, the influence of the national culture means that such changes are more likely to occur in some nations than others (Hofstede, 1991).

We can expect that different types of sport organisations will possess different kinds of cultures. For example, professional clubs and major national leagues are more likely to emphasise dispassionate business values, while smaller, not-for-profit associations are more likely to value participation and fun. Some sport organisations like Italian and Spanish football clubs are geared almost exclusively to winning and are prepared to go heavily into debt in order to do so.

Others, like the company Formula One Holdings, manage the commercial rights to major events and have little other interest than to make money. While the Fédération Internationale de l'Automobile seeks to regulate motor sport, others still, like the International Olympic Committee, are interested in developing sport around the world, and in so doing acquire vast sums of money and spend it liberally.

The commercial and competitive pressures placed upon sport organisations from local football clubs, universities and colleges, to professional leagues and teams, has encouraged sport managers to embrace business tools and concepts like organisational culture. Culture is important to sport organisations because a better understanding of it can help to bring about change. Since organisational culture is so influential on the performance of its members, it is critical that cultural traits are both appropriate and strong. In the case of sport, it is common to have strong cultures that have been forged by tradition and a fierce sense of history, but some cultural characteristics like excessive drinking and on-field violence may no longer suit the more professional management approach that needs to be assumed.

Commentaries on organisational culture, while as disparate as the number of researchers pursuing its investigation, generally emphasise its most superficial manifestation. Moreover, organisational culture is frequently seen as mono-cultural; that is, it is perceived at one level, and as one entity. The organisation is distinguished as a giant cultural mass, constructed equivalently throughout, and with little or no internal variability. However, this methodology is difficult to sustain when analysing a sporting organisation. Sporting club cultures are inherently poly- (multi-) cultural, and can be perceived readily at several levels, or as several entities. For example, as an organisational or administrative unit comparable to other business organisations; as a supporter organisation, whose aims, objectives and traditions may be different (such as winning matches in preference to making a financial profit); and as a player unit, where motivation may vary from glory to money. While a player may perform for a club because of loyalty or remuneration (or any number of other reasons), the supporters are usually passionately attached to the clubs' colours and traditions, expecting only on-field success in return.

SUB-CULTURES AND SPORT

In sporting organisational cultures there is the additional hurdle of translating and adopting a culture directly from traditional business theory. It is dangerously simplistic to assume that a sporting organisation should adopt the methods and practices of a traditional business without addressing the cultural variables. While business methods can be transferred to accommodate the organisational strategies of a sporting club, a direct transfer fails to confront the issue of what it is that makes the culture of a sporting organisation differ from that of a traditional business enterprise.

Ideal business culture tends to reflect a willingness by an organisation's employees to embrace a standard of performance that promotes quality in the production of goods and services, in the attempt to generate a financial profit. This cultural ideology, while cognisant of business necessities, is unable to cater for the more diverse structures that exist in a sporting organisation. In any business, fiscal realities must be acknowledged, but in a sporting business, additional behavioural variables require recognition and respect. While different businesses have different cultures, they are less variable than the cultural differences between individual sports. It cannot be assumed, for example, that a single unified culture exists for all sports.

Fighting during a sporting context is an example of the variability of sporting culture. While in just about every ball game it is illegal to punch people, it is acceptable behaviour in some cases. The situation could not be clearer in terms of official rules and regulations. An overt punch in soccer is an immediate red-card, sending-off offence. In contrast, a punch in rugby union will only get the player a warning, and the opposition a penalty in their favour. In soccer, punching is unacceptable. In rugby, it is merely discouraged. The identical behaviours have quite different cultural meanings. Furthermore, in ice hockey, fighting is virtually considered an inherent and accepted part of the game, and charging the pitcher, although illegal, is considered to be almost within the batter's moral right should they be struck by a wayward pitch in baseball. Consider the ramifications of a punch thrown at the Wimbledon Tennis Championships or on the eighteenth green of Augusta. Sport managers must be aware of the cultural nuances of their respective sports and the influence they have upon players, employees, members, fans and the general public.

Culture is not a simple matter within a single sport either. Professional players, for example, have a different cultural attitude from some amateurs and spectators. This variability of attitudes is symptomatic of a wider, more troublesome area: the clash of cultures within sports. This is illustrated best at an international level, where players from different countries have been brought up with profoundly different ideologies of the game, and how it should be played. Soccer – the 'world game' – is indicative of this culture clash, in addition to the immense cultural

195

significance inherent in the game. Like all living cultures, sport is incessantly changing, dynamic in nature and subject to constant reinterpretation by its participants and viewers. The only apparent consistency in sporting culture is the pursuit of competition, the love of winning, and the ability to summon strong emotional responses in both victory and defeat.

Clearly, there is a need to study organisational cultures, accounting for the effect of the sport itself. For example, in the same way that we might expect that accounting firms might share some cultural traits, so might we predict that judo clubs do also. Similarly, the tradition and discipline central to a judo club might be expected to encourage cultural characteristics different to the youthful and eclectic philosophy found in a BMX club. Furthermore, these cultural characteristics might seep into the executive officers and employees of the clubs. Since so many sporting organisations covet tradition and the accomplishments of the past, they also tend to be resistant to change. However, before any change can occur, an organisation's culture needs to be accurately diagnosed.

DIAGNOSING AND MANAGING ORGANISATIONAL CULTURE

The central problem is that in order to grasp the concept of culture and its relationship to the individual, the group, and the organisation, an in-depth approach is required. Sport organisations create intentions and atmospheres that influence behaviour, routines, practices and the very thought systems of people. These systems and processes subsequently form patterns that are acquired primarily through socialisation, or learning over time from the reactions and behaviours of others. In essence, individuals within an organisation are exposed to what researchers call 'culture revealing' situations, which might include the observable behaviour of other members, their organisational methods, 'artefacts' – the photos, honour boards and other memorabilia on show – and interactive communication, or the way in which individuals talk to each other. Some of these common superficial and observable representations of organisational culture are reproduced in Table 19.1. These are important to recognise because the driving values and belief systems behind them can never be seen as anything more than observable 'symptoms'.

Although the superficial aspects of culture can be observed, the difficulty comes in their interpretation because they are merely surface representations of deeper values. Thus, a useful cultural diagnosis will always seek to understand what drives the observable behaviour. For example, what does it mean if an employee

Table 19.1 Observable symptoms of sport organisational culture

Symptom	Explanation
Environment	The general surroundings of an organisation, like the building it is housed in and the geographical location, like the city or in a grandstand.
Artefacts	Physical objects located in the organisation from its furnishings to its coffee machine.
Language	The common words and phrases used by most organisational members, including gestures and body language.
Documents	Any literature including reports, statements, promotional material, memos and emails produced for the purpose of communication.
Logos	Any symbolic visual imagery including colours and fonts that convey meaning about the organisation.
Heroes	Current or former organisational members who are considered exemplars.
Stories	Narratives shared by organisational members based at least partly on true events.
Legends	An event with some historical basis but has been embellished with fictional details.
Rituals	Standardised and repeated behaviours.
Rites	Elaborate, dramatic, planned set of activities.

makes a mistake and is severely reprimanded by his or her boss? What does common jargon imply? Why are certain rituals typical, like the celebration of employees' birthdays?

The question remains as to how observations made translate into deeper values. Most researchers recommend some form of classification system that describes organisational culture in the form of 'dimensions', each one a deeper, core value. These dimensions reflect on particular organisational characteristics as an aid to categorising cultures. The summation of these characteristics is used to describe an organisation's culture, which can then allow for comparisons to be undertaken between varying organisations. For example, observable evidence in the form of an end of season awards night in a sporting club might be suggestive of the nature of the organisation's reward/motivation values. Enough observable evidence can lead a sport manager to make some tentative conclusions about each dimension. Table 19.2 lists some common dimensions used to describe organisational culture. They can be seen as continua, an organisation's position somewhere between the two extremes.

Table 19.2 Cultural dimensions

Dimension	Characteristics
Stability/changeability	Disposition toward change: Degree to which organisation encourages alternative 'ways of doing things' or existing ways.
Cooperation/conflict	Disposition toward problem resolution: Degree to which organisation encourages cooperation or conflict.
Goal focus/orientation	Clarity and nature of objectives and performance expectations.
Reward/motivation	Nature of reward orientation of organisational members: Degree to which organisation encourages seniority or performance.
Control/authority	Nature and degree of responsibility, freedom and independence of organisational members.
Time/planning	Disposition toward long-term planning: Degree to which organisation encourages short-term or long-term thinking.

Source: Adapted from: Smith, A. and Shilbury, D. (2004) Mapping cultural dimensions in Australian sporting organizations. *Sport Management Review*, 7(2): 133–165

Any analysis that captures the complexity of organisational culture may have great difficulty in separating the interwoven strands of organisational history and personal relationships. As a result, concrete conclusions may be difficult to establish. It is therefore important to take advantage of the symbolism created by myth, ritual and ceremony that is abundant in sport organisations in order to gain a complete understanding of the full range of human behaviour within a complex organisation. The traditions, folklore, mythologies, dramas, and successes and traumas of the past, are the threads that weave together the fabric of organisational culture.

A psychological approach is helpful in identifying and interpreting human behaviour in organisations as cultural phenomena. Psychologists, originally stimulated by the work of Carl Jung, suggest that there are different levels of behavioural awareness, from the conscious to unconscious. Organisational psychologists have appropriated this kind of thinking and transposed it to culture. The key analogy is that an organisation is like a mind.

From the psychological viewpoint, the readily apparent and observable qualities of a sporting organisation are the same as the conscious part of an individual mind. These include the physical environment, the public statements of officials, the way individuals interactively communicate, the form of language used, what clothes are worn, and the memorabilia that fills the rooms and offices. Another of the most important observable qualities involves the place of sporting heroes. They are culturally rich and are highly visible indicators of the culture that is sought. Heroes give an insight into the culture of an organisation, since they are selected by the rank and file as well as the power brokers. In addition, they indicate those qualities in individuals which are respected and admired by a wider audience. The hero is a powerful figure in a sporting organisation, and may be simultaneously an employee and ex-player. The hero may also be charismatic, entrepreneurial, or just plain administrative, which often characterises business enterprises. By understanding the orientation of hero figures, both past and present, it is possible to map the trends in cultural change. Heroes can be both reactionary and progressive. Heroes that reinforce the dominant culture will not change the values and attitudes that the culture emphasises. On the other hand, a hero that transcends and transforms the dominant culture will be a catalyst for change in the behaviours and values of a club. Often a hero is the most powerful medium for change management to be successful.

Tradition is another window into the culture of an organisation. Like heroes, traditions are readily observable through memorabilia, but it is important to note that the underlying values and assumptions that give meaning to heroes and tradition reside in the deeper levels of a culture. Tradition may on one hand be preserved by the present cultural identity, while on the other hand the sporting organisation may have developed a contemporary cultural personality. Thus, it is useful to acknowledge the importance of tradition and history to a sporting organisation because it may be a cultural linchpin, or a stepping stone from which their cultural character has launched itself.

In order to bypass the obstacles (in the form of stereotypical views and superficial signs) that can block an assessment of culture, it is essential to analyse and explore natural, observable outcroppings of culture; places where the cultural understandings can be exposed. By analysing these sites, it is possible to gain a practical insight into the underlying culture of the organisation. Thus, this level deals with organisational rites because, first, their performance is readily apparent, and second, in performing these rites, employees generally use other cultural forms of expression, such as certain customary language or jargon, gestures, and artefacts. These rites, which are shared understandings, are additionally conveyed through myths, sagas, legends, or other stories associated with the occasion, and in practical terms may take the form of barbecues or presentations. In order to actively assess this level of culture, not only must observational techniques be employed, but meanings must be attached to them. This requires more than a superficial level of analysis.

There are also 'unconscious' parts of organisations as well. In effect, it is the unconscious that controls the individual. This incorporates the beliefs, habits, values, behaviours and attitudes prevalent in a sporting organisation. An accurate assessment of this level of culture is difficult and fraught with danger. For example, how employees say they behave and what they state they believe, has to be compared to their actual behaviour.

CHANGING ORGANISATIONAL CULTURE

Cultural understanding stems from successfully translating information into meaning. Every aspect of a sporting organisation is symbolically representative in some way of its culture. All information is not equal, however, yet all possible data must be analysed in order to establish the most holistic representation possible of the existing culture. In order for a culture to be created and bolstered, shared values and beliefs must in some way be reinforced and transferred to organisational members through tangible means. A cultural map summarises the predominant features of a sporting organisation's culture, and provides a means in which raw data can be interpreted into measurable criteria. It works by providing sets of categories in which information can be collected and summarised with the intention of identifying the main themes that continually emerge. Some researchers believe that this approach can also be used in a more statistical form, the numbers attached to responses from questions derived from the dimensions and answered by organisational members (e.g. Howard, 1998).

While the range and diversity of information available for cultural analysis is profound, many cultural studies ignore all but the most apparent and accessible data. A holistic cultural analysis will utilise every available piece of information, with the more obvious elements becoming vehicles for the transmission of less tangible, more subjective facets of culture. However, the culture of any one sporting organisation cannot be classified into one of just a few categories, even though there are many models (e.g. Goffee and Jones, 1996) which offer four quadrants or divisions. There are as many organisational cultures as there are sporting organisations, and they cannot be generically categorised into one of a fixed number of groups. Sporting clubs are immersed in tradition, history, values, and myths, and these should figure prominently in any diagnosis. From an accurate diagnosis change is possible.

The main lesson for cultural change is that it cannot be tackled without a clear prior understanding of an organisation's chief cultural traits and how they are manifested. Once an accurate diagnosis has been undertaken, through

some form of formal or informal cultural map, elements of culture can be managed. Since a sport manager cannot literally change people's minds, they instead have to change people's actions. To some extent this can be imposed or encouraged, but it is a slow process. For example, new rituals can be introduced to replace older, less desirable ones, like a club dinner instead of a drinking binge. Entrenched values and beliefs can be extremely difficult to change, and even with the right introduction of new symbols, language, heroes, stories, employees, etc., genuine cultural change in an organisation can take a generation of members to take hold.

SUMMARY

In the world of sport management, organisational culture has gained prominence as a concept useful in assessing and managing performance. Sport organisational culture can be defined as the collection of fundamental values and attitudes that are common to members of a sport organisation, and which subsequently set the behavioural standards or norms for all members. The difficult is, however, that the deep values common to organisational members are not easy to access. As a way of getting around this inaccessibility problem, sport managers can use cultural dimensions which suggest some of the possible values that are present. Once a thorough diagnosis has been completed, sport managers can work toward adapting and replacing undesirable cultural characteristics.

REFERENCES

Goffee, R. & Jones, G. (1996) What holds the modern company together? *Harvard Business Review*, 74(6): 133–149.

Hofstede, G. (1991) *Cultures and Organisations: Software of the Mind*. London: McGraw Hill.

Howard, L. (1998) Validating the competing values model as a representation of organisational cultures. *International Journal of Organisational Analysis*, 6(3): 231–251.

Miles, R.E (1975) *Theories of Management: Implications For Organisational Behaviour and Development*. New York: McGraw-Hill.

Ogbonna, E. and Harris, L.C. (2002) Organisational culture: A ten year, two-phase study of change in the UK food retailing sector, *Journal of Management Studies*, 39: 673–706.

Pettigrew, A.M. (1979) On studying organisational cultures. *Administrative Science Quarterly*, 24: 570–581.

Schein, E. (1984) *Coming to a New Awareness of Organisational Culture*. San Francisco: Jossey-Bass.

Schein, E. (1985) How culture forms, develops and changes. In *Gaining Control of the Corporate Culture* (Kilman, R.H., Saxton, M.J. and Serpa, R. et al., eds). San Francisco: Jossey-Bass, pp. 17–43.

Schein, E. (1997) *Organisational Culture and Leadership*, 3rd edn. San Francisco: Jossey-Bass.

CHAPTER 20

LEADING CHANGE AND STRATEGIC PLANNING

Maggie Preedy

INTRODUCTION

In the fast-paced world of the twenty-first century, it is a truism that change is the only constant factor, both in our personal lives and in the workplace. The theme of this chapter is understanding and tackling change in the workplace, where the ability to handle change or innovation successfully is an essential skill, whatever your work setting is and your role within it. You may be employed by a large national leisure or fitness chain, or work as an independent coach or fitness trainer, or as a volunteer manager of a sports team. This chapter uses the term 'organisation' as shorthand to cover this wide range of workplace settings. The chapter is structured as follows: first, we look at various types of organisational change, then at some useful models for understanding change and the factors that need to be taken into account in ensuring successful innovation; finally, we briefly consider strategic planning, why it is important and how it takes place.

TYPES OF ORGANISATIONAL CHANGE

We can distinguish between various types of change.

Change may be *planned* – a deliberate alteration in policy or practice designed to improve organisational performance – or *unplanned* and unpredictable, for example the departure of a key member of staff. Innovation can be *proactive*, that is, taking the initiative, as for instance in creating a new pricing strategy to attract retired people as a new client group for a health and fitness club. On the other hand, it may be *reactive*, that is, introduced in response to changing customer demands or alterations in government policy and guidelines, such as a national policy initiative to encourage wider participation in sport and reduce obesity. Change may be *externally generated*, as in the example of the participation policy mentioned above, or *internally generated*, that is, devised by the managers and staff within the organisation.

Innovation may be *incremental* and gradual, as, for example, in the ongoing replacement of pieces of gym equipment as they wear out, or *radical*, involving major innovation, such as the complete redesign and refitting of the gym. It may be a *core* innovation, that is, a change in the central functions and processes of the organisation, such as introducing a new training programme for a hockey or netball team, or *peripheral*, such as an alteration in a leisure centre's recording system for customer data. Figure 20.1 shows the incremental/radical and core/peripheral dimensions of change in the form of a matrix. Analysing planned innovation in this way helps to give an indication of how easy or challenging it is likely to be to implement the intended change.

Changes in the top left-hand quadrant, introducing major alterations to core activities, are likely to be highly disruptive to the status quo and to provoke anxiety and possible resistance, and thus are highly risky and may be unsuccessful. On the other hand, changes in the bottom-right quadrant are likely to be much less contentious and problematic and can usually be incorporated relatively easily into the organisation's routine.

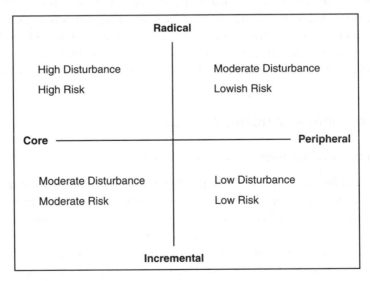

Figure 20.1 Types of organisational change

Source: Adapted from Pennington (2003)

maggie preedy

RATIONAL MODELS OF CHANGE

Traditional models of change, which are still dominant in practice and prescribed in management textbooks, treat organisational change as a process of careful analysis and planning. Typically they approach change as a linear sequence of stages, as shown in Figure 20.2.

Such approaches have a number of advantages. They provide a clear framework for planning, ensuring that all necessary stages are included. They also provide a logical and systematic guide to the change process, which can be followed both by those planning the change and those responsible for putting it into practice, thus reducing the chance of misunderstanding and lacking clarity about what is intended. Rational models are therefore useful where relatively little peripheral change is involved, such as alterations in technical systems and procedures, and

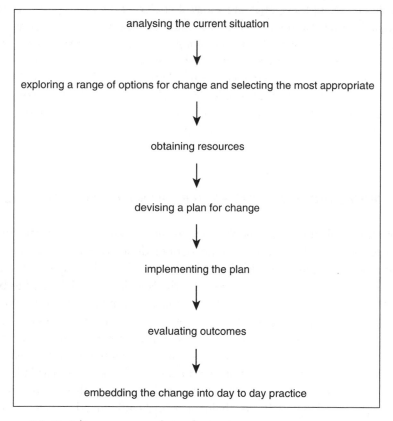

Figure 20.2 A linear approach to change

in situations where there is a relatively high level of certainty and agreement among organisational members about what change is needed and how it should be put into place.

However, studies of planning and implementation of change in a wide variety of organisations have shown that innovation plans very often fail to be put into practice – much planned change does not take place. In cases where it does, there is often a large implementation gap (Becher, 1989) between the intentions of planners and what is actually put into place. These findings have led to the questioning of rational models and discussion of their limitations.

Such models are highly normative and prescriptive, portraying what *should* happen, rather than what actually does happen in practice They assume that organisational goals are clear and agreed, that planning change follows systematic and logical steps, and that full information can be gathered on the range of possible change options, enabling a logical choice of the best option, to which all organisational members will be committed. However, organisations are in many ways 'non-rational' (Patterson et al.,1986; Carnall, 2007): goals and the means for reaching them are neither shared nor agreed, different people have very different objectives, evidence to provide the basis of rational analysis and choice is incomplete and unreliable, external pressures and demands impact on organisational decisions in unpredictable ways, and plans for change may be determined as much by individual and group interests as by organisation-wide plans.

INDIVIDUAL AND CULTURAL FACTORS IN SUCCESSFUL CHANGE

Given the limitations of rational models noted above, successful change strategies need to take into account the 'people' dimension of change, including organisational cultures and politics. 'Change is technically simple and socially complex' (Fullan, 2001). Change for individuals is difficult – it is hard to break out of established and familiar routines. Thus for example a high proportion of people who sign up at a gym for an exercise programme fail to continue with it beyond the first few weeks of enthusiasm. People also tend to oppose change that they are not in control of. In many cases change is planned by senior managers and implemented by more junior members of staff who have had little or no influence on the shape and scope of the plans for change. Also, in organisations that are part of a large multi-site chain, or strongly influenced by external forces

maggie preedy

(as in the case of public sector organisations which need to meet national and local government expectations), changes may often be externally initiated, and thus even senior managers may feel they have little or no control or influence on plans for change and how they are to be implemented. Organisational change is often assumed to be beneficial to all those concerned, but in altering existing arrangements it can be personally and professionally threatening and disruptive, and bring losses as well as gains. Any change, however small, is likely to disadvantage some individuals or groups involved and therefore to be resisted by them.

Thus individuals often have good reasons for resisting change in the workplace. Radical changes are likely to bring about alterations in individuals' status, job content, and the need to retrain, learn new skills and work with new colleagues. If the organisation is not prospering, people may be faced with more dramatic adjustments, for example, relocation, redeployment or redundancy. Changes which have a major effect on people's work will have an impact on both their performance and self-esteem. Thus the leadership of change needs to take into account and allow time and space for the various stages that people go through in adapting to change in the workplace. One way of representing these adjustment processes is Carnall's (2007) coping cycle, which has five main stages, outlined below.

1) Denial

When significant changes are first proposed, the initial response from staff may be to deny that innovation is necessary, and to suggest that current ways of working are effective, with comments such as: We've always done it this way; If it ain't broke, don't fix it; Why change things, we're successful/making a profit, aren't we?

2) Defence

At this stage people are coming to terms with the realisation that change is going to take place whether they like it or not. This can lead to feelings of depression and frustration, manifested in defensive behaviour where people seek to protect their own jobs and professional territory. This stage of the cycle provides scope for individuals to come to terms with the changes and what they mean for their own work and professional identity.

3) Discarding

Here, staff start to let go of the past and look forward to the future with more optimistic feelings as they recognise that the changes are both inevitable and necessary. This process can be greatly helped by support from colleagues and those leading the implementation of the changes.

4) Adaptation

People now engage in a process of adjustment and learning, trying out new behaviours and working out ways of coping with the changes. Colleagues, supervisors and managers all learn as the new arrangements are put into place and modified as necessary to ensure that they work effectively in practice. Individuals' performance and self-esteem start to recover.

5) Internalisation

Now the changes have been implemented, modified and accepted. Staff start to develop an understanding of new ways of working and new skills needed. The changes gradually become embedded and incorporated into day-to-day routine and people come to take them for granted as the normal way of doing things. As people learn to work effectively in the new situation, their self-esteem and performance continue to improve. The coping cycle is shown diagrammatically in Figure 20.3 (Carnall, 2007: p. 241).

Enabling people to have scope to work through their own meanings of the change and what it entails for their own job and professional identity is a central concern in the leadership of change. Other key cultural aspects that have been found to be essential for successful change are:

Staff ownership of problems and solutions. Those affected by the change need to share the perception that there is a problem requiring solution and that the proposed innovation will meet this need. This helps them to develop a sense of commitment to the change and to take responsibility for their own roles in ensuring its success.

Building a critical mass of staff support for and commitment to the innovation: once a majority of staff are in support of the change, dissenting voices are marginalised and the impetus to implementation becomes stronger and self-sustaining.

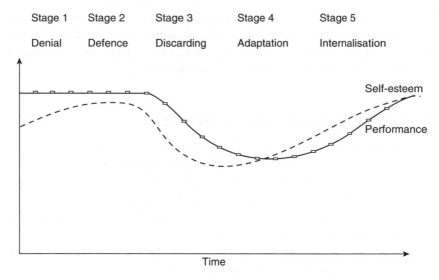

Figure 20.3 The coping cycle in organisational change

Ensuring people's understanding that the proposed changes are relevant and appropriate both to the organisation and to their own work, and are feasible, that is, will work well in practice. Portraying the benefits that will be brought about by the changes helps to develop a sense of their acceptability across the organisation, contributing to the critical mass of support mentioned above.

Negotiating with influential groups and individuals to ensure that their needs and interests are met and that they are therefore in support of the change. Negotiations may include strategies to minimise or compensate for the perceived losses of those who feel that they will not benefit from the change.

Linked to the above point, recognising that conflict and disagreement are both necessary and fundamental in organisational change. Since individuals and groups have different interests and understandings with respect to any proposed change, conflict and dissent are inevitable in the process of gaining majority agreement to the proposals.

ALTERNATIVES TO THE RATIONAL MODEL

While clear planning is important, organisational change cannot be seen as a purely rational process. Since individual and group reactions to change are diverse and complex, and cannot be tightly controlled or predicted, developing staff support across the organisation is vital. A widely used model for leading change is Kotter's (1996) eight-step approach, which builds in recognition of some of the non-rational aspects of organisational life.

EIGHT-STEP MODEL FOR LEADING CHANGE

1   Establish a sense of urgency, so that people see a clear need for change
2   Form a powerful guiding coalition to steer the change through
3   Create a vision of what the change will achieve
4   Communicate the vision so that it is shared by all staff
5   Empower staff to act and experiment, getting rid of obstacles to change, such as unhelpful structures and systems
6   Plan for and create short-term wins – visible improvements help to motivate and encourage people to continue the change
7   Consolidate improvements and produce the impetus to further change
8   Establish the change as part of day-to-day routine.

This approach was developed from Kotter's consultancy work with around one hundred companies tackling large-scale changes. It addresses the individual, cultural and political issues involved in bringing about change, which were discussed above, including the need to build a shared vision of and commitment to the proposed change, and to ensure the support of powerful groups in the organisation. This approach thus takes into account some of the realities and complexities of the change process which are neglected by rational models. On the other hand, Kotter's approach can be criticised on the grounds that change is better seen as a continuous ongoing cycle, rather than a linear process, and that he may underemphasise the challenges and difficulties of later stages of the process, presenting an unduly simplistic view of stages 6–8 (Cameron and Green, 2004). Other studies of organisational change (e.g. Fullan, 2001; Kanter, 2002) have highlighted the need for ongoing perseverance through later stages of implementation to ensure that the planned change is sustained and becomes embedded in day-to-day routine.

Recent approaches to leading change have been strongly influenced by ideas drawn from chaos and complexity theories, which point to the rapid and unpredictable changes and connectivities in the natural and human environments (turbulence in both these spheres, e.g. in weather patterns, and in global financial markets have been evident recently). These theories portray organisations as

maggie preedy

Table 20.1 Traditional and complex responsive system models of change

Traditional	Complex responsive system
Few factors determine outcomes	Many factors determine outcomes
The whole is equal to the sum of the parts	The whole is different from the sum of the parts
Direction is determined by design and the power of a few leaders	Direction emerges from various sources and the participation of many people
Individual and organisational behaviour is knowable, predictable and controllable	Individual and organisational behaviours cannot be known, predicted or controlled
Causality is linear – each effect can be traced to a cause	Causality is mutual – each cause is also an effect, and vice versa
Organisational relationships are directional	Organisational relationships are empowering
All organisational systems are essentially similar	Each organisational system is unique
Efficiency and reliability are the main measures of value	Responsiveness to the environment is the measure of value
Decisions are based on facts and data	Decisions are based on tensions and patterns
Leaders are experts and authorities	Leaders are facilitators and supporters

complex responsive systems which operate in paradoxical ways, pulled both towards stability and instability.

From this perspective, because of the complexity and unpredictability of what takes place within the organisation and the turbulence and uncertainty of external environmental influences, organisational leaders are unable to systematically control change or plan for organisational success. Control is dispersed throughout the system, and change is achieved by learning, evolution and adaptation. Table 20.1 compares traditional views of change with those in complex responsive systems (Olson and Eoyang, 2001).

This view recognises the limitations in what organisational managers can achieve in complex responsive systems, that tensions and ambiguity are important aspects of emerging change, and that managers act as facilitators and enablers, rather than the heroic 'great man/woman' leaders portrayed in traditional models of change.

STRATEGIC LEADERSHIP AND PLANNING

The final part of this chapter turns to look at *leading change* within the context of two important factors which we have given little attention to so far – the organisation's *future direction* and its *external environment*. This activity is usually called strategic planning. Change and creativity are important for all sport and fitness organisations, the basis for future success and growth. Strategic planning is a key leadership process which provides the organising framework for successful change and growth. Strategic planning involves looking at the medium- and longer-term direction of the organisation, mapping out an agreed vision of its future and how to get there, taking account of expected trends and developments in the external environment as well as internally. The objective of strategic leadership is to build the organisation's strengths so that it is able to meet customer or client needs more effectively than competitor organisations.

Apart from agreeing that strategy is essential and complex, there is considerable debate in the literature on strategy, about what strategic leadership entails and how strategic plans are developed. Sources differ in particular in:

> The extent to which strategy is seen as a rational planning process or as an evolutionary process that emerges through trial and error.

> The relative importance ascribed to internal and external factors in shaping strategy.

> How far the environment is seen as knowable, or predictable, or as uncertain.

> Whether organisations merely respond and react to external events, or whether their strategies can be proactive and imaginative in shaping external expectations and demands.

In an influential study, Hamel and Prahalad (1994) argued that strategies should not just seek to anticipate the future but to *create* it by being innovative – shaping the role of the organisation, and stakeholder and competitor perceptions of it.

There has also been debate on how far strategy is best undertaken as a top-down process, devising an organisation-wide plan that subunits then implement, or as a bottom-up process – building up a corporate plan from sub-plans developed at grassroots level by departments and teams. Much of the literature continues to emphasise a top-down approach – strategy as the business of senior managers. However, the position taken here is that strategy is or should be the concern of all organisational members. There are two main reasons for this. First, as indicated above, there are rapid changes in the environment, with external factors exerting increasing influence on the work of sports organisations. Boundaries between organisations and their external contexts have become more fluid and permeable, and it is thus important for all staff to understand and respond to environmental influences. Second, in order to be effective, strategic planning and innovation need the commitment and ownership of all staff, not just senior managers. This commitment is more likely to develop where staff have been involved in designing the strategy, rather than having it imposed from above.

One widely used approach to strategy which attempts to reconcile some of these differences in perspective, is that of Johnson et al. (2007). Their approach has three major stages, as shown in Figure 20.4 and explained in the text that follows overleaf: the *strategic position, strategic choices*, and *strategy into action*.

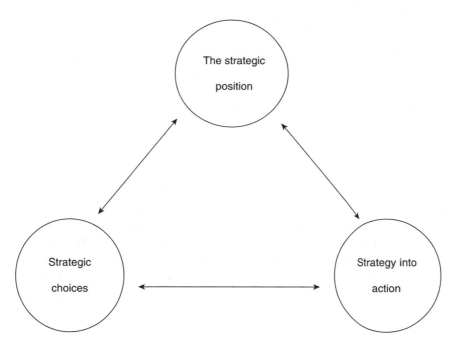

Figure 20.4 Strategic planning

Source: Adapted from Johnson *et al.* (2007)

The arrows are two-way in order to show that the process is not linear – the three elements are interlinked and overlapping.

The strategic position

This process is concerned with examining the current situation of the organisation:

- What changes are going on in the external environment, and how these will affect the organisation and its activities.
- The objectives and expectations of organisational managers and staff, and of customers and other stakeholders.
- The knowledge, skills and competences of the staff, and the technical and financial resources of the organisation.

Strategic choices

This stage involves looking at the possible choices for how the organisation can develop in the future – exploring the options for future strategy and direction, at the overall level of the organisation as a whole and for the sub-units within it and selecting the preferred option. This phase also includes making decisions about the direction of development and methods to be used. Thus, for example, choices may need to be made between developing the core business by expanding into new markets, or diversifying the range of products or services offered.

Strategy into action

This part of strategy development is concerned with implementing the selected strategy – the processes of leading and managing change that were discussed earlier in this chapter. This involves gaining staff commitment, implementing new ways of working and embedding new processes and activities into the day-to-day routine of the organisation. Another factor that is also important here is enabling success through ensuring that the organisational structure and culture support the chosen direction of strategy development, and that the strategy builds on and is supported by the four main organisational resource areas: people, information, technology and finances.

So far, this model for strategy development would seem to share many of the characteristics and limitations of the rational models of change discussed earlier.

However, Johnson (2007) suggests that strategy needs to be seen through different perspectives, or lenses, each providing an important, but partial view of how it takes place. The complexities of strategy development need to be seen through multiple perspectives, thereby giving a fuller picture.

The *design lens* portrays strategy development as the positioning of the organisation to meet specified purposes through a process of rational analysis and structured decisions. The *experience lens* sees strategy as the 'outcome of individual and collective experiences and the taken for granted assumptions' reflected in the organisation's culture. The *ideas lens* views strategy as 'the emergence of order and innovation from the variety and diversity which exist in and around organisations'. The design lens, which sees strategy development as a logical process, takes a view which is similar to the rational models of change discussed earlier. The experience lens highlights the individual, cultural and non-rational aspects of organisational life similar to aspects of the eight-step approach to change. The ideas lens has clear parallels with the idea of organisations as complex responsive systems. Table 20.2 provides a summary of the three lenses, their assumptions about organisations and implications for the leadership of change.

Table 20.2 Three strategy lenses

Lens	Design	Experience	Ideas
Strategy is:	Deliberate positioning through rational analysis and direction	Incremental and gradual development, through individual and collective experiences	Emergence of order and innovation through variety in and around the organisation
Assumptions about organisations	Hierarchical ordered and logical	Cultures based on history and past successes	Complex systems of variety and diversity
Role of leaders	Strategic decision-makers	Enactors of organisational experiences	Coaches and champions of ideas
Implications for change	Change = implementation of planned strategy	Change is evolutionary, with resistance to major innovation	Change is usually gradual but occasionally sudden

Source: Adapted from Johnson *et al.* (2007)

CONCLUSION

Different people in the organisation are likely to take different perspectives on the development of strategy and innovation, depending on their position, and degree of control and influence on what is planned. If you are asked to implement a top-down innovation that is strongly opposed by other colleagues in your department, your attitude and approach to what is happening will contrast with those of the senior managers who designed the innovation. The three strategy lenses suggest that we need to draw on multiple perspectives in understanding and tackling organisational change and strategic planning. The dominant rational models are important and necessary but not sufficient to gain a full picture of a complex process.

REFERENCES

Becher, T. (1989) The national curriculum and the implementation gap. In Preedy, M. (ed.), *Approaches to Curriculum Management*. Milton Keynes: The Open University Press.

Cameron, E. and Green, M. (2004) *Making Sense of Change Management*. London: Kogan Page.

Carnall, C. (2007) *Managing Change in Organisations*. 5th edn. Harlow: Financial Times/Prentice Hall.

Fullan, M. (2001) *The New Meaning of Educational Change*. 3rd edn. London: Cassell.

Hamel, G. and Prahalad, C.K. (1994) *Competing for the Future*. Boston: Harvard Business School Press.

Johnson, G., Scholes, K. and Whittington, R. (2007) *Exploring Corporate Strategy*. 8th edn. Harlow: Financial Times/Prentice Hall.

Kanter, R.M. (2002) The enduring skills of change leaders. In Hesselbein, F. and Johnston, R. (eds), *On Leading Change*. New York: Jossey-Bass.

Kotter, J.P. (1996) *Leading Change*. Boston, MA: Harvard Business School Press.

Olson, E. and Eoyang, G. (2001) *Facilitating Organisational Change: Lessons from Complexity Science*. San Francisco: Jossey-Bass/Pfeiffer.

Patterson, J., Purkey, S. and Parker, J. (1986) *Productive School Systems For a Non-rational World*. Alexandria, VA: Association for Supervision and Curriculum Development.

Pennington, G. (2003) *Guidelines for Promoting and Facilitating Change*. LTSN Generic Centre.

SECTION 5

PERSPECTIVES ON LEARNING AND INSTRUCTION

INTRODUCTION

If you casually observe at most sport or health clubs, you will no doubt see participants practising quite a wide range of physical skills and coaches/instructors using their experience to guide them; many of the physical and instructional skills that you don't often see performed in everyday life. How are such skills and competencies learned? Or perhaps more importantly, at least to a coach or instructor, how can you best help people to learn such skills? These are the questions addressed in this section.

The section begins by identifying and describing the different learning situations of how coaches/instructors learn their craft, then focuses more closely on what is known about how physical skills are learned. Attention is then focused on effective behaviours for coaches and instructors in leading this learning, with a final discussion of the nature of the professional knowledge, values and experiences of coaches and instructors.

Chapter 21 invites you to compare the interview descriptions of how intermediate-level sports coaches have learnt how to coach to your own experiences. Sources of coach learning are classified as formal, non-formal and informal with particular attention given to the role of the latter: the process of informally learning on the job through experience and use of the internet. It is drawn from a journal article originally written by researchers Trevor Wright, Pierre Trudel and Diane Culver from the University of Ottawa, Canada. The chapter was adapted for this text by Ben Oakley of the Open University.

In Chapter 22, Tom Power from the Open University summarises the different ways that people have tried to answer the question 'how do people learn physical skills?' as our knowledge of motor learning and psychology have developed over the previous hundred years. This chapter covers the main theoretical perspectives that currently dominate most physical instruction or sports coaching textbooks, and closes by briefly considering a new perspective that is beginning to enter the coaching and instruction literature.

In Chapter 23, Ben Oakley of the Open University moves our attention from learning to teaching, providing a practical four-step framework for instruction. The framework draws on the literature of good practice in coaching from international authors, many who contribute to 'coach education' programmes (e.g. UK, Australia, USA). In addition, the author draws on his own experience as a national coach to make connections between ideas and link to practice.

In Chapter 24, Terry McMorris and Tudor Hale, both academics from the University of Chichester, draw our attention to coaching and learning styles, helping us to identify the strengths and weaknesses of different styles, and to consider and evaluate alternatives.

In Chapter 25, we focus upon the professional knowledge of fitness instructors and sports coaches. Tom Power, of the Open University, presents a model for understanding the professional knowledge of coaches and instructors, which can be used to articulate the richness of current professional knowledge, as well as to identify areas that may benefit from further professional development.

CHAPTER 21

LEARNING HOW TO COACH[1]
The different learning situations reported by coaches

Trevor Wright, Pierre Trudel and Diane Culver,
adapted by Ben Oakley

INTRODUCTION

The development of coaches might initially seem straightforward. They undertake a course to become qualified and then 'work'. But in reality it is a more complex process with a number of different learning situations beyond formal training. Some of this learning is planned, some is not, and there is a lot of learning by experience. This has led some writers to describe typical coach development as 'ad hoc learning' (Nelson *et al.*, 2006: p. 174).

This chapter aims to identify and describe the different learning situations reported by coaches, and to gain some insight into their preferred sources of knowledge. It starts by outlining the background to classifying sources of coach learning as formal, non-formal and informal (Nelson *et al.*, 2006). The chapter then moves onto the main section which identifies the range of learning situations experienced by coaches. This section of the chapter draws heavily on a study that used 35 interviews of community youth ice hockey coaches in Canada (Wright *et al.*, 2007); the main issues identified in the Canadian study are transferable to other sports and settings. Quotes have been used from Wright *et al.*'s (2007) interviews for coaches to explain, in their own words, how they perceive their learning; in addition, edited sections of their explanatory text have been utilised and referenced throughout. The chapter concludes by considering the learning preferences of coaches from a *variety* of sports (Erickson *et al.*, 2008).

In essence, what follows is a summary of coach training and development that focuses on average intermediate level coaches, most of whom work in a

---

[1] Adapted version of Wright, T. Trudel, P. and Culver, D. (2007) 'Learning how to coach: the different learning situations reported by youth ice hockey coaches', *Physical Education and Sport Pedagogy*, 12(2), pp. 127–144.

voluntary role. The aim is that readers might compare the different learning situations to their own experience and reflect on their own learning pathway and the sources of knowledge they have found most useful in their role.

BACKGROUND

In an attempt to foster coaches' development, *formal* coach education programmes have been organised in many countries around the world to enhance safe and ethical working practice. Examples of these large-scale programmes are the National Coaching Certification Program (NCCP) in Canada, the National Coaching Accreditation Scheme (NCAS) in Australia, the National Coaching Certificate (NCC) in the UK, and the American Sport Education Program (ASEP) in the USA. These programmes share similar characteristics including: (a) being mainly classroom based; (b) having different levels; and (c) having well-defined content for each level (Wright *et al.*, 2007).

It may be assumed that learning to coach in formal coach education programmes is associated with acquiring a well-defined quantity of information that some experts have identified as what coaches should know in order to be certified. Given this view of learning, coach education programmes have concentrated on what Sfard (1998) calls the acquisition learning metaphor, where experts deliver information to their students/coaches who must acquire this information and then apply it in their own setting (Wright *et al.*, 2007). In recent years a number of Higher Education institutions have also offered formal degree programmes aimed at preparing and educating coaches.

Another type of learning situation coaches use is attendance at coaching conferences, courses or seminars which are organised educational activities outside the formal system designed to provide selected types of learning to particular groups (e.g. coaching the elite athlete) and not necessarily leading to certification (Erickson *et al.*, 2008). These have been termed *non-formal* learning situations (Nelson *et al.*, 2006).

Taking another perspective, researchers such as Wenger (1998) have reinforced the notion of learning through experience which could be called *informal* learning. Erickson (2008) defines informal learning in coaching as learning that occurs in situations that 'are self-directed and based on personal experience and activity' (Erickson *et al.*, 2008: p. 259). The process of learning through experience occurs through day-to-day activities and corresponds to learning through participation (Sfard, 1998), that is, recognising that people pick up things socially through participating and mingling with other people in a community of practice (Culver and Trudel, 2006). Previous studies such as Jones *et al.* (2004) have conducted in-depth interviews with elite coaches from England, New Zealand, and Australia. They found that their practical experiences, whether through observation and/or discussion with other coaches/mentors, seem to be more important than coach certification programmes in their progression toward becoming an elite coach (Wright *et al.*, 2007).

Reflection (or reflective practice), the process of using experience and a 'reconsidering of existing ideas' has been identified as central to this type of informal learning. Reflective practice is about 'squeezing more learning out of experiences' (Turner, personal communication) and is particularly useful for coach development 'as it could provide a bridge linking knowledge gained from ... experience, observations, coaching theory, and education' (Nelson and Cushion, 2006: p. 175).

Wright *et al.* (2007) suggest the internet is now challenging our traditional ways of learning, both formal and informal. The internet provides access to a huge amount of information. Some researchers in the field of education have indicated that the Web could be used as a resource to provide more interactive opportunities for students over a large geographical area (Spitzer, 1998) as well as providing more freedom to actively learn rather than acquiring passively an imposed curriculum in a traditional classroom (Barab *et al.*, 2001). However, internet-based learning might not facilitate the development of crucial interpersonal skills required in coaching but it could impact upon coach development, particularly in informal situations. Since the role of the internet in learning is not yet fully understood slightly more space is devoted to discussion of this learning environment.

Among the three main learning situations (formal, informal, and non-formal) for coaches to learn how to coach, formal coach education programmes have been, up to now, the only method recognised that leads to certification. According to Cushion *et al.* (2003) it is time to extend our conception of learning how to coach: 'if we are to develop imaginative, dynamic, and thoughtful coaches, we must widen the search beyond the "usual suspects" of content knowledge that has (sic) traditionally informed coach education programs' (p. 216).

LEARNING SITUATIONS IDENTIFIED

The distinction between different types of learning situations was the basis for the interviews which we quote from extensively in this section. Wright *et al.* (2007) interviewed coaches, asking them questions about learning through formal coach education programmes, on their learning outside of these programmes, and finally on their use of the internet. To maintain their anonymity the interviewees are referred to as Coach 1 (C1) to Coach 14 (C35).[2]

The learning situations identified in a number of studies (e.g. Nelson et al., 2006; Trudel and Gilbert, 2006; Wright et al., 2007), reveal seven different learning situations that fall into the formal, informal, or non-formal categories of learning. The seven learning situations are explained below in more detail and enhanced with some of the original ice hockey interview data.

Formal coach education training (formal)

Typically coach education is organised into 3–4 levels with level 2 being a required level of intermediate competency in some countries. The opinions of ice hockey coaches about this formal training varied somewhat. For some coaches, the content of the training course was what they were hoping for:

> It was useful, it gave me some concepts to think about. I think it was useful for practice preparation, also the parts on motivation and dealing with kids were good.
>
> (C29)

Other coaches mentioned that:

> There was too much repetition from the Coaching level 1 course.
>
> (C28)

Finally, there were some coaches who took their level 2 not because they wanted to, but because they were required to if they wanted to coach at a competitive level:

> I went there because I had to take it. That was the only reason I went.
>
> (C35)

Time and money are frequently barriers for coaches taking their level 3 although in the case of ice hockey those who took it mentioned several benefits:

> All of the information is pertinent.
>
> (C23)

---

[2] All references to ice hockey coaches are from Wright et al. (2007).

The Advanced I level gave me the opportunity to learn from a lot of the other people that were in the program.

(C5)

Coaching seminars (non-formal)

Besides learning through coach education training courses, some coaches attend other coaching development opportunities available in their community. An expert or a professional coach often instructs in a traditional format of information delivery. Wright *et al*.'s (2007) data showed that coaches seem to enjoy attending such seminars. For example, some coaches mentioned the benefits of listening to professional coaches, who address specific topics not taught in the formal programme in Canada (National Coaching Certification Programme):

One guy came in and explained the trap, and another explained the umbrella powerplay. The NCCP didn't do any of that.

(C22)

Mentoring (formal/informal)

Formal mentoring programmes are sometimes available for coaches but they are often rather optional or self-directed so they might be considered as an informal learning situation. Interestingly, if you formalise mentoring then you may well lose some of the power that results from its organic development due to deep compatibility (i.e. of personal qualities, attributes and values) (Turner, 2009, personal communication).

Observations from ice hockey coaches illustrate some different approaches to mentoring. One club had an individual in place who had been involved as a coach mentor for the past three years. In his role, he was responsible for monitoring each coach in the association, giving help if coaches needed it, and evaluating coaches based on observations of practices and games. His role involved one-on-one guidance with each coach, as well as monthly meetings for all of the coaches to get together over breakfast. Two quotes highlight differing issues:

I would ask him questions about systems and stuff. He would come out to my practices and give me constructive feedback after … He was available if you wanted him, but some coaches probably didn't use him like I did ... Coaches who didn't use him were probably limiting themselves.

(C28)

He [the mentor] has his different ideas, so is it the right way? I don't know, you run the risk of following one person's ideas, rather than a number of ideas.

(C34)

Some organisations appoint Coach Development Officers (CDOs) as a person in charge of coach development. This is what two ice hockey coaches had to say about the monthly meetings one such CDO organised:

It allows you to develop relationships with your peers so if there are times where you are looking for a specific aspect that you want to teach the children, then you'll know who some of the experts are that you can rely on. It helps you to build up your network of contacts that you can use for augmenting your own teachings.

(C11)

We have no reason to hold anything back in our association, we are trying to be as much like a club as we can ... we have to share things in our association. It's like our own little coaching community.

(C29)

A possible limitation of CDOs is the scheduling and number of the meetings is very important with volunteer coaches who have little free time.

Books/video (informal)

Coaches acquire a variety of information through books and video. The ice hockey coaches' perspectives varied depending on how experienced they were. Beginner coaches tended to consult books or videos that explained drills or sport specific issues:

I have read books and watched videotapes. I find them very good. I am always trying to come up with new drills and skills.

(C33)

trevor wright, pierre trudel and diane culver, adapted by ben oakley

More experienced coaches seemed to use books and videotapes for more advanced topics such as sport psychology, nutrition, and physical fitness, because they already have a large database of drills. Coaches often develop their own extensive personal libraries of resources.

Personal experiences (informal)

Other studies in this field (e.g. Erickson *et al.*, 2008) delineate this further into 'learning by doing', and 'observing other coaches'. Let's use the voices of ice hockey coaches to describe in their own words how their experience with others helped them.

> Coaching experience is number one. I think playing experience is overrated because the most important skills of a hockey coach are teaching and communication, just because you have played doesn't mean you can coach.
>
> (C33)

> I learned a lot from my dad … he taught us that it's not a life and death thing but it's fun, enjoy the experiences you have.
>
> (C4)

Interestingly, many coaches mentioned that their experiences at work have helped them to coach, particularly developing leadership skills:

> I'm a general manager of a trucking company, so there are some leadership skills that you develop there that you can bring into coaching hockey.
>
> (C6)

Interactions with other coaches (informal)

Direct interactions with other coaches and observation is often mentioned as an excellent situation to learn to coach. Ice hockey coaches reported having a great opportunity to learn:

> The fact that I was an assistant coach with a number of coaches along the way, and they weren't necessarily good coaches, I learned a lot.
>
> (C5)

We talk all the time. You learn by listening to people, asking them questions, and then by observing people. I wouldn't call them coaching mentors but they are similar to that.

(C33)

Amongst the ice hockey coaches they often consulted elite coaches and if they did not know any elite coaches well enough to communicate with them, they could go and observe games and practices:

I spend a lot of time going to practices and you see the drills and the flow.

(C22)

Finally, there was the possibility of watching professional games which, with some existing grounding in coaching, was viewed by some as being useful:

I watch professional hockey. I don't watch it for the entertainment. I watch it from a coaching perspective and see how they play in the defensive zone, neutral zone, just always dissecting the game.

(C14)

The internet (informal)

In the Wright et al. (2007) study coaches were asked questions regarding the internet and if they believed it could be used as a learning resource. The ice hockey coach interviews indicated that the internet was most commonly used to interact with people via computer-mediated communication (CMC – email and online forums) tools, and to access information via the Web.

The majority of ice hockey coaches used email for personal communication with parents and players, to give information like team schedules, competition information and to exchange information regarding the preparation of their practices. These coaches were also aware of the threaded discussions (otherwise known as online forums), via the Web. A number of coaches (n = 18) said they had visited coaching websites with threaded discussions but had decided not to post anything. Only five coaches had posted a message on a threaded discussion dedicated to hockey.

Some coaches expressed concern about the quality of information obtained on threaded discussions, because of anonymous postings that might not be trusted.

trevor wright, pierre trudel and diane culver, adapted by ben oakley

Some also made reference to a threaded discussion that went out of control and became a venting place for people. A limit of interacting through both email and threaded discussions seemed to be the coaches' preference for face-to-face interactions, rather than computer-mediated interactions:

> I don't think it's a good way to communicate because it's very impersonal and a lot of the times things can get misinterpreted when they are typed. When you talk to someone face-to-face you get a greater understanding of the information that is being conveyed.
>
> (C15)

With regards the use of the Web:

> I know a lot of associations have coaching textbooks on the Internet and everyone clicks and gets a drill or something.
>
> (C26)

Using search engines (e.g. Google), some coaches visited coaching websites that offered a variety of drills that coaches could access for free. The frequency with which these coaches accessed drills often depended on their experience. Coaches who were relatively new (1–4 years) to coaching tended to search for drills more often than experienced coaches. However, the need to keep one's programme interesting by bringing in new ideas was a concern for other experienced coaches. For example:

> If I was not to have the Internet as a resource my program would be pretty old quickly.
>
> (C5)

Fourteen coaches searched the Web for advanced information such as nutrition, sport psychology, and physical training. The coaches underlined a few limits of using the Web. Reading information on a computer screen is perceived differently than reading on paper. Finding information through the Web could also be difficult at times and become time-consuming for coaches who do not have a lot of free time:

> It becomes very cumbersome trying to find out what is good and what is bad because you have to read through so many sites.
>
> (C14)

LEARNING PREFERENCES

Recognising that people have different learning styles (see Chapter 24) recent attention has focused on gaining insight into the preferred sources of coaching knowledge (Erickson et al., 2008). Erickson et al.'s (2008) interviews were conducted with 44 intermediate coaches from a variety of sports, again in Canada. This is only one study so there should be some caution in assuming the results apply in all other settings. The top three sources of coaching knowledge were reported as 'learning by doing' (identified by 58% of coaches), followed by 'formal coach education training' (43%) and 'interaction with peers' (33%). The other remaining sources of knowledge all had much lower proportions of mentions with little to choose between them.

When the coaches were asked how they would prefer to gain coaching knowledge, formal coach education was mentioned most frequently, followed by mentoring. Erickson et al. (2008) concluded that 'it appears coaches actually learn, and prefer to learn from a variety of sources' (p. 536). And, 'in particular, the inclusion of formal ... learning opportunities as preferred sources of knowledge, in addition to more experientially-based modes, cautions against swinging too far' (p. 536) from a balance and blend of sources.

CONCLUSIONS

In this chapter, Wright et al. (2007) and others have identified the different situations in which coaches learn to coach. Although these situations were categorised into formal, informal and non-formal, the objective was not to promote one over the other. As Erickson et al. (2008) suggested, each situation seems to have a unique role in the development of a coach and coach education should include a combination of all seven learning situations, instead of focusing on one. Future efforts should concentrate on investigating the complementary potential of these learning situations and what can be done to make each of these situations more appealing for coaches. This is particularly so as new technologies emerge that make distance learning and the sharing/communication with a distributed group of coaches far easier than in the past.

REFERENCES

Barab, S.A., Thomas, M. and Merrill, H. (2001) Online learning: from information dissemination to fostering collaboration. *Journal of Interactive Learning Research*, 12(1): 105–143.

trevor wright, pierre trudel and diane culver, adapted by ben oakley

Culver, D. and Trudel, P. (2006) Cultivating coaches' communities of practice: Developing the potential for learning through interactions. In R. L. Jones (ed.), *The Sports Coach as Educator: Reconceptualising Sports Coaching*. London: Routledge.

Cushion, C.J., Armour, K.M. and Jones, R.L. (2003) Coach education and continuing professional development: experience and learning to coach. *Quest*, 55: 215–230.

Erickson, K., Bruner, M., MacDonald, D. and Cote, J. (2008) Gaining insight into actual and preferred sources of coaching knowledge. *International Journal of Sports Science and Coaching*, 3(4): 527–538.

Jones, R.L., Armour, K.M. and Potrac, P. (2004) *Sports Coaching Cultures: from Practice to Theory*. London: Routledge.

Nelson, L. and Cushion, C. (2006) Reflection in coach education: the case of the National Governing Body Coaching Certificate. *The Sport Psychologist*, 20(2): 174–183.

Nelson, L., Cushion, C. and Potrac, P. (2006) Formal, nonformal and informal coach learning: a holistic conceptualisation. *International Journal of Sports Science and Coaching*, 1(3): 247–259

Sfard, A. (1998) On two metaphors for learning and the dangers of choosing just one. *Educational Researcher*, 27: 4–13.

Spitzer, D.R. (1998) Rediscovering the social context of distance learning. *Educational Technology*, March–April: 52–56.

Trudel, P. and Gilbert, W. (2006) Coaching and coach education. In D. Kirk, M. O'Sullivan and D. McDonald (eds), *Handbook of Physical Education* (pp. 516–539). Sage: London.

Wenger, E. (1998) *Communities of Practice: Learning, Meaning, and Identity*. New York: Cambridge University Press.

Wright, T., Trudel, P. and Culver, D. (2007) Learning how to coach: the different learning situations reported by youth ice hockey coaches. *Physical Education and Sport Pedagogy*, 12(2): 127–144.

CHAPTER 22

LEARNING PHYSICAL SKILLS – THEORETICAL PERSPECTIVES

Tom Power

INTRODUCTION

If you are a fitness instructor or sports coach, then it is almost certain that you already have some understanding of 'how people learn physical skills'. You may feel a little uncomfortable with 'theories', preferring 'practical' things, but what you believe to be true about the way people learn physical skills determines the way you go about instructing or coaching. Every aspect of the way you organise your athletes' training and practice, the way you talk, the kind of tasks you set, and how you feed back, draws upon your ideas about how people learn physical skills.

Your own ideas, your personal 'theory' or theories may be explicit and clear; they may draw upon training courses or materials you have already engaged with, or they may be 'intuitive' and implicit, but these ideas determine your professional practice and engagement with your athletes, day by day and minute by minute.

The purpose of this chapter is to help you to pause for a moment and consider your ideas about how people learn, in the light of a hundred years of research. It summarises the main ways of answering the question 'how do people learn physical skills' that have developed over the previous century. Two of the perspectives considered dominate most physical instruction or sports coaching textbooks at present. A third is a new perspective that is just beginning to enter the coaching and instruction literature in the new millennium.

As you read this chapter, you may find support for many of your own ideas and practices; you may 'fit' some of these ideas into a bigger picture, or perhaps your may find some new ideas that you want to explore in your professional practice.

BEHAVIOURIST PERSPECTIVES

Early in the twentieth century, behaviourism was the dominant theoretical perspective in modern psychology. Behaviourism concerns itself mainly with a person's behaviour. Behaviourist approaches are typically experimental, exposing subjects (often animals) to specific environmental conditions (stimuli) then observing the subject's behaviour (responses). This might almost be described as a 'black box' approach to learning.

'Black box' is a technical term for a way of studying almost any device or system (such as a clock or a person), where the study focuses upon the inputs (what you do to the system) and outputs (what the system does in response). What happens between the input and output is unknown, as if the workings took place in a black box we cannot see into.

For example, you might take a 'black box' approach to car mechanics when learning to drive, saying 'If I put my foot down on the accelerator (input), the engine goes faster (output). I don't need to know what happens under the bonnet (in the black box) to make that happen' (see www.en.wikipedia.org/wiki/Black_box).

Classical conditioning

The Russian psychologist Pavlov carried out some of the earliest and best-known behaviourist work, at the dawn of the twentieth century. In the presence of food (stimulus), dogs normally begin to salivate (response). Pavlov found that, by ringing a bell prior to presenting dogs with their food, eventually the dogs would begin to salivate when the bell was rung, even if no food was presented. The dogs had learned to associate the sound of a bell with the imminent arrival of food (Figure 22.1).

This kind of learning through association is called 'classical conditioning' and was used in schools and the military for 'drill training', where athletes repeatedly carry out a physical skill in response to an audible stimuli (such as the commands of the sergeant, or the sound of a whistle). Eventually, after much practice, the response becomes conditioned and automatic.

> ... which was the way in which physical activities were conducted in the early decades of this [twentieth] century. In education, the physical training syllabus of 1919 aimed to accustom the body to

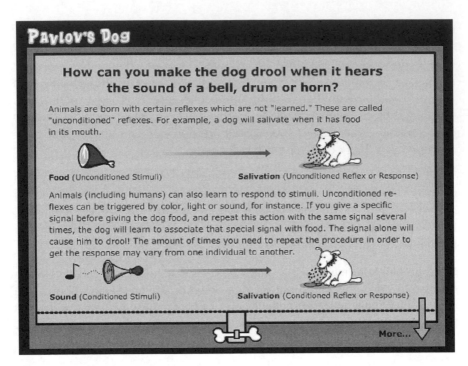

Figure 22.1 Pavlov's dog

Source: www.nobelprize.org/educational_games/medicine/pavlov/pavlov.html

'external suggestions and stimuli'. In drill training, the children stood in rows, facing the teacher, raising their arms or knees, stretching upward, bending the trunk forward and so on.

(Woods, 1998: p. 66)

Thorndikes laws (connectionism)

Thorndike studied how connections are made between stimulus and response; his theory (connectionism) consists of three primary laws (Thorndike, 1931):

- The law of readiness: the subject must be physically and psychologically ready to learn/perform the task.
- The law of effect: responses to a situation that result in rewards (success) are likely to strengthen the stimulus-response bond and become habitual. Responses that lead to unpleasant effects (failure) are likely to lead to that response being avoided.

- The law of exercise: regular practice strengthens the bond between stimulus and response.

We can see how these laws can be applied to the learning of a physical skill, such as a child learning a tennis serve.

The law of readiness makes us ensure the child is old enough to hold and strike with the tennis racquet, that they can understand what they are being asked to do and that they are neither too tired nor hungry to participate.

The law of effect tells us that we should ensure that attempts to perform the desired response should result in success, encouragement or reward.

The law of exercise tells us that they must practise the desired response regularly for it to become habitual.

Operant conditioning

Skinner further developed Thorndike's law of readiness in his theory of operant conditioning (Skinner, 1938). Skinner argued that it was not 'our environment' per se that we were responding to or learning from, but rather the effects of our actions (operations) in the environment. Essentially, operant conditioning means learning from the consequences of our behaviour.

Skinner identified several ways in which we learn from our behaviour:

- *Positive reinforcement* increases the probability of a behaviour being repeated because the behaviour results in pleasant consequences, such as scoring a goal or being praised by peers.
- *Negative reinforcement* increases the probability of a behaviour being repeated because the behaviour results in something that was unpleasant stopping, such as a ballet dancer practising pirouettes finding that she no longer gets sick or dizzy when she uses the correct technique for moving her head.
- *Punishment* decreases the probability of a behaviour being repeated due to unpleasant consequences of the behaviour, such as the use of yellow or red cards in football.

Summary of behaviourist perspectives

Behaviourism was the dominant theoretical paradigm for understanding learning, including learning of physical skills, from the 1900s to 1950s. Much of what was learned through the behaviourist studies is still informative today, and some research still carries on in this tradition.

However, by the 1960s, there was an increasing desire to 'open up the black box' and begin to explore the mechanisms at work in our minds and bodies as we were making these behavioural choices.

COGNITIVE PERSPECTIVES

Information processing theory

In the 1960s, the emerging field of computer science was beginning to impact upon psychology, giving birth to information processing theory.

Like behaviourist models, information processing starts with environmental stimuli (input) and ends in action (output). However, as Figure 22.2 shows, information processing opens up the black box to theorise about what might be going on in between.

Although significantly simplified, Figure 22.2 shows many of the features common to most models of information processing.

There are a great many sensory inputs we receive at any given moment, particularly in the context of sporting activity: which do we attend to as

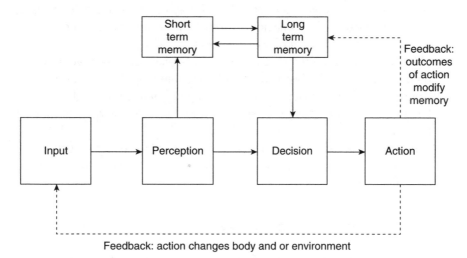

Feedback: action changes body and or environment

Figure 22.2 A simplified model of information processing

Source: Adapted from Welford (1968)

meaningful information carriers and which do we ignore as irrelevant? Perception is the process of paying selective attention to these various inputs.

What we perceive to be happening in the environment is passed onto short-term memory (e.g. where everyone is on the pitch now) and compared with long-term memory (have I been in situations like this before? What happened next? What worked before? What didn't?).

Both our perceptions and our memories inform our decisions about what course of action to take.

When we act, the position or motion of our body changes, being fed back along with any subsequent changes in the environment, as new input. The outcomes of our actions also become part of our memory, providing a further feedback mechanism to influence future decisions.

From a practitioner's point of view, one key feature of this model is the emphasis on perception – making sure that the athlete is attending to the appropriate stimuli within the environment. Another is that in this model, learning may be seen as primarily brought about through remembering and applying previous learning experiences.

Motor programmes and schema theory

When we have decided to execute a particular action, there is still the process of carrying it out, which becomes much easier, quicker and smoother the more often we have practised a particular action. How does practice improve these actions?

One early explanation was that we develop a set of mental blue-prints or 'motor programmes' (Keele, 1968) for each action: 'a set of muscle commands that allow ... the movement [to] become automatic'. The idea was that a set-piece of movement was remembered and stored, including the sequence, timing and extent of muscle contractions and limb movements, from beginning to end of the piece. Such set-pieces could then be carried out automatically once the athlete had decided to initiate the motor programme.

Two problems presented themselves to this explanation. First, because each motor programme would only be useful under exactly the same conditions as it was learned in, a staggeringly vast number of motor programmes would be needed to cover all the variations of movement required by the athlete.

Second, observation showed that athletes do not repeat movements at exactly the same speed, or in exactly the same way.

Schema theory (Schmidt, 1975) proposed a far more flexible and efficient mechanism for developing these swift, automatic movements. Athletes do not store 'complete sequences' of every variation of a particular movement, rather, they abstract general rules about how to perform a group of movements, which are flexible enough to allow variation in pace, power, and position.

Information processing theory has dominated research and practice into the learning of physical skill in the latter decades of the twentieth century. Both the models of information processing and applications to practice have become highly detailed and refined (Schmidt and Wrisberg, 2008: p. 325).

Three-stage theory

At around the same time as Keele was formulating the notion of motor programmes, Fitts and Possner (1967) were also considering the fast, smooth, accurate movements of well-practised athletes, how different these were to the movements of novices, and how novices progressed to become well-practised athletes.

They proposed a three-stage theory of learning physical skills:

- The cognitive stage.
- The associative stage.
- The autonomous stage.

In the *cognitive stage*, the athlete is focusing upon understanding 'what' has to be done, or 'how' the movement is performed. You might say they are trying to develop a mental model of the process they are trying to learn. In this stage, they are likely to be very verbal – asking a lot of questions about what bits go where and how.

The physical movement is likely to be slow and difficult, with a relatively low likelihood of successfully completing the process.

In the *associative stage*, the athlete begins to be able to perform the technique. The emphasis of effort now moves from building a mental model of the movement or performance, to refining the process of the movement or performance. This is done through becoming aware of and eliminating mistakes in the performance, and through strengthening associations between the critical aspects of the performance that lead to success.

In this stage, the likelihood of successfully completing the movement is much higher; though the athlete may still need to focus significant mental effort on how they are performing the movement, and it may still be relatively slow and difficult, they are now able to perform the technique with a greater chance of success.

In the *autonomous stage*, the athlete is able to perform the movement with very little conscious effort (e.g. the autonomous nervous system governs things that we do automatically, without having to think about them, such as breathing. When we have learned to walk, this becomes an autonomous skill that we can carry out without conscious effort).

In the autonomous stage, the athlete has a very high certainty of being able to carry out the movement; repeated practice means that the movement is carried out very quickly and smoothly and with relatively little effort.

Adaptive Control of Thought (ACT) theory

In a similar vein, ACT theory (Anderson, 1982) suggests there is a progression from:

- *Declarative knowledge*, learning what to do, and being able to 'declare' or say it,

  to
- *Procedural knowledge*, being able to carry out the technique or procedure.

As well as relating to acquiring physical skill, ACT also speaks to the development of tactical skill, arguing that being able to 'declare' what their tactics would be in various situations helps athletes carry out the right technique when it is required.

Whilst it seems clear that knowing what to do and being able to do it isn't the same thing, it doesn't automatically follow that if you are able to do something, you can also 'declare' what you are doing.

In other words, it is possible to have an 'implicit' knowledge of how to do something, and to be able to do it well and regularly, without having ever stopped to make this knowledge explicit, or something you could 'declare' to another person. For example, you may find it much easier to actually ride a bike or to swim than to explain how to do either of these to a young child.

Table 22.1 Theoretical depictions of stages of motor learning

Theorists	Early stage of learning	Later stage of learning
Fitts and Possner (1967)	Cognitive (mental modeling)	Autonomous (easy, automatic movement)
Adams (1971)	Verbal motor (more talk)	Motor (more action)
Anderson (1982)	Declarative (can say it)	Procedural (can do it)
Newell (1985)	Coordination (acquiring movement pattern)	Control (adapting movement pattern to circumstances)

Source: Adapted from Schmidt and Wrisberg (2008): p. 13

Summary of cognitive perspectives

The cognitive perspectives explore what happens between the external stimulus of the environment and the physical response of the action. They are concerned with how patterns of motor movement are acquired and selected, and the processes that athletes go through in developing autonomous patterns of movement.

There are now several cognitive theoretical depictions of stages of motor learning summarised in Table 22.1.

Cognitive perspectives have formed the dominant paradigm for understanding the learning of physical skills since the late 1960s.

SOCIAL LEARNING/SITUATED PERSPECTIVES

All of the perspectives so far have tended to look at the learning of physical skills as an essentially individual activity, looking at physical behaviours (the ability to perform certain techniques) in response to certain environmental stimuli.

Bandura (1977) was one of the first to raise the importance of the social dimension to learning physical skills, suggesting we copy the behaviour of people who matter to us. These role models may be people who:

- Are similar in some way to us (in age, gender, or abilities).
- Have high status (parents, coaches, sports heroes).
- Are rewarded for their behaviour (by winning competitions, or praise).

More recently, some (Culver and Trudel, 2006; Glipeau and Trudel, 2006; Jones *et al.*, 2004) have begun to apply Lave and Wenger's (1998) social learning theories to sports teams and athletes.

One of the key organising concepts for Lave and Wenger is that learning should not be thought of as an exclusively individual process, but rather as a process of social participation, taking place within a community of practice: a group of people 'who share a concern, a set of problems or a passion … and who deepen their knowledge and expertise in this area by interacting in an ongoing basis' (Wenger *et al.*, 2002: p. 4).

In such an understanding, learning may be viewed as the process of moving from legitimate peripheral participation at the edges of such a community to being fully involved in the centre of practice.

For example, a girl moving from primary to secondary school and joining the secondary school hockey club with the 'big girls' might initially attend training sessions but not compete. She will need to form relationships with the rest of the team and the coach, learn how the team and the league work, perhaps going along to support them at matches. Over time, she may join the competition squad and eventually become a key member of the team.

In this example, the hockey club is a 'pedagogic setting': an enduring context for teaching and learning hockey. From a social learning perspective, the pedagogic setting is not just the physical place (the gym or sports club) where learning takes place. It also includes all the people, roles, relationships, and the things that hold these together.

> Participants create, enact, experience – together and separately – purposes, values and expectations: knowledge and ways of knowing; rules of discourse; roles and relationships; resources, artefacts and the physical arrangement and boundaries of the setting. All of these together and none of these alone [compose the pedagogic setting].
>
> (Leach and Moon, 1999: p. 268)

Within a pedagogic setting, it is possible to observe dimensions such as:

- learning activities;
- assessment activities;
- roles and relationships.

These are often carried out, or mediated, by using specialist:

- language (special terms or ways of speaking);
- tools and artefacts (such as training equipment, organisational charts, posters).

All these observable dimensions are informed by:

- goals and purposes (what are people trying to achieve?);
- views of learning (how do people learn?);
- views of successful learning (what kind of performance counts as success?).
                              (Adapted from Leach and Moon, 2002: p. 23)

So, in the example above, the process of learning hockey and playing for the school team, is not simply about learning a series of discrete physical skills, such as how to 'bully-off' or perform an 'Indian dribble'. It is also about learning how to participate in the activities of the club (training, practice, competition); it is about understanding the various team and club roles (formal and informal) and developing relationships; it is about learning to use the language and tools of the club, and about developing shared goals, purposes and values.

Ultimately, from this perspective, learning is about developing identity, such that the young girl may one day say 'I'm a hockey player' or 'I'm club captain'.

Summary: Social learning perspectives

Social learning is at present a relatively new theoretical perspective from which to consider the learning of physical skills; apart from reference to Bandura, it is almost unmentioned in most textbooks.

However, it has become one of the major theoretical perspectives for learning in general, and both work based and informal learning in particular. Within the research community, this perspective has just begun to cross over into the domains of sport and fitness. For example, see work now emerging from Loughborough (Cushion, 2008).

Social learning perspectives offer insights that are rich and complex, which is both their strength and their weakness. As we move into the coming decades, such perspectives may possibly become established as a new paradigm for understanding the acquisition of physical skills.

CONCLUSION

Over the course of the last hundred years, there have been very different ways of framing the question 'how do people learn physical skills'.

The answers put forward in response have also changed quite dramatically, as different theoretical perspectives have developed. It is not so much that earlier answers were 'wrong' and newer answers 'right', but rather that a more rounded picture has developed as we have found new points of view from which to consider the question.

It is precisely because there is no single, simple answer that the process of coaching and instruction, like teaching, is considered to be as much of an art as a science. Therein is its challenge and its reward.

REFERENCES

Adams, J.A. (1971) A closed-loop theory of motor learning. *Journal of Motor Behavior*, 3: 111–150.

Anderson, J.R. (1982) Acquisition of cognitive skill. *Psychological Review*, 89: 369–406.

Bandura, A. (1977) Self-efficacy: Toward a unifying theory of behavioural change. *Psychological Review*, 84: 191–215.

Culver, D.M. and Trudel, P. (2006) Cultivating coaches' communities of practice. Developing the potential for learning through interactions. In R.L. Jones (ed.), *The Sports Coach as Educator. Re-conceptualising Sports Coaching*. London: Routledge.

Cushion, C. (2008) Clarifying the concept of communities of practice in sport: a commentary. *International Journal of Sports Science & Coaching*, 3: 4.

Fitts, P.M. and Possner, M.I. (1967) *Human Performance*. Belmont, CA: Brooks/Cole.

Glipeau, J. and Trudel, P. (2006) Athlete learning in a community of practice. In R.L. Jones (ed.), *The Sports Coach as Educator. Re-conceptualising Sports Coaching* (pp. 77–94). London: Routledge.

Jones, R.L., Armour, K.M. and Potrac, P. (2004) *Sports Coaching Cultures: from Practice to Theory*. London: Routledge.

Keele, S.W. (1968) Movement control in skilled motor performance. *Psychological Bulletin*, 70: 387–403.

Lave, J. and Wenger, E. (1998) Legitimate peripheral participation in communities of practice. In B. McCormick and C. Paechter (eds), *Learning and Knowledge*. London: Paul Chapman.

Leach, J. and Moon, B. (1999) Recreating pedagogy. In J. Leach and B. Moon (eds), *Learners and Pedagogy*. London: Paul Chapman.

Leach, J. and Moon, B. (2002) Globalisation, digital societies and school reform: realising the potential of new technologies to enhance the knowledge, understanding and dignity of teachers. *2nd European Conference on Information Technologies in Education and Citizenship*. Barcelona.

Newell, K.M. (1985) Coordination, control and skill. In D. Goodman, R.B. Wilberg and I.M. Franks (eds), *Differing Perspectives on Perception and Action* (pp. 295–317). Hillsdale, NJ: Erlbaum.

Schmidt, R.A. (1975) A schema theory of discrete motor skill learning. *Psychological Review*, 82: 225–260.

Schmidt, R.A. and Wrisberg, C.A. (2008) *Motor Learning and Performance. A Situation-based Learning Approach* (4th edn). Champaign, IL: Human Kinetics.

Skinner, B.F. (1938) *The Behaviour of Organisms*. New York: Appleton-Century-Crofts.

Thorndike, E.L. (1931) *Human Learning*. New York: Appleton-Century-Crofts.

Welford, A.T. (1968) *Fundamentals of Skill*. London: Methuen.

Wenger, E., McDermott, R. and Snyder, W.M. (2002) *Cultivating Communities of Practice: A Guide to Managing Knowledge*. Boston, MA: Harvard Business School Press.

Woods, B. (1998) *Applying Psychology to Sport* (1st edn). London: Hodder & Stoughton.

CHAPTER 23

WHAT MAKES SUCCESSFUL SESSIONS?

Ben Oakley

In this chapter we focus on instructional sessions such as those in which techniques or technical skills are introduced or refined. What makes successful sessions is answered by the presentation of a practical four-stage framework for leading these types of sessions, emphasising constructive instructional behaviours within each stage. The framework synthesises and draws on the literature of good practice from academic and coaching authors, many who contribute to 'coach education' programmes (e.g. Sports Coach UK, Australian Sports Commission and the American Sport Education Programme). In addition, the author draws on his own experience as a national coach to make connections between ideas and link to practice. Much of the advice from the literature applies equally to anyone instructing physical skills, from Pilates and swimming teachers through to gym instructors and rugby coaches. It is recognised that instruction and teaching represent a narrow conception of what some coaches actually do, particularly at higher levels, and that coaching is often more complex and less episodic than it is made to look in this chapter.

One of the implicit threads running through the four-stage framework introduced in this chapter, is the need for coaches to consider the context and setting of their own practice so that the advice is adapted to their own circumstances. By coaches comparing and contrasting their own approach to the framework presented here it should assist them in understanding, and perhaps adapting, their own practice to what makes a successful instruction session.

The four-stage framework we present below closely mirrors the recommendations of Miles (2004: p. 43) who stated that when initiating a new activity the coach should:

1   Introduce and contextualise.
2   Demonstrate and explain.

3   Guide practice.
4   Analyse and provide feedback.

We realise that many sessions start with a warm-up and/or may include a physical conditioning segment; advice about these activities is not in the scope of this chapter. Note that the participants in instructional sessions are termed 'athletes' throughout the text. So let's see what the coach education literature says about successful instruction in these four stages.

STAGE 1 – INTRODUCE AND CONTEXTUALISE

Much of the literature rather skips over the importance of the first few minutes of a session and the first impressions athletes have of the session. This is because the topic of effective communication is often, as in this book, addressed in other parts of the coaching literature. The nature of introducing a session is partly about you, the coach, conveying enthusiasm and motivating athletes but also about clarity in expressing the aim of the session. So, simple language is needed and, if appropriate, a sense of energy and purpose. You should use brevity and keep an introduction short, perhaps a few minutes (Martens, 2004). If you already know the individuals or group you are working with they will be familiar with the way you work, but if not, you are shaping the atmosphere of your learning environment in these initial encounters.

Christina and Corcos (1988) suggest a good 'introduction should tell your athletes what they will be learning and why it is important: in addition, it usually prepares them for the explanation and demonstration that follow' (p. 31). They emphasise the role of regular routines in getting athletes' attention and arranging them so all can see and hear. Perhaps something can be learned from commercial health and fitness instruction in which the advice is that individuals should be visually greeted, including eye contact, as they enter a gym/class and the instructor should introduce themselves, for the benefit of newcomers (Dalgleish and Dollery, 2001).

Simple, commonsense principles are advised such as:

> Make sure the background your athletes see behind you is free from visual distractions ... do not make your athletes face the sun
>
> (Christina and Corcos, 1988: p. 32)

ben oakley

increase your athletes' *motivation* to learn the skill by not only explaining its value but also pointing our well-known or successful athletes who use the technique

(Christina and Corcos: p. 33)

naming technical skills is important so that you can make quick reference to them … and how it fits into the total plan for playing the sport, the easier it is for them to develop a mental plan for learning it

(Martens, 2004: p. 200)

This leads towards the next stage in the four-stage framework.

STAGE 2 – DEMONSTRATE AND EXPLAIN

Cognitive perspectives of learning (see Chapter 22) address how patterns of motor movement are acquired and selected, and the processes that athletes go through in developing autonomous patterns of movement. Visual demonstration, supported by explanation is one of the main ways patterns of movement are presented. Douge (2001) terms this 'modelling' and points out that coaches do not always have at their disposal someone who can demonstrate good skills. Two alternatives are for the coach to demonstrate, provided they have excellent techniques, or to use video/DVD footage to help athletes develop a mental plan of the activity. From the author's experience even still images have a role to play in providing added insight and variety, especially if attention is drawn to a specific element by the coach. For example, 'look closely at the foot placement in these examples'.

Visual demonstrations are generally more effective than verbal instructions (Abernethy, 2001; Martens, 2004). Consider how difficult it is for words to convey the complex movements and intuition in physical movement, in fact too much verbal explanation is often counter-productive. The following points summarise the main advice about good demonstrations (advice about the verbal aspect follows later).

As with the stage 1, gain the attention of performers and position so all can see, hear and be seen,

(Sports Coach UK, 2003)

Demonstrate the whole technique several times showing how to perform it from different angles. Front and side views are often best.

(Martens, 2004)

In some indoor situations, for example, gymnastics or dance-related skills, using *mirrors* can provide information that helps imitate a certain form or stance

(Christina and Corcos, 1988)

Teaching athletes about the mechanical principles underlying the skills being learned can often be helpful at more advanced levels, e.g. centre of gravity,

(Abernethy, 2001)

If the technique is complex, demonstrate the major parts separately and at a slower speed if it involves rapid movement

(Martens, 2004)

Ensure successful features of performance are highlighted to athletes to encourage them to learn from each other in the practice stage

(Sports Coach UK, 2003)

Wrisberg (2007) suggests that research indicates that learners benefit more from demonstrations when they ask for them, perhaps because people are motivated to watch something they have requested – therefore, as part of a cooperative learning environment, encourage athletes to ask for demonstration or use of video/DVD when they think it might be useful.

Demonstrations can be undertaken in silence to enable athletes to take in what they see but advice contained in most coach education focuses on verbal explanations which support a demonstration. There are two common aspects that are emphasised.

Link to previous experience

Either before or after the demonstration build on athletes' own experience and skills by linking to previous skills whenever possible (Sports Coach UK, 2003). The cognitive perspective of learning suggests athletes develop general rules about how to perform a group of movements, which are flexible; so, by linking to previous experience you are encouraging transfer of these rules of movement. For example, if you are teaching the tennis serve, tell and show your athletes how this skill is similar to throwing a ball (Martens, 2004).

Keep it short and simple

Explanations should be restricted to providing only a few key cues or phrases – the skills for the coach are to decide what the two or three key elements or teaching points are at each stage of learning (Abernethy, 2001). The information provided to someone at the cognitive stage of learning will differ markedly to that provided at the autonomous. Specific *symbolic communication* and *learning cues* can often be used to good effect to enhance communication: this can be applied to both explain demonstrations and in the practice stage that follows.

Each sport has examples of *symbolic communication* which can often signifi-cantly reduce the time taken to learn a movement (Douge, 2001: p. 22). These are also known as analogies and are often used to show an athlete how to visualise and feel a movement. For example, one sometimes used in skiing is 'imagine you are squeezing a large balloon between your knees' or Douge (2001) gives an example relating to the release of the disc in the discus throw: 'imagine that you are quickly and tightly twisting a lid onto a jam jar' (p. 22).

So, *symbolic communication* is one way of keeping explanations short and simple; another is the use of *learning cues* to focus athletes' attention on specific aspects of movement at a particular moment. Wrisberg (2007) gives an example:

> A short precise statement such as 'stay smooth and follow through' would be more helpful for a basketball player attempting a free throw than 'Keep your weight evenly distributed, shooting elbow in, eyes on the rim, knees bent and shoulders relaxed'
>
> (p. 99)

He goes on to give a few examples from different activities, including: swimming ('keep the legs tucked in' – on the tumble turn); tennis ('hit the ball on the rise' – for ground strokes); and weight training ('keep the weight moving with a smooth action').

There are two final aspects of this stage worthy of note. First, the idea of congruence or making sure that the explanation matches what is being demonstrated. Put simply, the visual model that athletes are being shown needs to agree with the verbal explanation otherwise the messages you are transmitting will be confused.

Finally, as with all coach–athlete interaction it is worth *checking for understanding* at the end of a demonstration and explanation. Paraphrasing the main points and inviting and asking questions are essential aspects in closing this stage of the session. The skills of active listening and effective questioning discussed in Chapter 12 are highly relevant in this checking for understanding.

STAGE 3 – GUIDING PRACTICE

The way athletes practise has a strong influence on their learning and it is often the coach that guides this practice. However, in some activities much of the practice is done by individuals working alone and in this case they will be drawing on some of the ideas and learning cues they may have received in earlier contact; perhaps this would be via a coach.

It is worth drawing attention to the diversity of contexts under discussion here. At one end of the scale there might be a closed skill such as a new type of exercise in a gym environment to the other end of the scale say, a complex new pattern of play in a team sport involving open skills.

There are three groups of coaching decisions applicable to this diversity of contexts and the task of guiding effective practice.

1   Practice of the parts or whole skill being learned.
2   The structure of practice.
3   Principles of effective practice.

1. Parts or whole?

Some skills are so complex that it is difficult for athletes to assimilate all the information into a mental plan (e.g. a new pattern of play in a team sport or the pole vault). In this case the whole-part-whole method is recommended (Martens, 2004; Wrisberg, 2007). This involves the whole skill being practised in its entirety, then it is practised in parts and then the parts are put back together into the whole for further practice. Examples of complex skills where this approach might be used are a hockey or cricket shot, a tennis serve or a complex exercise class routine for those athletes in the first (cognitive) stage of learning. Most skills have preparation, action and follow-through phases which are used to break down the skill. Indeed most National Governing Body (NGB) coaching schemes advise coaches and instructors of the recommended sequence of movements and practice drills for their particular sport. Slow-motion practice of new plays or strategies is also another way of focusing on the constituent parts.

However, one aspect lost in breaking down skills into parts is the timing and dynamics of the entire action and attention should focus on re-establishing the timing aspect when the parts are combined back into the whole.

2. The structure of the practice

Two types of practice structure are often referred to in the coaching and skill acquisition literature: blocked and varied practice. This applies far more readily to competitive sport than gym-based activities. A blocked practice structure involves repeating the same skill many times and it should only be used sparingly since research suggests that in sport this repetitious form of practice seldom produces the same kind of results in competition (Abernethy, 2001). It might be of value in helping shape a skill in its early stage (e.g. heading a ball) or for refining a small point of technique at a more advanced level if there is a sound level of existing technical proficiency (e.g. a lob shot in racket sports). Consider how this might relate to how some people can perform well in a golf driving range or cricket 'nets' but struggle in the more varied environment of competition.

A far more recommended form of practice is in providing a range of different practice conditions (variable practice) since it prepares athletes for the variety they may face in their activity. Wrisberg (2007) uses an example in volleyball in which, a *blocked* structure might require players to dig 10 times, then pass 10 times, then block 10 times, and then spike 10 times instead of practising a *variety* of movement patterns (e.g. digging, passing, blocking, and spiking) in a random order of 40 attempts. Although the same number of repetitions might have been undertaken 'a considerable amount of research indicates that' (p. 106) more random and variable practice produces superior learning. It should also be noted that, in sport, practice sessions that closely mimic competition also help develop perceptual and decision-making skills.

3. Principles of effective practice

In this section we draw on the literature in developing five principles of effective practice.

Are your athletes learning the right things?

The ways in which practice is conducted and the choice of practices used are all subject to coaches' beliefs regarding effective and appropriate coaching behaviour gleaned from previous playing, coaching and associated educational experiences of how coaches should coach. Effectively this is an image that newer coaches might aspire to, consciously and/or subconsciously (Potrac et al., 2008). Many coaches therefore use exercises and practice routines mainly due to use by their own coaches in the past which may be outdated. Therefore, it is important to be open minded to new approaches and to question/analyse the practices you use and whether athletes are learning the right things.

Judge athletes' attention and interest

This principle is particularly relevant to newcomers learning a new technique who are likely to tire quickly. Martens (2004) suggests short frequent drills interspersed with rests or practice of another technique that uses different muscle groups and demands less effort. Other authors are slightly less specific but address the same theme – for example, 'good coaching sessions include a lot of variety' (Cox, 1999: p. 92). The message is clear: keep your athletes interested.

Interest is also maintained by making practices fun, using enthusiasm and aspects such as skills 'challenges', changing the ways you do things or getting participants to try out new team positions or use of different types of training aids or equipment. Maintaining athletes' attention and interest is also enhanced by having clear goals for the session: an aspect addressed in a subsequent section.

Manage your resources

Resources for coaching sessions can be viewed as the resources of time, facilities, equipment and, if available, additional people's expertise. Martens (2004) focuses on time and identifies obvious time wasters such as:

- Coaches who talk too much.
- Activities in which most of the athletes' times are spent waiting.
- Dealing with misbehaviour.
- Not having facilities or equipment ready.

There is not scope in this chapter to discuss these issues in detail but clearly organisation and planning are pre-requisites to manage efficient use of resources. Cox (1999) advises encouraging interested families and friends to make a positive contribution to sessions if appropriate: they represent a potentially useful resource.

Also consider the contributions of other coaches or experienced performers who may provide another insight or perspective on particular issues. A fresh voice in a session helps to maintain athlete interest provided the opinion does not contradict the main communication messages.

Structure practices so athletes can see their own improvements

Performers learn best when they are interested and motivated and this is stimulated by the satisfaction of seeing their own improvements, not just physically, but also in feedback received (Sports Coach UK, 2003). Therefore, think carefully about how practices can be structured for athletes to experience a reasonable amount of success: this is particularly important for coaches of children (Martens, 2004). Progress need not just be about performance but also to do with recognition of improvements of other important attributes such as fitness, cooperation with others, attitude and awareness.

Of course athletes' perceptions of improvement will largely depend on their expectations. You can influence this since ideally 'excellent coaching sessions involve each athlete in goal-setting' (Cox, 1999: p. 79). This is challenging with larger groups but a coach can perhaps set time aside to meet athletes individually or set realistic group goals.

With specific reference to children, Whitehead (1993) advises that coaches need to organise sessions that recognise the blend of contrasting goals amongst children, younger children in particular. She identifies the common features of three different types of goal: 'pleasing others' relates to approval goals, 'personal progress' relates to process goals, and 'superiority over others' relates to outcome goals. Most of the coaching education literature stresses the need to focus on process goals, that is on what athletes actually do when performing their activities so success is largely under their control. 'If process goals are well set by coaches, children can feel some success even when they lose' (Whitehead, 1993: p. 113). Therefore, it is often about aspects of performance rather than the final outcome.

Generate as much feedback as possible

Feedback is included in this list of principles of effective practice since it is an overarching theme of 'good' practice sessions. In the stage that follows, feedback is addressed in detail.

STAGE 4 – ANALYSE AND PROVIDE FEEDBACK

The behaviourist perspective of learning (Chapter 22) underpins much of what follows about the role of analyses and feedback. A person practising alone will make some progress in perfecting a skill using their own evaluation of how close to the desired performance they are, but they will learn quicker with other sources of feedback, particularly with more complex skills and performances.

The observation and analysis of athletes and the identification of the causes of sub-standard performance represents one of the core skills of good instruction. The process of analysis can either be carried out systematically with the aid of technology or, more often at grassroots level, in an ad hoc manner using visual judgement. Different coaches can observe different things and there is a tendency for people 'to see what they expect to' based on their particular background and experience (Sports Coach UK, 2003). NGBs attempt to educate would-be coaches and instructors of the typical faults to expect in an activity but there is no substitute for knowledge, experience and reflective practice in developing the coaching craft of observation. The use of match analysis in team sports or, more commonly, film analysis provides valuable additional data on which to base a considered judgement about what needs to be adjusted and the feedback that might be given.

A general principle of the amount of feedback is outlined below:

> … research suggests that the quality of feedback provided is more important than the quantity. In other words, you should consider how and when to give feedback rather than assume that more is better
> (Wrisberg, 2007: p. 114)

The types of feedback can include a comment from the coach, a sensation from the equipment and/or body or an evaluation of the performance outcome. Douge (2001: p. 24) describes examples of other options available to collect useful information about performance:

- Heart rate monitors can be used to gather data about effort and physiological responses.
- Sprint or distance coaches can use timing devices to provide information about speed or splits in different sections of a performance.
- Coaches can use questioning techniques to help athletes construct their own feedback – questioning helps athletes identify for themselves what is and isn't correct.

Feedback principles

The following six principles and subsequent discussion provide a useful guide to reviewing and checking your existing knowledge about feedback.

1   Give only one or two pieces of information at a time so they can be absorbed more readily; make it simple and precise

(Douge, 2001; Martens, 2004)

2   Help the athlete appreciate that adjustments resulting from feedback may result, in the short term, in a poorer outcome

(Douge, 2001)

3   When using video playback with novices, you may need to direct their attention to the most important visual cues in the playback

(Wrisberg, 2007)

4   Athletes should be allowed the opportunity to evaluate their own performance and if appropriate their peers (Wrisberg 2007) – in fact there is a danger that if athletes only get feedback from the coach then it may create reliance and negate the development of independent learning and athlete autonomy that are the features of elite performance

(Magill, 2004)

5   Give feedback immediately after performance, rather than during it or sometime after it has been completed

(Cox, 1999)

6   Learning is more effective when an athlete attempts to correct only one error at a time, which means if there are several errors you must decide which to correct first

(Martens, 2004)

The following discussion moves on to address principles of *how* feedback is presented which is just as important as *what* is said. Empathy and well-developed communication skills help here but what is needed is the patience and predisposition to be able to give feedback sensitively about what is correct or positive as well as what is incorrect. An approach which will be familiar to many features in both more academic- (e.g. Wrisberg, 2007) and practitioner-based texts (e.g. Sports Coach UK, 2003): the 'sandwiching' of feedback. This phrase describes the basic tenet of sandwiching corrective feedback with a positive statement about performance before the feedback advice and ending with further positive encouragement. This is a way of conveying feedback that is as non-threatening as possible and framing it in a way that is factual and not personal (i.e. about the performance rather than about the person).

A further important principle is to consider avoiding giving corrective advice in the presence of others (Douge, 2001). This is a particular issue in team or group situations when taking an athlete to one side or substituting them, as an activity continues is often more appropriate (Martens, 2004). The behaviour of some coaches on the sidelines, of team sports in particular, needs to take into account that feedback can be a distraction, rather than an encouragement, if it is given during performance (Cox, 1999).

CONCLUSION

This chapter has provided practical advice, grounded in the coaching literature, of what makes successful instruction sessions. The guidance applies to many of the concepts identified in other chapters of this book, including techniques of communication, motivation and theories of learning physical skills. The four-stage framework presented may not occur in every instructional session but the principles are transferable to a range of settings.

REFERENCES

Abernethy, B. (2001) Acquisition of skill. In F.S. Pyke (ed.), *Better Coaching*, 2nd edition (pp. 161–170). Lower Mitcham, Australia: Human Kinetics/Australian Sports Commission.

Christina, R.W. and Corcos, D.M. (1988) *Coaches Guide to Teaching Sports Skills*. Champaign, Illinois: Human Kinetics.

Cox, R. (1999) Psychological considerations of effective coaching. In N. Cross and J. Lyle (eds), *The Coaching Process: Principles and Practice for Sport* (pp. 67–90). London: Butterworth Heinemann.

Dalgleish, J. and Dollery, S. (2001) *The Health and Fitness Handbook*. In H. Frankham (ed.), Harlow: Pearson/Longman.

Douge, B. (2001) Coaching methods. In F.S. Pyke (ed.), *Better Coaching*, 2nd edition (pp. 15–26). Lower Mitcham, Australia: Human Kinetics/Australian Sports Commission.

Magill, R.A. (2004) *Motor Learning and Control Concepts and Applications*, 7th edition. London: McGraw-Hill.

Martens R. (2004) *Successful Coaching*, 3rd edition. Champaign: Human Kinetics.

Miles, A. (2004) *Coaching Practice*. Leeds: Sports Coach UK.

Potrac, P., Jones, R. and Cushion, C. (2008) Understanding power and the coach's role in professional English soccer: a preliminary investigation of coach behaviour. *Soccer and Society*, 8(1): 33–49.

Sports Coach UK (2003) *The Successful Coach: Guidelines For Coaching Practice*. Leeds: Sports Coach UK.

Whitehead, J. (1993) Why children choose to do sport – or stop. In M. Lee (ed.), *Coaching Children in Sport* (pp. 109–121). London: E & FN Spon.

Wrisberg, C. (2007) *Sports Skill Instruction for Coaches*. Champaign: Human Kinetics.

CHAPTER 24

COACHING AND LEARNING STYLES[1]

Terry McMorris and Tudor Hale

In this chapter, McMorris and Hale draw our attention to the contentious area of 'styles'. If a coach consistently uses a particular strategy for making and communicating decisions, or organising a training session, this could be said to be their 'coaching style'. The notion of a 'style' implies a behaviour that has some degree of consistency across time, with different athletes and settings, or learning different skills. The 'style' of the coach may almost be seen as 'the way they do things'.

Similarly, it has been argued that different individuals (athletes, in our context), have different preferred ways of learning, or learning styles. Again, the notion of 'style' implies a degree of consistency to this preferred modality of learning.

Considering coaching or learning styles can help us to identify the strategies that we may tend to rely upon in instructing and developing our athletes' or teams' performance. It helps us to identify the strengths and weaknesses of these approaches, and may also cause us to consider and evaluate alternatives.

Coaching styles are linked to leadership behaviours. Unlike leadership, very little has been examined with regard to coaching styles. This is, in fact, so much the case that in this chapter I have borrowed from work on teaching styles in physical education. At one time teaching styles would have been seen as having no bearing on coaching. Teaching was seen as being concerned with the development of the individual as a whole, while coaching was thought to be concerned only with outcome, that is, winning and losing. This attitude has changed greatly over the years and coaches perceive their roles as being concerned with the individual's welfare as well as their performance. In reality,

---

[1] Edited from McMorris, T. and Hale, T. (2006) 'Coaching and Learning Styles' in *Coaching Science*, pp. 55–66, Chichester: John Wiley & Sons Ltd.

the gap between what was considered to be purely the domain of physical education and that which was looked on as being concerned with coaching has merged.

COACHING STYLES

One of the early attempts to highlight coaching styles was undertaken by Rainer Martens (1987). Martens divided coaching into two styles, *command* and *cooperative*, although he accepted that, to some extent, it is a command–cooperative continuum. The command style is characterised by the coach taking responsibility for all aspects of learning and performance. The athletes simply have to do what the coach tells them. The coach organises practices, team tactics and motivation. Such coaches are thought to favour extrinsic motivation and use many reward and punishment systems. Also, they tend to place outcome as being the most important of their goals. Cooperative coaches are almost the opposite. They see their role as that of a facilitator, making it possible for the athletes to achieve their goals. They prefer to develop intrinsic motivation and put the athletes' welfare ahead of outcome. This does not mean that they are not interested in winning but that they see social factors as being the more important.

Martens believes that there are personality reasons for coaches adopting each of the styles. He believes that cooperative coaches are high in self-esteem and are able to empathise with their athletes. One would have to have high self-esteem to let the athletes have the major say in training and practice sessions, and team tactics. The coach, when using such a style, has to be willing to 'take a backseat' and not be in the limelight. To Martens, the command style coach is low in self-esteem, hence the need to be seen to be in control. Often such coaches will try to take the praise for performances. Also, they are low in the ability to empathise with their athletes.

More recently, John Lyle (1999) has taken a similar stance to that of Martens. Lyle divided coaching styles into *autocratic* and *democratic*. He claims that it is possible to be democratic with regard to communicating with athletes (the leadership role) while being autocratic during practice and training sessions (the coaching role). The autocratic style is like Martens' command style. The coach is 'in charge' of everything. Practice and training are organised by the coach and the coach tells the athletes what to do. They have no say in the matter. The democratic style is similar to Martens' cooperative style, with the coach involving the athletes in organisation and decision-making concerning what is to be done and even how it is to be done.

COACHING STYLES BASED ON MOSSTON'S TEACHING STYLES

The physical educationist Muska Mosston identified nine teaching styles used in physical education (e.g. Mosston and Ashworth, 1994). Observation of these styles shows that they are also employed by coaches. In this section, I have adapted Mosston's teaching styles to a coaching role. I have also taken the liberty of simplifying some of the concepts, particularly those that are more involved in educating the person as a whole. Table 24.1 outlines each of the styles and gives their major characteristics. Here I will expand a little on the content of the table.

The *command* style is almost identical to Martens' command and Lyle's autocratic styles. The coach is very much in charge. Content is chosen by the coach and the methods of practice and training are decided solely by him/her. There is no ambiguity in the role of the coach, assistants and individual athletes. This style can be particularly useful when the activity involves an element of danger, for example, coaching the javelin or discus. It also has some advantages with large groups. One of its major advantages is that it is the easiest of all of the

Table 24.1 Mosston's teaching styles

Style	Description
Command	Coach makes all decisions and instructs learners during practice: everyone practises the same tasks, at the same level of difficulty
Practice	Coach makes all decisions but learners progress at own rate depending on their ability level
Reciprocal	Athletes coach one another
Self-check	Athletes assess their own success and failure
Inclusion	Athlete and coach decide on what is to be learned and the coaching methods to be used
Guided discovery	Athlete makes all decisions guided by the coach
Divergent	Coach sets problems for athletes to solve
Individual programme-learner's design	Learner decides on what is to be coached
Learner's initiated style	Coach only helps when asked
Self-teaching	Athlete takes sole responsibility for all aspects of learning

styles in which to maintain discipline. Coaches who feel threatened by a lack of athlete discipline often resort to this method of coaching. Obviously its lack of input from the athletes can alienate some of them. For coaches to use this style successfully they need to be particularly well respected for their knowledge. The style has major limits if the athletes are at different levels of ability and development. It tends to be a style more suitable for homogenous groups.

Mosston claims that, for this style to be successful, the coach must be aware of the emotional state of the athletes. If the athletes are getting bored or not achieving success they are powerless if the coach is using such a style. Coaches who successfully use command style, and there are many, constantly monitor their athletes and alter practices, or even abort them, when they feel that it is necessary. Perhaps the most successful users of this style are individuals who have strong and charismatic personalities, what some people call the 'X' factor. In reality though, I think that few coaches actually use a pure form of command style. Most seem to include other styles as well.

Most coaches who believe that they use the command style in fact use the *practice* style. As with the command style, the coach is very much in charge. The athletes do what the coach tells them. However, the speed and type of progression during the session will vary from athlete to athlete depending on their ability levels. Unlike in the command style, not everyone is practising and progressing at the same rate. This is called *differentiation*. The coach lets the athletes practise as individuals, or in groups, and goes round providing individual and small group coaching. This style does allow for small inter-individual differences in ability and developmental stage.

The *reciprocal* style is sometimes called *peer coaching*. The coach sets the agenda, that is, chooses the topic or topics to be coached, but splits the team up into groups of twos or threes and so on. Then each group goes off and practises. They provide one another with feedback. It can be particularly useful when the athletes know the tasks well and can help one another. Some athletes like this because they feel that making mistakes will not lead to the coach seeing them as being poor performers. Good coaches will move around the groups, as with the practice style. Athletes can progress at their own rate and each can work on aspects of their own performance rather than simply everybody doing the same thing. Obviously this can only be used if there is good discipline and the athletes have a sound knowledge of the activity. Care must be taken with choice of groups. Individuals who do not get on together can end up arguing in such situations, while some athletes will not be critical of people whom they see as being better than themselves.

The *self-check* style is similar to the reciprocal style in that the coach sets the agenda but, instead of being 'coached' by a peer, the athletes actually 'coach' themselves. The athletes practise by themselves, or in small groups, and assess their own success and failure. They attempt to put problems right and try out changes in technique or tactics. The coach can go around checking on them. As well as allowing the athletes to work on their own problems and progress at their own rate, it increases athletes' self-esteem and independence. This can be very important. Many individual athletes, in particular, need to learn to compete without their coaches being there to give them feedback. With beginners, who have little knowledge of the activity, this can end up as being trial and error learning. With more advanced performers, however, the athlete has some knowledge to draw upon and the trials will be more than hopeful guesses.

The *inclusion* style is the first of Mosston's styles that involves the learner in the decision of what to learn. The learner and coach together agree on what the athlete should work on, the level at which they should begin and the rate of progress they should make. Thus this level takes care of individual differences with regard to ability level and experience. However, lazy athletes can opt for an easy time. The coach needs to be a good communicator to get success. They must be good motivators. Some athletes want to do too much. The coach needs all of his/her diplomacy skills with such an athlete to get them to work at a more suitable level. This must be done without damaging the athlete's self-esteem. Not an easy task.

The *guided discovery* style requires the coach to help the athlete to make the correct decision concerning what they are to practise, how they are to practise, what the results of the practice tell them and how they are going to change in order to perform better. This sounds like a difficult task for the coach and it is. It is far easier to take a command approach and tell them that they have done this incorrectly and this is how to improve. It is more difficult to get the athletes to work it out for themselves. However, the ability to come to the conclusions yourself, albeit under a lot of guidance, means the learner is not only finding out how to do something but also why it should be done this way. More parts of the brain are involved and reasoning is deeper. All of this aids learning.

The *divergent* style could be termed a *problem-solving approach*. The coach sets a problem, or task, and lets the athletes work out a solution or solutions for themselves with or without help from the coach. The use of this style demands a great deal of self-esteem from the coach, as the coach is letting the performers 'take charge' of their own learning. It does, however, lead to some great moments of innovation. It also allows for an increase in independence and self-esteem in the athlete. Where the athletes have developed a tactical ploy of their own they are more likely to want to implement it than one that has been forced upon them by the coach. In team sports different parts of the team can be working on different problems. I have seen this style used extremely successfully in professional football. The main issue for the coach is to set realistic problems and to explain the scenario succinctly to the athletes. Players do need a lot of experience to use this method successfully.

The *individual programme-learner's design* refers to where the learner decides on the main area to be practised, for example, receiving serve in tennis. In many individual sports this is very common. Many tennis players and golfers highlight their strengths and weaknesses then decide what they wish to work on and go to a coach for help. The coach takes care of the actual practice. The *learner's initiated* style takes the individual programme-learner's design a stage further, with the coach merely giving advice when asked. The athlete decides not just on the area to be worked on but also the type of practice to be utilised. Mosston's final style is the *self-teaching* style, which does not require a coach.

LEARNING STYLES

While coaching styles are very important, so are the styles used by the learner. Furthermore, as we will see in the final section of this chapter, the interaction between coaching and learning styles is an important one. There are four types of learner, *activists, reflectors, theorists* and *pragmatists*. Activists, sometimes called *accommodators*, are characterised by open-mindedness and a willingness to became involved immediately in trying out the new skill. They like to be given a challenge and love to 'have a go'. Activists are not afraid to make mistakes. Males tend to be more activist than females.

Reflectors, or *divergers*, prefer to think through a problem before trying to perform a skill. They are willing to listen to what the coach has to say about how to perform a skill. They tend to be cautious in approach but will work out alternative methods of performing a skill. They like to work in small groups or pairs. Females tend to be more reflectors than males. Theorists, or *assimilators*, are similar to reflectors and like to take their time in working out how to do something. They are more analytical than reflectors but less cautious, although they will only try out movements that theory suggests will work. They like to work alone. People using a pragmatic, or *convergent*, style are more like the activists, in that they enjoy trying things out without too much reflection or theorising.

However, they use some theorisation in that they like to see if ideas will work. However, unlike the theorists and reflectors they are willing to do this with a minimal amount of cognitive questioning. These people like to find out the answers using action rather than reflection.

PRACTICAL IMPLICATIONS

I will be surprised if any coaches are out and out autocrats or democrats. I will be even more surprised if they are very accurate in knowing which style they actually use. Thinking about how you deal with coaching sessions and how you behave during competition will help you make an educated decision on your style. However, research has shown that coaches are notoriously poor at actually knowing how they behave. Finding out is simple. You can make up a checklist. You can divide activities into those that would be displayed by an autocrat, for example, giving instructions and commands; and those that a democrat would use, for example, asking questions, listening to suggestions. Get someone to observe your coaching and put a tick or cross next to each of the types of behaviour as you use them. Table 24.2 gives an outline of autocratic and democratic behaviours that you could use to help you make up your checklist. There are now sophisticated computer packages such as *Sports Coach*, which use video evidence and computer print-outs to determine your coaching style. In essence, they are only checklists using technology. However, they are useful in that you can see yourself doing the coaching. Not always a pretty sight.

Mosston does not recommend one style over another; he says that the style used should depend on the interaction between the coach, the athlete and the task. For many people, reacting to different tasks and athletes is not too difficult; they

Table 24.2 Behaviours used by autocratic and democratic coaches

Autocrats	Democrats
Decide what is to be coached in each session	Discuss with athletes their needs and agree on content of session
Tell athletes what to do and how to do it	Provide options on the best ways to perform a skill
Have all athletes working on the same task and progressing at the same time	Use differentiation based on individual abilities
Dictate tactics	Discuss with athletes the tactics to be used

will naturally empathise with nervous athletes or be more patient with beginners than experts.

In one of our coaching courses at Chichester, the staff deliberately try to adopt a specific coaching style in order to give the students an example of what it looks like in practice. We all find this very difficult to actually do. I normally choose to use a command style. This you would think is easy but I always find myself drifting into guided discovery and problem-solving (divergent style) approaches.

While guided discovery is my favourite style because it gets the learners to think their way through a problem, it may not be the best with tasks that have an element of risk. For example, letting people try to work out how best to pack down in a rugby scrum is inappropriate. At the other extreme, I have often seen people use command or practice styles when teaching dribbling in hockey, football and basketball or running past defenders in rugby. Dribbling is a skill that depends on the person using their own strengths to outwit an opponent. Moreover, great dribblers are innovative. How can you be innovative if someone is telling you what to do? Two of the best runners with a Rugby ball are Shane Horgan and Brian O'Driscoll but they go past defenders using different strategies and styles. Horgan attacks at speed and begins his move a comparatively long way in front of the defender. He swerves around the defender while already running at speed. O'Driscoll gets closer to the defender before beginning his move and relies on his ability to change direction and accelerate in limited space. To teach Horgan and O'Driscoll to use the same strategies would be stupid.

The importance of motivation cannot be underestimated. Highly motivated individuals will spend long periods of time doing what, to others, is repetitive and boring practice. They can, and will, work alone. They are able, and willing, to use the individual styles set out by Mosston (individual-learner's design and learner's initiated styles). The coach must be careful, however, and take into account the skill level of these athletes and the task they are learning. The great ice hockey player Wayne Gretsky spent hours, as a child, practising by himself. Learning the basic skills using this individual approach was fine, even for a child. However, more advanced skills may need greater input from a coach, especially with younger performers. Experts may be best left to themselves and may well come up with something new when left alone in these situations. Innovative plays in many sports have come about from this kind of practice. Similarly, some of the best vaults in gymnastics and jumps in trampolining are the result of such practice.

So far, we have not talked about the role of the athlete's learning style in the decision of how to coach. While there are questionnaires that can be used to determine individuals' learning styles, these are designed for classroom studies and may be inappropriate. More importantly, in team games, players are reluctant to give such information to coaches who select the team. With individual athletes the coach can find out how the athlete learns by simply talking to them about the process. In team situations, it may be safer to assume that all of the learning styles are represented; therefore, variety in your use of style will help. When introducing a new skill activists like to 'have a go' before any instruction is given. This can unnerve reflectors and theorists, however. When dealing with males I tend to let them have a go first because males are more likely to be activists than females. With females, I point out what we are going to do and why. Pragmatists also like the idea of having a go but they want some time to work out an answer for themselves. Activists do not mind having a go then being stopped, told how to do it and then returning to the practice. Activists, and to a lesser extent pragmatists, are happy with command and practice styles of coaching. Pragmatists prefer self-check and inclusion. They also do not mind reciprocal coaching but that will also depend on their relationships with the others in the group.

I must say that I am not keen on reciprocal coaching. I have seen it work very well with experts but have major problems using it with beginners. Mosston included it in his teaching styles because, as an educational tool, it is useful in helping the peer 'coach' to understand the skill better. However, if the peer does not get it right the coaching is incorrect. Reflectors and theorists are happier with guided discovery and problem solving. Coaches can set problems and help the athletes to solve them. Many reflectors and theorists like to spend time inactive physically but very active mentally. Activists hate this and even pragmatists are not too happy. These differences can cause problems in teams.

SUMMARY

Martens and Lyle identified coaching styles along a continuum from autocratic to democratic. The physical educationist Mosston saw teaching styles as falling into very similar types. Unlike Martens and Lyle, he divided teaching styles into 10 subgroups, ranging from command (autocratic) to self-coaching, which goes even further than a democratic style. More importantly, Mosston claimed that the style of choice should be made depending on the coach–athlete–task interaction. One of the factors that coaches should take into consideration concerning the athlete is his or her learning style. Although four styles have been identified, in essence one could argue that there is a continuum from the activist to the theorist. Males tend to be more activist and females more theoretical in approach.

264

The difficulty in adopting different coaching styles to suit different situations is the coach's personality. Can he/she really change? This appears to be possible for some but not for all.

Schmidt and Wrisberg (2008) advocate a 'problem-based approach' to teaching physical skills, in which practice is organised in response to three key questions:

- Who is the person learning the skill?
- What is the skill being learned?
- Where is the person required to perform the skill?

In this chapter, you may see that such questions provide a useful framework for evaluating the appropriateness of a particular coaching or instructional style, in a particular situation:

- Is the style of instruction appropriate to the person learning the skill?
- Is the style of instruction appropriate to the skill being learned?
- Is the style of instruction appropriate to the context in which the athlete has to perform the skill?

This chapter also hints at a fourth question, 'is the style appropriate to me' as a coach or instructor? Is this a style of coaching that I can believe in and practise?

This depends to a large extent upon your professional knowledge, your values and beliefs about coaching or instruction, upon who you are as a coach or instructor, and what you bring to that role. Developing an understanding of this is the subject of the final chapter in this section.

REFERENCES

Lyle, J. (1999) Coaches' decision making. In N. Cross and J. Lyle (Eds.), *The coaching process: Principles and practice for sport* (pp. 210–232). Butterworth Heinemann: Oxford.

Martens, R. (1987) *Coaches Guide to Sport Psychology*. Champaign, IL: Human Kinetics.

Mosston, M. and Ashworth, S. (1994) *Teaching Physical Education*, 4th edn. New York: Macmillan.

Schmidt, R.A. and Wrisberg, C.A. (2008). *Motor Learning and Performance*. Leeds: Human Kinetics.

CHAPTER 25

COACHING AND INSTRUCTION
Understanding and developing professional knowledge

Tom Power

The purpose of this chapter is to explain a model for understanding the professional knowledge of coaches and instructors, which can be used to articulate the richness of their current professional knowledge, as well as to identify areas which may benefit from further professional development.

PROFESSIONAL KNOWLEDGE

In this chapter, we focus upon the professional knowledge of fitness instructors and sports coaches; not upon personality traits or behaviours, but upon knowledge. What do you need to know to be a good fitness instructor or sports coach?

You might like to think about that for a few minutes before reading any further, or perhaps try discussing this apparently simple question with a few colleagues.

If you are a fitness instructor, you may have considered consulting the content of REPS courses, to see if they shed light on what constitutes professional knowledge. If you did this, you may well have found information indicating a range of 'things you need to know about' including:

- Types of exercise (such as gym or water-based, yoga or Pilates).
- Clients groups (e.g. older adults, children and young people, pre- and post-natal).
- Specific medical issues (heart disease, metabolic syndrome, after-stroke care).

(REPS, 2007)

Alternatively, if you are a sports coach, you may have explored the SCUK site; SCUK is just beginning to codify its answer to the question 'what does a coach need to know?' in the UK Coaching Framework. At the time of writing, it has identified that for coaching to be recognised as a profession, coaches will require:

- a professional education;
- a specialised body of knowledge;
- professional practice;
- explicit systems of ethics and values.

(SCUK, 2008)

These represent two quite different approaches to describing 'what you need to know', and if you wrote your own description, it is likely to be quite different again. This may be, in part, because of the complexity of the role and the broad range of settings in which it is practiced: what are the features that are common and important across different disciplines of instruction in sport or exercise?

There is as yet 'no theoretical framework' (Côté et al., 1995) for understanding the key areas of knowledge required for effective coaching and physical instruction, or how such areas of knowledge might relate to one another. Although 'sports psychology' and 'sports pedagogy' are well-established disciplines, the literature on what constitutes 'professional knowledge' for coaches or instructors remains sparse.

Over recent years, the author has talked with many employers and industry bodies in the UK, discussing 'what does a good fitness instructor or a good sports coach need to know?', in order to inform the design of professional development courses in this sector.

In general, those in the industry have found it easier to pin down what many described as the 'hard' knowledge and skills, such as how to correctly use a piece of gym equipment, or the particular techniques or rules of a certain sport; these things typically form the core of many sports and fitness organisations in-house training schemes or awards.

It is usually much harder to pin down what many described as the 'soft' knowledge and skills: how to communicate effectively with different groups, or in different contexts; how to motivate and inspire; how to really teach techniques and strategies effectively. Yet this 'soft' knowledge was often seen as key to professional practice, to determining the quality of the experience of those we coach and instruct, and to the employability of coaches and instructors (SkillsActive, 2006). These areas of 'soft' knowledge and skill form some of the key themes of this book: motivation, communication, leadership, and the focus of this section: learning and instruction.

This chapter attempts to suggest a structure, or model, for organising our understanding of the different dimensions of professional knowledge required for effective professional practice. The model can be used as a framework for answering the question: 'what does a good sports coach or instructor need to know?', for articulating what coaches or instructors already know, and for identifying areas for further professional development.

A MODEL OF PROFESSIONAL KNOWLEDGE

In contrast to the situation in the sports and fitness sector, the process of 'professionalisation' has been going on in relation to school teaching for the best part of a century. Teaching in schools is different to fitness instruction because of the emphasis on motor skills in the latter, the distinctive features of which have already been discussed in previous chapters. Fitness instruction is also different from coaching, because coaching has not only an emphasis on motor skills, but also tactical skills (Martens, 2004) and competition (Côté et al., 1995).

Yet, despite these differences, it is possible that many commonalities remain in the nature of professional knowledge required for good practice, between teachers, instructors and coaches. In this chapter, I explore this by adapting a model for 'teacher professional knowledge' (Banks et al., 1999) and applying it to the context of sports coaching and fitness instruction (Figure 25.1).

Banks et al. (teacher educators and educational researchers at the Open University) originally developed this model in 1996 to help show the complexity of a teacher's task, and it has subsequently been used extensively to support the design and implementation of professional development courses. Teachers and trainee teachers in the UK and other parts of the world, such as Spain, the Netherlands, Sweden, Egypt and South Africa (Banks et al., 1996; Leach and Banks, 1996; Leach et al., 2006; Power and Thomas, 2007) have used the model to help them explore the different and wide-ranging aspects of knowledge they already have – as well as to decide what knowledge they would like to develop in the future. Most recently, the model has been used by student teachers from a number of different countries to articulate their developing professional knowledge (Banks, 2008).

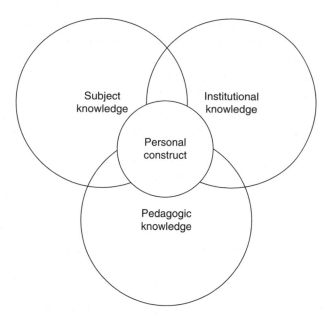

Figure 25.1 A model for the professional knowledge of sports coaches and fitness instructors

Source: Adapted from Banks *et al.* (1999)

Despite the model being used in a broad range of contexts, the reactions to it have usually been remarkably similar:

- Teachers recognise the different categories of knowledge in the model and see them as meaningful distinctions.
- Teachers were often excited by the model, valuing the ease with which it helps them articulate what they know and what they do.
- The model can be interpreted on different levels, both as a tool for developing personal understanding, and as a mechanism for planning professional development within institutions.

I have tried to outline below how this model could be adapted and applied to the context of Sports Coaching or Fitness instruction.

Sport and fitness (subject) knowledge is the underlying knowledge we need to have about our particular form of exercise or sport. For example, in fitness instruction, it might include knowledge of anatomy and physiology, as well as techniques and principles for a range of exercise activities or disciplines (such as

269

gym routines, circuit training, spin cycling or yoga and so on). In sports coaching, it would include your knowledge of the rules of the game, as well as strategies and tactics for successful performance or competition. It includes all the specialist terms of the sport, their meanings and concepts; the physical techniques and mental models that give rise to proficiency and skill.

Institutional knowledge is that knowledge that we need in order to practise effectively within the particular settings in which our work is situated.

Institutional knowledge includes the part of our subject knowledge we teach and pass on, transformed and applied to the context of the organisation in which we practise. As leaders, coaches or instructors, our sports and fitness knowledge may be very sophisticated. There is the process we have to go through to transform such knowledge, in order to make it teachable to the people we instruct or coach. For a fitness instructor, this may mean selecting the appropriate piece of anatomical or physiological knowledge to pass on to a club member, in order to help them understand the key aspect of an exercise and perform it correctly.

Institutional knowledge also includes knowledge that is specific to the particular club or centre that you train in, such as:

- tools (what resources are available for training?);
- language (what do we call things in this club?);
- practices (the systems, procedures and customs of the institution);
- roles and relationships (who does what?);
- values (is there an esprit de'corps, a specific outlook and purpose within an institution?).

As well as the transformed aspects of our personal sport and fitness knowledge, institutional knowledge may also refer to the knowledge frameworks of the awarding bodies for our sport.

For example, a children's gymnastics coach needs to know what skills need to be covered for each of the 'badges' that children train for, and how developed participants' skills need to be, for them to achieve success at the appropriate level. Governing bodies may specify other aspects of institutional knowledge, such as the terminology that should be used, or formal value systems that coaches should operate within.

So institutional knowledge includes:

- our sports and fitness knowledge transformed to the context of our practice;
- things we need to know to function within our club or centre;

■   things we need to know to function within the frameworks and institutions that shape the organisation of our sector.

Such institutional knowledge is essential for effective professional practice within your club.

Pedagogic knowledge is our understanding of how to teach something: it underpins the choice of appropriate strategies to develop the required skills and capabilities in those we coach or instruct.

Pedagogic knowledge provides you with a range of techniques from which you choose appropriately to make training and practice fun, active, enjoyable and successful for participants. It includes the way you communicate and motivate, how you assess progress and identify areas for development. It is the knowledge that enables you to use a diverse range of practices and processes to help participants and teams achieve their goals.

The *personal construct* is placed at the centre of the model, as it draws upon all other areas; also because it may be seen as the most important aspect of the model.

Your personal construct includes your values, making the personal construct closely related to the notion of a personal 'philosophy of coaching' (Lyle, 1999).

> Coaching behaviour reflects a set of values about coaching, sport and human relationships more generally. This set of values ... has been termed a 'coaching philosophy' ... Values are the means through which individuals evaluate their experiences and lead to some things being regarded more highly than others. A complete set of values provides a meaningful context for an individual's activities ... values legitimate behaviour.
>
> (Lyle, 2002: p. 165)

Martens (2004) argues that being explicitly aware of your coaching or instructional philosophy, having clear guiding principles, can bring greater clarity to many of the day-to-day decisions and response we are called to make.

> If you give the same amount of time to the development of your philosophy as you do to the development of your technical knowledge of the sport, you will be a better coach.
>
> (Martens, 2004: p. 5)

271

What do you think makes a great sports person, or a good instructor? What do you hope to achieve through your instruction? Why does sport or fitness matter to you? The values that you hold will affect who you are as a coach or instructor, what you praise or strive for, and how you interact with those you lead. Though not often explicitly expressed, or even consciously considered, your 'coaching philosophy' will be implicit in almost everything you say and do as a coach or instructor.

However, the personal construct goes beyond a personal philosophy of coaching or instruction: a young male Jamaican athletics coach and an older female Scottish swimming coach may possibly have very similar philosophies of coaching, were they to take the time to sit down and make these explicit. Yet, even so, their different lived experiences are likely to lead to them being very different people.

This 'being who you are', this 'you' that has been constructed over the course of your life and defines what makes you 'you', is the heart of the personal construct.

It is likely that your experience of sport and fitness has had a significant impact upon your self-image and your enjoyment of life: what excites you about sport and fitness and fires you up to pass that onto others? What special experiences, skills and understandings do you bring to training session?

Are you an expert on game strategy, or the psychology of winning? Perhaps you are a great exercise class leader because of a background in dance and a love of music and movement. Maybe there was a special area of study you have done, or particular experiences you have, that let you bring some unique knowledge to your practice.

The personal construct can also be influenced by the values and cultures of our organisations, if we appropriate them personally. On the other hand, Sports Coach UK points towards the way in which the cumulative effect of many people's individual values and experiences gives vitality and life to the institutional culture:

> The structure of sports coaching in the UK is based on a system whose cultural characteristics are fundamentally premised on volunteerism. In the desire to professionalise the occupation and its working practices, therefore, we must not lose sight of the importance of historical qualities, the role of mutual support, and the strong sense of belonging built upon the love of sport.
>
> (SCUK, 2008: p. i)

Finally, as the last point illustrates, it is important to emphasise that the model is not describing discrete, static categories of knowledge: categories overlap and relationships between categories are dynamic, with knowledge in one category interacting with knowledge in other categories.

POSSIBLE APPLICATIONS OF THE MODEL

The first application is to give a coach or instructor a framework for considering and discussing their own professional knowledge; the framework provides a means to being more specific and explicit about what constitutes our professional knowledge and skills.

The model can also be used for planning opportunities for professional development, and considering staff deployment. To illustrate this, I will give a few brief scenarios followed by an outline of how the model might suggest areas of professional knowledge for development.

Scenario 1: Competitive athlete moving into coaching for the first time

Here we see that the new coach is likely to have strong *subject knowledge* (having competed at an elite level of the game, they will have a clear understanding of the rules, techniques and tactics that can bring success).

However, whilst they have experienced being coached for a long time, they have not yet practised the art of coaching.

If the new coach is beginning coaching in the same institution as they trained in as an athlete, many aspects of *institutional knowledge* will be strong: they will have a clear idea of the roles and relationships, customs and practice in the institution, as well as the training tools that are available, and how these can be used. However, other aspects of institutional knowledge may need developing – particularly, if the new coach is starting out with 'novice' athletes: they may need to work at mediating their 'elite' subject knowledge into a form that is accessible and teachable to 'novice' athletes. They may also need to become re-acquainted with the 'curriculum' of different levels of novice award associated with their sport, and the performance criteria required for success at each level.

Perhaps most importantly, the new coach will need help in developing their *pedagogic knowledge*. They will almost certainly benefit from the guidance of a more experienced coach who can help them identify a range of teaching strategies for developing the particular skills they are working on, and to choose the ones which are most appropriate for the particular athletes they are working with.

Finally, consideration must be given to the *personal construct* of the new coach. How do they see themselves in this transition from competitive athlete to coach? What is it they value about their own experience and about their sport? If they are highly competitive and value winning over participation, they may be better suited to coaching athletes who have begun to participate in competitive events, rather than more participatory 'outreach' coaching activities. Alternatively, they may see the sport as having been a key part of their personal development, and may relish the opportunity to help young athletes develop too.

Scenario 2: An experienced fitness instructor whose previously local authority gym is coming under the management of a private sector company

In this scenario, the instructor's *subject knowledge* should be satisfactory, although if they have been instructing for a long time, it may be necessary to check that their knowledge is up to date: when was their last formal training or professional development opportunity? How have they kept abreast of recent developments in exercise techniques and injury prevention?

The instructor's *pedagogic knowledge* should also be satisfactory, as they have a long-standing experience of instruction to draw upon, though again, it would be sensible to check what opportunities they have had to keep this knowledge updated and current. Perhaps there may be changes in the target client group as a result of the new ownership; the instructor may have to adapt some of their pedagogic knowledge and practices to suit the needs of any new client groups.

The *institutional knowledge* is likely to be the major area requiring training and support, for even if the premises and many of the colleagues are familiar, the new management is likely to result in substantial changes to procedure, as well as possible re-alignment of roles and responsibilities. It is quite likely that there will also be some changes to language and terminology with the transition from public to private sector. If the fitness centre is refitted, there may also be a need for further training in the new work stations and other equipment that is introduced.

What about the instructor's *personal construct*? What are the values that motivated them in their previous circumstances, and (how) do they translate to the new situation? Are they perceiving the new situation as an opportunity to enhance their professional practice, or is there conflict between their personal values and beliefs and the market/profit orientation of the new management? If there is conflict, are there aspects of their personal philosophy of being a good instructor that can find expression and provide motivation in the new workplace?

SUMMARY

The conceptual understanding of the professional knowledge of fitness instructors and sports coaches is currently under-developed and under-researched, though this is likely to change over the coming decade, with the increasing move to professionalisation within the sector.

The Banks, Leach & Moon model of teacher professional knowledge has been used extensively within teacher professional development and research contexts, where it is recognised as both meaningful and useful.

In this chapter, we have presented an outline of how the model may be adapted to describe the professional knowledge of sports coaches and fitness instructors, together with two cameos showing how the model helps us elucidate and describe areas of strength and weakness in that knowledge.

The model has not yet been adapted to take account of the distinctive features of motor-skill learning, nor the tactical or competitive aspects of sports coaching; these being areas for further consideration.

To know whether the model offers the same 'grasp' on the complex realities of sports coaching and fitness instruction as it does for those of school teaching, will require further research and development with participatory researchers from the sector.

REFERENCES

Banks, F. (2008) Learning in DEPTH: developing a graphical tool for professional thinking for technology teachers. *International Journal of Technology & Design Education,* 18: 221–229.

Banks, F., Leach, J. and Moon, B. (1999) New understandings of teachers' pedagogic knowledge. In Leach, J. and Moon, B. (eds), *Learners and Pedagogy*. London: Paul Chapman.

Banks, F., Leach J. and Moon, B. (1996) Knowledge, school knowledge and pedagogy; reconceptualising curricula and defining a research agenda. ECER conference, Seville, Spain, September 1996.

Côté, J., Salmela, J.H., Trudel, P., Baria, A. and Russell, S.J. (1995) The coaching model: A grounded assessment of expert gymnastics coaches' knowledge. *Journal of Sport and Exercise Psychology*, 17: 1–17.

Leach, J. and Banks, M. (1996) Investigating the developing 'teacher professional knowledge' of student teachers. BERA conference, Lancaster, UK, September 1996.

Leach, J., Ahmed, A., Makalima, S. and Power, T. (2006) DEEP IMPACT: an investigation of the use of information and communication technologies for teacher education in the global south. Researching the issues. DFID Research Series No. 58. Available online: www.dfid.gov.uk/pubs/files/ict-teacher-education-no58.asp (accessed 31 March 2009).

Lyle, J. (1999) Coaching philosophy and coaching behaviour. In Cross, N. and Lyle, J. *The Coaching Process: Principles and Practice for Sport* (pp. 25–46). Oxford: Butterworth-Heinemann.

Lyle, J. (2002) *Sports Coaching Concepts*. London: Routledge.

Martens, R. (2004) *Successful Coaching. America's Best-selling Coach's Guide*. Champaign, IL: Human Kinetics.

Power, T. and Thomas, R. (2007) The classroom in your pocket? *The Curriculum Journal*, 18(3): 373–388.

REPS (2007) *The Fitness Industry Qualifications and Career Framework*. The Register of Exercise Professionals, September 2007. Available online: www.exerciseregister.org/custom/documents/QualMap2007.pdf (accessed 31 March 2009).

SCUK (2008) *The Professionalisation of Sports Coaching in the UK: Issues and Conceptualisation*. Bill Taylor & Dean Garret, February 2008. Available online: www.sportscoachuk.org/research/Research+Publications/Professionalisation+in+Sports+Coaching.htm (accessed 31 March 2009).

SkillsActive (2006) *SkillsActive Higher Education Conference: The Challenge of Employabililty*. 15th March 2006, Leicester, UK. Available online: www.enhancingemployability.org.uk/_get_file.php?file=34_1_***skillsactive_he_conference_2006.pdf&cat=events (accessed 31 March 2009).

SECTION 6

YOU AND YOUR CUSTOMERS

INTRODUCTION

The purpose of this section is to stimulate understanding and thinking about the issues, concepts and working practices surrounding you and your relationship with your customers. The authors provide a range of voices ranging from self-employed to public/private organisational perspectives. The section starts by defining terms and coming to a clearer understanding about the nature of customer relationships and customer satisfaction. The following chapters develop the reoccurring themes of understanding customers, scheduling time use effectively and the way in which communication elements contribute to the customer relationship.

Chapter 26 adapts existing material from the Open University Business School Management courses in order to help you focus on the main issue of understanding customers. In this chapter, Ben Oakley of the Open University and Martin Rhys, Staff Tutor in the Faculty of Education and Language Studies at the Open University, consider how customers are defined and can be identified in both voluntary and public/private sectors. They explain who customers, consumers and stakeholders are and how an understanding of customer expectations is crucial in explaining customer satisfaction.

Chapter 27 is written by three authors with very different backgrounds: Sean McQuaid, Manager of Edmonton Leisure Centre, in a London Borough, Ben Oakley of the Open University, and Paul Weighton, Manager of David Lloyd Leisure, Birmingham. They discuss how to get the most out of a sport facility in terms of the programming of sport and fitness activities to make effective use of space, time and resources. They work through the planning process comparing and contrasting the different approaches used in the public and private sector and give a number of examples.

Chapter 28 by Simon Rea of the Open University considers programming and scheduling from a different perspective – self-employed coaches and instructors. Drawing on his own fitness background and interviews with other sport and fitness workers he identifies the main influences that shape a self-employed person's schedule and how they go about managing their programme of appointments.

Chapter 29 is written by Maria Hopwood, Associate Professor in Public Relations at Bond University in Queensland, Australia. Her research in marketing communications and being a keen fan of cricket and rugby is evident in this chapter in which she explains the components of effective marketing communication with customers. The idea of a distinct sport marketing communications mix is developed in which relationship building is a key component, along with the more traditional tools such as advertising, publicity and personal contact. For a range of reasons, audiences nowadays are proving increasingly difficult to reach, so it is a constant challenge for organisations to try and make and stay in contact.

CHAPTER 26

IDENTIFYING CUSTOMERS AND THEIR EXPECTATIONS[1]

Ben Oakley and Martin Rhys

INTRODUCTION

You will know from your own experience that understanding any individual is a complex process. Once you have achieved an understanding you are able to adapt your behaviour in order to produce a particular effect on that individual – to please them or annoy them. Even when you think you have the measure of someone, they may still be capable of surprising you with a change of behaviour or attitude even after several years of relative predictability. The more important the relationship, the more important the understanding in order to sustain it.

For those working in the sport and fitness industry, whether in a paid or volunteer role, there can be few more important professional relationships than the one they have with their participants or, as we shall call them, 'customers'. Without customers, there would quite simply be no role to play. To get customers, and more importantly to keep them, we have to understand them – their needs, their expectations, their attitudes, their behaviours, their tolerances. Once this understanding is achieved, it becomes the key driving force behind the improvement of provision.

You'll see that this chapter often refers to sport and fitness organisations, but the principles it outlines will apply just as relevantly to all those involved in sport and fitness, including the self-employed or volunteers.

But who are these customers? For a self-employed sports therapist or sports shop owner, a customer may simply be someone who buys their services or products.

---

[1] Adapted version of 'What is a customer?' and 'Understanding customers in sport and fitness' in *The Sport and Fitness Sector: An Introduction* (2008), Oxford: Routledge, which were themselves adapted from the OU Business School Certificate in Management Programme, B630 *Managing Customers and Quality*, Book 1 *Understanding your Customers*, and Book 2 *Meeting Customer Needs* (2001), Milton Keynes: The Open University.

For others in the sport and fitness industry, the business of identifying who the customer is can be a little more complex.

This chapter therefore starts by exploring the question of identifying customers, consumers and stakeholders with an outline of the exchange process. It then moves on to explore ways in which a diverse range of people can be segmented into groups so as to target efforts at providing more effectively for their needs. Finally, in order to begin to understand customer satisfaction the nature of customer expectations is explored. This includes a brief consideration of how the brands aim to fulfil expectations by providing consistency.

THE EXCHANGE PROCESS

In the exchange process an organisation offers a product or service and the customer typically offers a sum of money in return. The amount of money is nearly always determined by the organisation, and the customer must decide whether they think the product or service is worth what is being asked. So a gym will set a monthly membership fee for usage of its facilities, and customers will decide whether they are willing to pay that fee.

The assumption is that both the customer and the organisation value what the other has to offer. If they did not, then one or other would go elsewhere, if they could. The essence of the exchange is mutual value; there must be a belief on both sides that the exchange is fair and equitable. If the customer does not perceive it as such, they are unlikely to take part in the exchange. It is also possible that a customer will take part in the exchange but decide later that it was not fair or of mutual value, in which case they will be unlikely to come back to the organisation in the future.

Of course it's not always this simple. A customer living in a centre of high population will have plenty of choice regarding which facility or sports club to use, some even with specialist features. Someone living in a more rural area with one facility within 25 miles will see their choice reduced to either joining or nothing.

There is inevitably a tension in this exchange. The organisation will try to provide what the customer wants and values at the lowest cost to itself. It will not try to provide more than it needs to, as this will be likely to cost it more for no greater return. If the customer will buy something without any extra features, such as specialist coaching, there is little point in the organisation adding them.

However, the customer often looks for better value, and if another organisation offers it, the customer may be encouraged to change supplier. So an organisation must always try to keep the exchange balanced, but also make sure that the exchange it offers is better value than any offered elsewhere. This idea of mutual value, or balance and equity, in the exchange is likely to lead to customer satisfaction and possible repeat use and purchases. However, many organisations recognise that they may need to do more to encourage customers to buy from them on a regular basis.

This idea of exchange also operates within organisations. How often have you heard people at work complaining about the service offered by another department? Often these conversations end with someone saying, 'we'd be better off doing it ourselves'. The same principle of exchange is at work here so that within organisations there are 'internal' customers. If you are not providing something of value, and your customers do not perceive that there is a fair exchange, they may look elsewhere.

If you work in a public sector or non-profit organisation (e.g. a Leisure Trust or a sports club), you may think that customers will continue to come to you and your organisation because they have no choice. However, the local authority, or club members, may decide that you are not delivering what they want. They could choose to stop funding the service or pay some other organisation to provide it. Thus the principle of an exchange process remains valid: in this case it is between those who hold the resources and those who provide services that meet their needs.

CUSTOMERS, CONSUMERS AND STAKEHOLDERS

We have already established that it is not just the people who buy a product who need to be considered as customers. This chapter will use the general term 'customer' to include two kinds of people:

- *Customers*, who buy or pay for the products and services an organisation provides, although they may not use them themselves.
- *Consumers*, who use an organisation's products and services, but do not buy them.

Most commercial organisations tend not to make a distinction between customers and consumers. This is because they have to satisfy the needs of both groups with their products or services. Those providing swimming lessons for children, for instance, have to make sure that their lessons are fun and effective for children, and they also have to package the product and present it in a way that is attractive to parents. The distinction is still important as it is the parent (the customer) who has to be encouraged to complete the exchange process with the organisation, and they may want something different out of the exchange from the child (the consumer). In this case the parent would perhaps be particularly concerned about safety.

It is worth mentioning that any organisation will have a number of different customer groups. Finding a way to categorise and identify different groups of customers is very important. However, for some organisations it is very simple. Consider a small business managed by the owner, providing physiotherapy for sports injuries. Her customers are sport participants to whom she provides her services. She does not have any employees, and only works with individuals in her treatment room, which is at the front of her family home, so she deals directly with the end customers, with no one between her and them. Situations are not always this straightforward.

Consider a leisure centre and ask yourself who the customers are. In broad terms, the customers are the people from the local area who come to use the facilities; however, these people can be divided into those who come for team games and those who come as individuals, for example, to use the gym. The leisure centre could also identify the children who come with their parents and need to be kept occupied, and the parents who come to watch their children play. Another group might be the babies and toddlers for whom a crèche is provided so that their parents can take part in sports. Each of these groups of customers needs to be identified and what they want from the exchange process worked out, so that products and services can be developed which will suit them.

So, organisations will have several different groups of customers, who all expect different things from their relationship an organisation. We can take this even further and introduce other parties who neither buy nor directly use an organisation's services. We use the term 'stakeholder' to mean those who have an interest in an organisation because they can affect, or be affected by, what is done by the organisation.

Doyle (1998) argued that the survival of an organisation depended on its effective management of a broad range of stakeholder interests. He pointed out that satisfying the multiple and often conflicting stakeholder expectations is the role of every manager within an organisation. He identified stakeholders and their expectations in the model shown in Figure 26.1. Note that

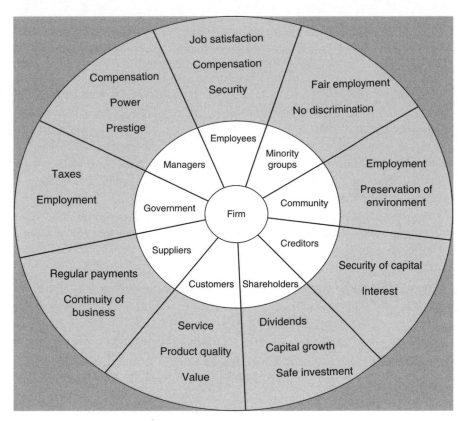

Figure 26.1 Stakeholders and their expectations

Source: Doyle (1998), p. 12

in the figure, 'compensation' covers salary, wages and other remunerative benefits.

As you can see from the figure, stakeholders include a number of groups of people whom we would not call customers in the sense we have been using. In other words, 'stakeholders' is a much broader term, which encompasses, but is not limited to, customers.

Stakeholders can also be defined as those who have a stake in and/or an influence over the organisation's performance or development. For instance, two important stakeholders for an organisation wishing to develop a town's sport or fitness facilities are the local community and local/national government since they both can strongly influence local planning and design consents.

SEGMENTATION

In the previous section we discussed the diversity of customers and thus there are many influences which affect the choices they make. We implied that if customers all behaved in the same way, or had certain characteristics in common, this might lead to their having similar needs for particular products. Some examples may help:

- People of similar ages might want similar products. For example, people in their 30s with young children might be interested in sport or fitness facilities that provide some form of children's play area or crèche.
- Young people may purchase the same brands of designer trainers.
- People with a high level of disposable income and an interest in slightly adventurous activities may purchase skiing holidays.

Segmentation thus involves breaking down the total spectrum of customers into groups. It can be defined as:

> the process of splitting customers, or potential customers, within a market into different groups, or segments, within which customers have the same, or similar requirements satisfied by a distinct marketing mix.
>
> (McDonald and Dunbar, 1998: p. 15)

It is worth highlighting three important aspects of this definition. First, it identifies that customers can be grouped together in various ways so as to help organisations meet their common needs. This focus can save money and time and increase effectiveness. Second, the definition suggests that managers can use the information about their customers to design a marketing mix (identifying the blend of factors that are important for marketing) which will attract a particular group of customers more than their competitors. Finally, it implies that customers' needs can be explained by and even predicted from information about what they have in common with others.

Organisations are likely to use a combination of characteristics or segmentation variables to develop easily identifiable segments or groups of customers. Using a range of segmentation variables makes it possible to identify the types of people who will seek particular benefits from a product. The following extract (example 26.1) (edited) from *Marketing Week* is a good example of how markets can be segmented by lifestyle.

284

EXAMPLE 26.1

Recognising grey matters

There is a fundamental change occurring in the structure of the UK population. By 2020, nearly half the population will be over 45, while the proportion of under 25s will drop to just 25 per cent.

Studies of the over 55s – commonly referred to as the 'grey' market – conclude that this group is experiencing a new sense of emotional and financial freedom …

Despite [the impressive size of this market] the commercial opportunities presented by the grey market remain largely untapped. Marketing and advertising tends to focus on younger markets, while the over-55s, who constitute one-third of the total UK population, are largely ignored.

Understanding the mind-sets and motivations of target markets lies at the heart of successful marketing and advertising. The reason the grey market has so far been ignored suggests a lack of willingness rather than a lack of ability on behalf of marketers. Misconceptions about their lifestyles, ranging from bus passes and bingo cards to dentures and dementia, perpetuate the problem.

The reality is somewhat different. Carat Insight concludes that for many over-55s approaching retirement, an important personal objective is to secure good physical and mental wellbeing by engaging in active lifestyles. This can involve sports and leisure activities, as well as community issues and local affairs. Contrary to the belief that many older people are couch potatoes, the Carat Foretel Attention Study observed that only 30 per cent of over-55s watch TV for the sake of 'wanting something to do'.

A 'young at heart' attitude is a key trait of the grey market and this is not only reflected in active lifestyles, but also in the desire to experiment and to continually learn. For example, Carat states that few older consumers are truly 'fearful' of technology and constitute almost ten per cent of all UK Internet users …

Despite their propensity to experiment, greys are more experienced and wiser in their purchasing behaviour. Being 'time rich' allows them greater freedom to inspect the market and they prefer more informed purchases rather than impulse buys. Saga Services has found that over-55s view the information gathering process as an enjoyable activity.

> [...] Overall, the over-55s exhibit a vast disparity in health, wealth and social circumstances. Consequently, classifying all 19 million greys as a single audience ignores the rich diversity in personality, character and psychological make-up.
>
> (Rakhia, 1999: pp. 28–29)

We can see from this that the main segmentation variable used here is age, but it is linked to lifestyle. The over-55s are seen as an exciting group of customers who need to be further analysed and divided into smaller groups, depending on the activities they like doing, and their attitudes and motivations.

In most cases a combination of different segmentation variables is used, for example, of age and lifestyle, as in the example above, or of age and attitude. Organisations need to find meaningful ways of dividing up potential and existing customers for their products so that they can develop products which will appeal to a particular group. For instance, large public sector leisure centres try to appeal to a very wide range of segments but they try and target certain groups to help generate off-peak usage. Typically, this might be the over-55s, the unemployed and, where possible, school groups.

Having first identified and then researched the various market segments, it then becomes possible to consider in detail the needs and expectations of these segments, which is further explored in the next section. Understanding customer expectations is also the basis for managers selecting the appropriate blend and timing of activities that are provided in sport and facilities (see Chapter 27).

CUSTOMER EXPECTATIONS: THE ZONE OF TOLERANCE

Customers have expectations of services and the task of organisations is to make sure that they meet, or even exceed, those expectations. If they do this, we assume that the customers will be satisfied, and that if the expectations are not met, the customers will be dissatisfied. There are three elements which contribute to a customer's expectations, and we show them in Figure 26.2.

This model shows how a customer's expectations and perceptions of the various aspects of a service will affect their final quality assessment. The model suggests that a customer forms expectations before purchase. These arise from word-of-mouth recommendation, past experience, external communications and the customer's own needs. The customer will then assess these expectations in the light of their experience of the purchase. They will assess both the process and the output. In other words, they will consider the way the product or service has

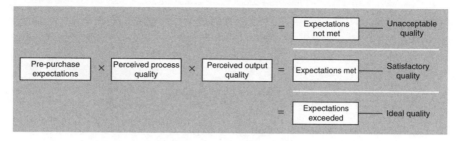

Figure 26.2 The roots of customer satisfaction

Source: Adapted from: Berry *et al.* (1985), p. 47

been delivered to them, and – particularly in a health and fitness setting – the role of the staff in that delivery (the process) They will also evaluate the way in which it meets their goals, for example, to lose weight, to tone up and/or to meet other people (the output). The relative importance of each of these elements will depend on the product and on what the customer perceives to be most important. The outcome will be one of three states:

- Expectations met – the customer will be satisfied.
- Expectations not met – the customer will be dissatisfied.
- Expectations exceeded – the customer will be very satisfied, but will probably increase their expectations to take into account the new level of quality they have received. In future, the customer will probably need to perceive that the product is being delivered to this new level of quality just to be satisfied.

Parasuraman *et al.* (1991) showed that customers have two levels of expectation, adequate and desired: the first is what they find acceptable, and the second is what they hope to receive. The distance between the adequate and the desired levels is known as the *zone of tolerance*, and this can expand and contract according to circumstances. The two levels may vary from customer to customer, and from one situation to another for the same customer, depending on what else has happened to them that day, whether they are in a hurry, and so on.

You can probably remember situations in which you have accepted services or products which, in other circumstances, you would have refused or been disappointed by. The zone of tolerance is shown in Figure 26.3.

If we accept that this is how customers subconsciously evaluate products and that there is some tolerance in their evaluation, we can start to see what is meant by responsiveness to customers. Ideally, organisations or those who are

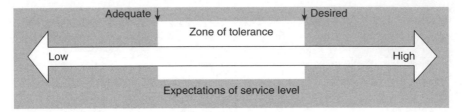

Figure 26.3 The zone of tolerance

Source: Parasuraman *et al.* (1991), p. 42

self-employed, will always try to operate within a customer's zone of tolerance. To do this, all staff need to understand is what customers want from their organisation and whether or not their customers' expectations are being met.

If a person realises that a customer is dissatisfied, they should, if they are responsive to the customer's needs, attempt to 'recover' the situation. Of course, it is not always possible to rectify the situation immediately: other people may need to be involved, or the resources may not be available. However, even if the response cannot be immediate, it is important that the organisation encourage feedback from staff and customers, so that lessons can be learnt.

Therefore an understanding of customer expectations lies at the heart of providing a good service and keeping customers satisfied. This is why large fitness operators for instance, strongly encourage their staff to follow a set of procedures and behaviours which try to ensure customers remain within their zone of tolerance. In a very different setting, it is equally important for a coach at a local tennis club to understand the expectations of their members.

We now consider another perspective of customer expectations: how brands aim to fulfil expectations by providing consistency.

CUSTOMER EXPECTATIONS: BRANDS AND BRAND VALUE

A brand name and identity can be a good way of differentiating a product or service. If two products are similar, customers are more likely to buy the product with the brand name they know, rather than the one they have not heard of, as a surer way to having their expectations fulfilled.

An interesting example of how important brand image can be seen is from taste tests carried out by Coca-Cola and Pepsi Cola. Respondents were asked to decide which of the two cola drinks they preferred. When they were allowed to see the brand of the drink there was a marked preference for Coca-Cola – 65 per cent preferred it. However, when the respondents were blindfolded the distinction between the two brands was reduced significantly. In this test 51 per cent of testers preferred Pepsi (De Chernatony and McDonald, 1998: p. 11). The differences between the two sets of results suggest that customers 'taste' both the drink and the brand image. The brand image adds value to the product or service in the mind of the customer.

Branding can provide benefits for both buyers and sellers. Customers benefit because they can immediately identify specific products that they do and do not like. Without brands, product selection would be quite random, with customers having to investigate each product and how it matched with what they wanted. Creating brand loyalty permits companies to charge more for a product (think of the Cola example above compared with other brands).

Another aspect of brands that relates to the service industry in particular is the variability in services. Unlike, say a pair of running shoes which conform to the same specifications, most services are delivered by people to people and because people are all very different in their personalities and ways of dealing with others, it is difficult for service companies to ensure that each customer's experience is the same as the previous customer's.

Service companies spend a lot of time trying to guarantee consistency in the provision of their services by means of an effective human resource policy of staff selection and training. Branding is another way of helping achieve more consistency especially in the perception of customers.

The most successful brands have an appeal that can cross borders and cultures and combine physical, rational and emotional appeal. The blend must be distinctive and, particularly in sport and fitness, it must have a clear identity which offers benefits of value to customers. A member of a David Lloyd club in one town will quite rightly expect the same standards and quality of provision if she or he uses the same club in a different location. The brand aims to consistently live up to expectations and reliably deliver the required provision.

SUMMARY

A successful operator in the field of sport and fitness must put successful customer relationships at the top of their priority list. In order to achieve this success, the operator must first be able to identify the customer and understand the nature of the exchange that takes place between them. Different customers have different needs and expectations and these can often be successfully segmented so that the various needs can be more efficiently met. Meeting the needs of customers involves operating within the customer's zone of tolerance, thereby adding worth to the brand, which in turn comes to represent consistent value in the eyes of its customers.

REFERENCES

Berry, L.L., Zeithaml, V.A. and Parasuraman, A. (1985) 'Quality counts in services too'. *Business Horizons*, May–June, pp. 44–52.

De Chernatony, L. and McDonald, M. (1998) *Creating Powerful Brands in Consumer Service and Industrial Markets*. Oxford: Chartered Institute of Marketing/Butterworth Heinemann.

Doyle, P. (1998) *Marketing Management Strategy*, 2nd edn. Hemel Hempstead: Prentice Hall Europe.

McDonald, M. and Dunbar, I. (1998) *Market Segmentation: How to Do It, How to Profit from It*, 2nd edn. London: Macmillan.

Parasuraman, A., Berry, L. and Zeithaml, V.A. (1991) Understanding customer expectations of service. *Sloan Management Review*, Spring, pp. 39–48.

Rakhia, R. (1999) Recognising grey matters. *Marketing Week*, 22(27): 28–29.

CHAPTER 27

GETTING THE MOST OUT OF A SPORT AND FITNESS FACILITY

Ben Oakley, Sean McQuaid and Paul Weighton

INTRODUCTION

It is not often that those who manage sport and fitness facilities get the chance to plan the activities and scheduling of what happens from scratch; normally facilities use an established format of activities which is incrementally adjusted year by year. In this chapter, though, we will start with an imaginary 'empty' facility and discuss the various factors that determine what activities could be provided. This planning process is known as facility programming. A facility's programme is typically represented to customers in brochure and/or online indicating the availability of different activities and services sometimes in a table format. Behind the scenes the planning of this programme is a complex process: this chapter aims to explain the process and decision-making involved.

Understanding such programming issues is important not just for those who work full time in such settings but also for those who may occasionally book and use such venues. For example, consider the following different group users of a facility: clubs, tournaments, instructional classes or workshops, children's parties. They all have different needs such as timing, equipment and convenience yet the facility also has to continue to satisfy individual members or casual users. In essence, programming is about balancing resources in a way that satisfies the needs of a range of users whilst also remaining financially viable.

It is assumed that readers have prior knowledge of the principles of market segmentation (see Chapter 26) since understanding the needs and expectations of different user groups is an essential prerequisite in catering for them and designing an effective programme. Indeed, some facilities will have a different philosophy to others and target certain market segments more than others. For example, public facilities owned by local authorities or local leisure trusts will have a different focus to private sector facilities. In fact, one of the themes running throughout the chapter is the comparisons and contrasts drawn between these two types of facilities (public/private).

The chapter is organised in the following way. In order to discuss a specific facility case, first, we outline the components that make up an imaginary centre whose programme has yet to be developed. From now on this case study is referred to as 'E-Leisure'. Following this, the general *influences on planning* are identified under different sub-headings including a section on its own right on the important controlling factor of *facility design*. Then *programme design* is addressed from the perspectives of both the public and private sectors; sometimes these approaches coincide but often they differ. Finally, short sections on *communicating the programme* and *evaluation and measurement* discuss aspects connected with implementation. With such a structure, general sport and fitness programming issues will be highlighted as well as the specifics of programme design from different sectors.

To illustrate the potential differences between the two sectors sample programmes for E-Leisure from the public and private sector are referred to in the text and these are in Appendix 1 (public) and Appendix 2 (private). A full week of a possible public sector programme is included in Appendix 1 whilst for brevity only a Friday and Saturday are included for the private sector example; this will show the main differences between week day and weekend schedules and the private/public contrast.

THE E-LEISURE CENTRE

The imaginary E-Leisure centre represents a typical facility in a town with a reasonable catchment area. At the outset we deliberately have not stated if this facility is in the public or private sector since the different approaches will be addressed later in the chapter. In addition to reception and changing provision the E-Leisure centre has the following facilities:

- One sports hall (six badminton court size)
- One swimming pool (25 metres, six lanes)
- One activity pool (12 metres with movable floor)
- One gym (medium size with resistance/free weights/cardiovascular areas)
- One dance (group exercise) studio
- One bar/food area

In the planning for the E-Leisure centre the activities that might be possible to provide in such a centre are outlined in Box 27.1 under the headings of 'dryside' and 'wetside'. Such a list might be arrived at in the real world if a group of experienced professionals drew on previous experience in facility management. Therefore the contents of Box 27.1 provide a tentative 'menu', which is by no means definitive but is aimed to stimulate thinking about what could be provided

---

BOX 27.1: PROMPTING LIST OF ACTIVITIES THAT COULD BE PROVIDED IN A SPORTS CENTRE

Dryside	Wetside
Sports hall	*Swimming pool*
*Badminton	*Lane swimming
*Table tennis	*Family swim sessions
*Netball	*Canoeing sessions
*Volleyball	*Underwater hockey
*Basketball	*Inflatable sessions
*5-a-side football	*Water polo
*Circuit training	*Ladies-only sessions
*Group exercise classes	*50 plus sessions
*Children's parties	*Disabled sessions
*Trampoline	*Children's parties
*Basic gymnastics	*Swimming galas
*Dance	*Swimming club training sessions
*Community non-sporting events	*Lifesaving/water safety sessions
(e.g. book festival)	*Swimming lessons
*Music events	*Sub aqua/snorkelling sessions
Gym	*Diving/learners pool*
*Group rowing or cycling ('spinning')	*Swimming lessons
*Circuits	*Aqua aerobics
*Group and individual inductions	*Scuba diving lessons
*Personal training	*Synchronised swimming
	*Antenatal sessions
Group exercise studio	
*Dance	
*Boxercise	
*Martial arts (wide range)	

in such a centre. This chapter will outline how the choices from such a menu are made.

It is recognised that the contents of Box 27.1 are not just determined by the facility space, such as a sports hall, but also about the additional equipment that makes different options possible, for example, a trampoline or martial arts mats. Furthermore, this chapter does not have space to also consider the important staffing or financial resource implications of activities choices.

With the specific scenario of the E-Leisure centre in mind we now turn to thinking about how the planning process might fill the various sports facility 'spaces' with appropriate activities.

INFLUENCES ON PLANNING

1. Organisational purpose and philosophy

As a first step in creating a programme there is a need to identify the main purpose and philosophy of the organisational environment. The *purpose* can be defined as the organisation's main reason for existence, for example, to make a profit (private or commercial) or provide a service to the community (public or leisure trust). The philosophy can be viewed as the framework of principles, attitudes and ideals guiding the organisation, such as: a certain rate of return per activity; or minority group participation being encouraged; or membership being required prior to entry (Badmin, 1988).

2. Community needs versus return on investment

Community-based leisure facilities often emerge from the desire of a local area's population to have a certain type of facility within their location. Local needs and ideas are expressed by the grassroots and influence those in power. Funding for these types of facility often comes from public/private partnerships or community-focused funds/grants, such as the National Lottery.

For example, school and leisure centre use are often combined to form 'dual-use' centres often on school premises. In situations like this, school use may be specified before a certain time (e.g. 6 pm), followed by community use in the evenings and at weekends. There may also be agreements in place (such as a Sports Development Plan) with the funding providers which may identify key sports that should be targeted during the programming of the facility.

Indeed, some centres may be required to provide for non-sporting community events (e.g. a book fair).

In contrast, the private sector consists largely of operators who have become specialists at building and operating certain types of facilities and delivering *their* choice of activities to a local area. Ideas or policies are derived from the management of a central organisation using their established business model to supply local people.

In many cases, private operators with a number of private leisure facilities have a fairly homogeneous product and a national brand identity (e.g. Fitness First). The facilities on offer in the private leisure centre will be based around getting a maximum return on capital employed (ROCE). For example, the percentage of ROCE in recent years amongst private operators has been 10–20% for every million pounds invested. Therefore, high participation numbers in each part of the facility or 'sweating the asset' is important.

Using Table 27.1, a centre that contains a swimming pool, keep fit/aerobics, weight training gym, and has an outdoor football pitch would stand a better

Table 27.1 Most popular sports and recreational activities for those 16 years or over

Rank	Activities taking part at least once a week	% of the adult population
1.	Recreational walking	20.0
2.	Swimming (all locations)	13.8
3.	Gym (including exercise machines)	11.6
4.	Recreational cycling (30 + mins)	7.8
5.	Football (all locations)	7.1
6.	Running/jogging	4.6
7.	Golf/pitch and putt	3.6
8.	Badminton	2.2
9.	Tennis	2.1
10.	Aerobics	1.5
11.	Yoga	1.4
12.	Squash	1.2
13.	Keep fit/sit-ups	1.1
14.	Bowls (all)	1.0
15.	Horse riding (Any)	1.0

getting the most out of a sport and fitness facility

Table 27.1 (Continued)

Rank	Activities taking part at least once a week	% of the adult population
16.	Weight training	1.0
17.	Cricket	0.9
18.	Fishing (all)	0.7
19.	Basketball	0.7
20.	Pilates	0.7
21.	Rugby Union	0.7
22.	Athletics (track and field)	0.6
23.	Dance exercise	0.5
24.	Netball	0.4
25.	Snooker	0.4
26.	Table tennis	0.4
27.	Weightlifting	0.4
28.	Boxing	0.4
29.	Aquafit/aquacise/aqua aerobics	0.4
30.	Hockey-field	0.3
31.	Martial arts	0.3
32.	Conditioning activities/circuits	0.3
33.	Tenpin bowling	0.3
34.	Skiing	0.3
35.	Darts	0.3
36.	Rugby League	0.3
37.	Tai Chi	0.3
38.	Pool	0.2
39.	Rock climbing	0.2
40.	Trampolining	0.2

Notes

i) To be included, recreational walking had to be continuous for 30 minutes and had to be at least moderate intensity, that is, described by the respondent as either 'a fairly brisk' or a 'fast pace'.

ii) To be included, recreational cycling had to be continuous for 30 minutes and had to be at least moderate intensity, that is, 'enough to raise the breathing rate'.

Source: Adapted from Sport England (2006)

chance of high participation levels, and therefore profit, than one which contains martial arts, squash, rugby and basketball.

However, to achieve a suitable return on investment private operators very carefully evaluate where to build in the first place. They evaluate the potential catchment area of a site undertaking demographic analysis in order to see to what extent the catchment area matches their business requirements and target market segments. If the demography of the local area is good then the operator will carry out a full competitor analysis looking at the saturation of the market. For example, a town or city with a strong demographic profile may have four or five leisure, health, fitness and racquet clubs already in operation. The operator will then have to look at how diluted the market is and whether they have a significantly differentiated product or more accessible site or can compete on price in order to take enough business from these established operators in order to make the investment worthwhile.

3. Project viability and focus

Research in the service industry has shown that customers divide products into three defined categories (Slack, 1994). These are as follows:

- Order winners: these factors are always considered by customers in their decision to purchase from or remain with a business. For example, when considering the E-Leisure centre swimming pool the order winners may be adult lane swimming and family swim sessions. These cater for the needs of most customers.
- Qualifying objectives: things that are less important but help the decision-making process when the customer chooses to purchase – in the case of E-Leisure swimming these may be aqua aerobics, diving and children's swimming lessons.
- Less important objectives: these were those objectives that were not normally considered by customers to be important, such as: canoeing, scuba diving and inflatable sessions.

From a private sector perspective, Slack (1994) suggested that a business analyses which of their potential facilities/activities are order winners and which are qualifying or less important objectives. It is really important that the private operator programmes effectively and concentrates on giving outstanding service in 'order winning' areas. There are many factors which are deemed to be 'qualifying objectives'; often the private operator cannot be good in all of these areas and must look at these carefully to see on what they wish to focus.

FACILITY DESIGN

1. Capacity

The capacity of the facility will have a major influence on the centre's programme. There are for instance a number of programme combinations that the E-Centre's six badminton court sports hall can accommodate. These are demonstrated on the E-centre (public) programme. The standard of hall, the markings and equipment (see below) will all influence the hall's capacity.

2. Equipment and set-up time

The length of time, level of difficulty and number of staff it takes to set up equipment can have major consequences for the programme of a centre. Set-up and set-down periods always need to be included in a programme. In some instances it may be possible, for efficiency, to programme activities requiring similar equipment to be set up together to prevent additional set-up/ set-down periods. For example, see how in the E-centre (public) programme, gymnastics has been programmed for last thing on a Friday evening and first thing on a Saturday morning. This minimises the need to set up and set down equipment.

The equipment fixings also need to be considered when programming. For instance, in the case of gymnastics, it would be advantageous to have the majority of the equipment floor fixings to be based on one side of the hall so that the other side of the hall can be used for other activities during gymnastics training sessions. Cross-court basketball net fixings and five-a-side football goal fixings will also mean that other activities can take place on the other half of the hall. This in turn maximises income and attendance figures. Note how, on a Tuesday, the E-centre (public) has five-a-side football on one half of the hall whilst badminton and taekwondo are on the other half of the hall.

The following observation from one of the authors, a private sector manager, emphasises efficiency concerns and the effectiveness of resource use: changeovers between activities need to be minimised in order to maximise participation and limit down time. This helps to minimise costs and increase participation time.

Programming in the private sector will therefore be geared around activities that are simple in structure and do not require too much equipment. This is why activities such as trampolining and gymnastics are rarely provided in the private sector.

3. Flexibility

The flexibility of a facility can often determine which groups of users can be catered for in the facility and what activities can be provided. For instance, in a Sports Hall portable 'rebound' boards mean that five-a-side football can take place on one half of the sports hall whilst badminton takes place on the other side. Dividing nets also make it easier to host different activities in the same hall whilst providing minimal disruption to each activity.

In a swimming pool a movable floor means that an activity pool can be catering for swimming lessons in shallow water followed by a scuba diving or canoeing session in deep water later in the day (e.g. Wednesday evening on the E-centre [public sector] programme). Architectural design is therefore a key concept employed at the planning stage of a facility to enable facilities to attain their true value.

One of the authors, a public sector manager comments: blinds around certain areas (e.g. swimming pool) may mean that a ladies-only session for Muslim ladies may take place. The flexibility of the facility in this instance will mean that other users can attend other activities in the centre without compromising the religious beliefs of others.

Without built-in flexibility within facility spaces, programming is far more limited. The speed at which these spaces can be converted to accommodate diverse activities will also be a consideration during programming.

4. Storage

Storage is always a big issue in leisure facilities with staff often complaining about the lack of storage areas. This can often be as a result of leisure providers trying to maximise the amount of income generation facilities. Storage can often be seen as not being a priority because it does not generate income directly.

However, if a quick set-up/set-down of activities is to be maintained, then equipment needs to be easily accessed by staff and easily stored away to minimise the inconvenience to customers and to maximise the amount of programming time that can be provided.

PROGRAMME DESIGN

General

There are a number of core issues that are common to the public and private sectors when programming a facility:

1   In a number of centres, the majority of its core, regular income base may be related to direct debit membership packages. So any programme needs to consider the *impact on these core customers*. When a membership is purchased, a number of customers will expect facilities to be very accessible at convenient times. For instance, the availability of a swimming pool, sauna or steam room. If this is not the case, then they may well choose to join a competitor.

2   *Target audiences* need to be considered when programming. For example, children's activities should be programmed at appropriate times whilst activities for parents and toddlers should take into consideration other family commitments. In this case, the 'school run' period should be avoided. Toddlers may also attend afternoon or morning pre-school classes so options should be provided, as illustrated by the choice of Monday or Friday pool sessions on the E-centre (public) programme.

3   Consideration needs to be given for *planned maintenance and training* schedules within the facility. For instance, in the case of a swimming pool, when will the pool floor be vacuumed/swept each week? Also, when will staff training take place and will it be at a time (i.e. a break in the overall programme) that will allow as many staff as possible to attend? In the E-centre (public) example, 3 pm Monday and 2 pm Thursday, respectively, are set for these types of sessions.

4   Often, programming will be influenced by attempts to *save on energy* consumption/costs (Wileman and Wright, 2006). An example of this is where a pool may have its temperature raised to accommodate a disabled group. Other sessions that require warmer water, such as parent and toddler sessions, may be programmed close to the disabled session to minimise the number of times the temperature needs to be raised and dropped. This is demonstrated on the Monday morning in the E-centre (public).

5   Where there are multi-activities taking place in the hall, consideration needs to be given to where each is placed to *minimise the disturbance* caused by customers accessing their area. For example, it may be considered less disruptive to have two badminton customers passing through a badminton court of 30 martial arts students than vice versa.

6   *Noise pollution* can often play a major part in programming. Noise can determine what activities can share the same area. For instance, in a:

  ▪   Swimming pool – it would be problematic to programme a noisy children's fun session next to children's swimming lessons. The noise created by the fun session would distract and hinder the delivery of the swimming lesson.

  ▪   Sports hall – an aerobics session with loud music in half of the sports hall would cause major problems for any instructor trying to deliver a coaching session (e.g. martial arts) in the other half of the sports hall. Similarly, a dance studio located next to a 'health and beauty room' providing massage and relaxation, might cause some issues unless the area is well sound proofed or activities are programmed accordingly. Often facilities have a policy on which style of music is played and at what volume and where it is used.

One of the biggest problems within a private centre regarding noise pollution is noise generated from children's activities. Effective programming can mitigate this but there may be restrictions put in place such as adult-only sessions or compulsory supervision in places such as bar or eating areas.

PUBLIC SECTOR INFLUENCES

In a number of instances within the public/leisure trust sector, the leisure operator will be managing the facility to the contract specification established between the local authority and operator. This will in many instances stipulate a requirement for the leisure operator to work under some specific programming conditions. These may include, for example, setting aside a specified section of the weekly programme for school or local authority swimming lessons. Such activities need to be reserved on the facility's programme at the very start of the planning process.

The programming of the different recreational spaces is a delicate balancing act where a number of aspects need to be taken into consideration if income is going to be maximised whilst also satisfying social objectives. If an organisation has a number of centres within an area, consideration should be given to the programmes linkages with the other centres so that the programme across all of the centres is coordinated. For instance, if there is Pilates at 6 pm on a particular day at one of the centres, then it may be beneficial to put it on at a different time at the other centres. That way, members of the centres experience a more varied programme whilst also being able to find their desired activity at one of the centres at a given time.

Sometimes it may be beneficial to consider limiting the number of clubs offering a specific activity in a centre (e.g. martial arts). If too many clubs offer the same 'product' then often they can work against each other and also take up time that other activities could use within the facility.

Furthermore, in some instances, the equipment used by private hirers or clubs may influence where they are placed in the programme in relation to other activities. A good example of this is groups such as cheerleaders/baton twirlers/martial arts weapons in which there are safety and welfare considerations that impact on their programming with any adjacent users.

One of the biggest challenges facing the public programming is how to maximise the usage and income during *off peak times*. There are a number of ways that this can be done:

a Target establishments or groups who are able to access the centre at off peak times, for example, colleges, schools, nurseries, special schools.
b Form *partnerships* with organisations that may be able to assist in providing an activity that might benefit both parties (Nolan, 2006). In some cases, funding may be available to deliver an activity for a specific group at off peak times. For instance, projects to meet 'social agendas' such as where a geographical area has a concentration of an ethnic minority group that demonstrates a high level of incidences of heart disease. In such a case funding from a Primary Care Trust can create opportunities to overcome the barriers to participation and, in turn, tackle the low exercise participation rates that are demonstrated by this group and hopefully improve health. In a similar instrumental way, police forces often fund projects to encourage youngsters to participate in organised activities during their free time. The police hope that this, in turn, will reduce levels of crime in an area.
c On some occasions it may be beneficial to provide a *loss leader* at an off peak time. For instance, an activity (e.g. 50+ day) may be put on for a group where very little income is made but a 'social agenda' objective may

be achieved. Monday has been dedicated to the 50+ programme in the E-centre (public).

PRIVATE SECTOR INFLUENCES

There are two main strategic influences on private sector programme design. First, private leisure provision tends to be more orientated towards a monthly or annual *membership structure* than the public sector. In most cases the vast majority of income will come from membership fees. This helps the private facility reduce much of the income risk associated with seasonality and variations in usage patterns. The membership structure and pricing structure has a profound impact on programming decisions. The income streams can be divided into two categories: those facilities which are available within the membership fee and those facilities which involve an additional payment.

Facilities included within standard membership fees are, as a general rule, 'order winners' (Slack, 1994). You will recall from earlier in the chapter that these are high participation activities which will always be considered important by customers when making a purchasing decision. Within the E-leisure facility the ability to lane swim, use the gym, take part in classes and play badminton would all fall into this category.

Facilities which require an additional payment will often be those which fall into the qualifying or less important objectives. These are more often specialised activities which may require a specialised coach or involve other costs.

Table 27.2 gives an indication of how the payment structure at the E-leisure centre may be arranged if it were a private club.

Many facilities will allow members to sign in guests at a standard guest fee, which in effect makes their guest a member of the club for that particular day and gives a club an opportunity to sell to a new customer. Perhaps the major difference between private and public facilities is that third party organisations, such as schools and clubs, generally do not hire out or use the club's facilities.

The second main strategic influence is a more systematic use of 'time-targeted customer programming'. Programme design at a private club deliberately aims to reach different target markets throughout the course of each day. To some extent, programme design at a private club is simpler than at a public facility. The aim is threefold: (i) to provide a wide range of popular activities; (ii) to programme so that different user groups can use the facility at a time most suitable to them; (iii) to get members together in groups so that they meet one

Table 27.2 Typical membership structure for a private sport and fitness facility

Facilities included in membership fee	Paid for in addition to membership
Badminton general play	Specialised badminton coaching courses
Badminton club night	Junior and senior swimming lessons
Basketball sessions	Diving lessons
Lane swimming	One-to-one personal training sessions
Family swimming	Other sports coaching clinics
Aqua aerobics	Food and beverages in the bar
Diving pool	
Use of gymnasium	
Group exercise classes	

another and develop clubs within clubs. Research has shown (IHRSA, 2004) that adults will stay longer at a facility if they are included in group activities and attempts to stimulate clubs and groups are encouraged. A typical week day would be structured as in Table 27.3.

Table 27.3 A typical week day

Time target market	Time user profile
6 am to 9 am	Corporate and adult members
9 am to 12 noon	Mums with pre-school children, 50+ members
12 noon to 2 pm	Lunches, corporate, mums with pre-school children, 50+
2 pm to 3 pm	50+ and families
3 pm to 5 pm	Mums, families, older children, 50+
5 pm to 8 pm	Families, older children, adults

This changes significantly at weekends to a structure which is dominated by families and junior activities earlier in the day. The E-leisure (private) programme shows this time-targeted customer programming strategy using shaded bars against the timings each day; a more complete explanation of the five main customer groups (Corporate, Adults, Mums with pre-school children, 50+, Families) is provided in Appendix 3.

COMMUNICATING THE PROGRAMME

To implement the programme it needs to be communicated to customers and established onto the organisation's computerised booking system. Normally it would be advertised to the public on notice boards, leaflets and the centre's website. However, high customer usage needs people to fully understand what is on offer and advertising can be supplemented by a good induction to the club. Communication then continues in two ways: internally within the facility through items such as programme leaflets/notice boards, and verbally through staff at the club (particularly through reception). The facility should also communicate externally through e-mails, texts and direct mail shots which can promote and highlight adjustments to the programme.

Effective communication helps to drive participation into facilities programmes and monitor and increase usage. One advantage that a private club may have over a public facility is that they have more customer data detailing when each customer visits and which sessions they have previously booked. If used properly, this data can help the private club to be very effective in its communication, promotion and development of the club's programme.

EVALUATION AND MEASUREMENT

Once the programme is established, it is important that the programme continues to develop and evolve. In order to do this it is vital that the centre receives feedback on how the current programme is performing and what could potentially be introduced to the programme. By continuously reviewing the programme, it means that the centre never becomes complacent and keeps up with the latest sport/fitness trends and developments, and trying to meet customer demands. A number of measures and evaluation devices are used.

Typical public sector measures

The obvious measurement, and one of the easiest figures to collate, is attendance numbers and income figures. These only give part of the overall picture and additional information should feed into programme evaluation with data provided by:

- Customer satisfaction surveys.
- Non-user surveys can provide an insight into why potential customers do not use the centre and what programme changes they would like to see.
- User forums, customer enquiry cards and comment books give customers the opportunity to provide their own suggestions.

Often, local authorities will have set targets for attendances for specific groups, and information will need to be collected to monitor the progress in attracting such groups (e.g. under-19 year olds). Performance indicators can also be established to see how attendances relate to other areas or even nationally. Often, indicators are established to determine how the usage of the centre reflects the profile of the local community. Such benchmarking schemes have been established nationally (e.g. by Sport England) which can provide valuable feedback in how the programme is performing compared to similar centres.

Traditionally, the public sector has concentrated predominantly on the above measures to determine a programme's success. However, a greater emphasis is now being put on centres to measure success by the same measures described in the private sector section below.

Private sector measurement and evaluation

Private clubs (and increasingly public sector facilities) use a number of performance indicators to measure programme success. These can be divided into process and outcome measures.

The *process* measures consider the 'look and feel' of the site and the satisfaction of its customers and staff. Examples of these measures that relate to programming are listed below:

- Health and safety – audit on compliance to company standards
- Standards audit – 'mystery shopper' or brand standards audits
- Customer satisfaction surveys (as for public sector)

Outcome measures are the 'end result' performance indicators. A private company can operate with poor results in the process measures; however, if outcome measures are poor, the business could close due to lack of financial viability. Examples of outcome measures that closely relate to programming are:

- Membership sales – how many new members join the club
- Membership leavers – how many members leave the club
- Income – how income compares to the projected budget and to previous year
- Costs – how costs compare to the projected budget and to previous year
- Profit – how profits compare to the projected budget and to previous year

Other factors will also influence the outcome measures above (e.g. the upkeep and decor of the facility) but it is the combination of process and outcome measures which will help highlight the role of programming in making the facility attractive to customers and financially viable.

CONCLUDING COMMENTS

Throughout this chapter the fact that the public sector has social objectives as well as financial objectives to consider has been highlighted. Public sector facilities are encouraged to provide opportunities for all sections of the community and to tackle some of the wider social issues that effect that community. The gap between the public and private sectors is, however, closing rapidly as budgetary pressures mean that the public sector increasingly has financial considerations at the forefront of its operations and often has to compete with the private sector for business. With this in mind, public sector managers increasingly have to adopt a commercial attitude towards the programming of their centres.

This commercial approach is dominated by the need to remain profitable in order to survive. Profit is the number 1 objective in private facilities. In order to maintain a healthy profit private clubs must offer a popular product mixed with good service at an affordable price for the market. The membership structure is perhaps the biggest differentiator between the sectors and it is this that helps private clubs maximise revenue as well as maintain income through seasonally quiet times.

Programming in the private sector focuses on popular activities, which will appeal to mass markets and lead to high participation. Private clubs will rarely accommodate specific niche groups or activities. Rather than simply offer facilities to non-members at quiet times, the private club will programme towards specific groups at certain times of the day and aim to grow the membership at quiet times through effective targeting of new and existing customers.

The private market is moving towards a position where large chains will tend to offer a homogenous product and service strategy similar to any large service company with multiple outlets. Such principles are also influencing the programming approach of public sector operators but they often offer a more eclectic mix of services to cater for community and social needs.

REFERENCES

Badmin, P. (1988) *Leisure Operational Management*. Harlow: Longman. IHRSA (2004) *IHRSA's Guide to Membership Retention: Industry Lesson on*

What – and What Not – to do, 1st edn. Boston, MA: International Health, Racquet and Sportsclub Association (IHRSA).

Nolan, S. (2006) *Institute of Sport and Recreation Management (ISRM) Seminar, The Effective Management of Sports Halls*. Loughborough University, Friday 3 November, (Session 2) from Vision to Provision – Flexible Sports Hall Programming For Events. Available online: www.isrm.co.uk/news/event_story.php?event_id=4 (accessed August 2008).

Slack, N. (1994) The importance-performance matrix as a determinant of improvement priority. *International Journal of Operations and Production Management*, 14(5): 59–75.

Sport England (2006) *Active People Survey Headline Results: Sport by Sport Fact Sheet*, 7th December 2006. Available online: www.sportengland.org/061206_sport_by_sport_factsheet_embargo_7_dec_final.pdf (accessed August 2008).

Wileman, J. and Wright, P. (2006) *Institute of Sport and Recreation Management (ISRM) Seminar, The Effective Management of Sports Halls*. Loughborough University, Friday 3 November (Session 4), Sports Hall Programme Development. Available online: www.isrm.co.uk/news/event_story.php?event_id=4 (accessed August 2008).

APPENDICES

APPENDIX 1: E-LEISURE (PUBLIC) PROGRAMME

Timing header: 06.00 | 07:00 | 08:00 | 09:00 | 10:00 | 11:00 | 12:00 | 13:00 | 14:00 | 15:00 | 16:00 | 17:00 | 18:00 | 19:00 | 20:00 | 21:00

Monday

Sports Hall (Court 1–Court 6): CLOSED — 50+ Badminton/Bowls/Circuits/Table Tennis — After School Club — Public Badminton

Dance Studio: Pilates — 50+ Pilates — Total Work — Fit Pilates — 50+ Group — After School — Supple Strength — Latino Fiesta — Body Con.

Main Pool: Adults Only — Public — Adults Only — Pool Vacuum — Public Swimming — Swim Club — Adults

Activity Pool: Parent & Toddler Lessons — Disabled Group — Public — 50+ Aqua Fit — Learn To Swim — Aqua Fit

Tuesday

Sports Hall (Court 1–Court 6): CLOSED — Taekwondo — Public Badminton

Dance Studio: School — After School Club — Football

Main Pool: Adults Only — Keep Fit — Fat Attack — 50+ Group — Public — Junior Circuits — Aerobics — Supple Strength — Boxercise — Swim Club

Activity Pool: School Swimming Lessons — Learn to Swim — Public — Adults Only — School — 50+ Group — Public — Adult 2 Lanes — Learn To Swim — Swim Club — Learn To Swim — Swim Club

Wednesday

Sports Hall (Court 1–Court 6): CLOSED — Taekwo — Badminton — Karate — Public Badminton — Gymnastics

Dance Studio: Pre School Gymnastics — Fat Burn — Supple Strengt — Aerobics — Pilates — Kai Bo — 20-20-20 — Body Cond.

Main Pool: Adults Only — School Swim (1 Lane) — Public — School Swimming — Public Swimming

Activity Pool: School Swimming Lessons — Learn to Swim — Public — Learn To Swim — Karate — Aqua — Sub Aqua

Thursday

Sports Hall (Court 1–Court 6): CLOSED — Public Badminton — Taekwondo

Dance Studio: Adults Only — Yoga — Aerobics — Gentle Work — Body Con — School — Total Work't — Cardio Kick — Yoga

Main Pool: Public — School Swimming — Staff Train — Learn To Swim — Swimming Club — Swimming Club

Activity Pool: Learn to Swim — Public — Staff Train — Learn To Swim — Sub Aqua

	Timing:	06.00	07:00	08:00	09:00	10:00	11:00	12:00	13:00	14:00	15:00	16:00	17:00	18:00	19:00	20:00	21:00
Friday	Sports Hall — Court 1–6	CLOSED				Pre School Gymnastics						Table Tennis		Public Badminton			
	Dance Studio				Body Pump	Legs Bums Tums	Total Work't	Core Stab				Junior Street Dance	Circuits	Gymnastics / Street Dance			
	Main Pool			Adults Only	School Swim (1 Lane)			Public	School Swim			Public Swimming		Public	Learn To Swim	Adults Only	
	Activity Pool				School Swimming Lessons			Public		Parent and Toddler Lessons		Learn To Swim				Canoe Club	
Saturday	Sports Hall — Court 1–6	CLOSED			Council Indoor Cricket			Birthday Parties			Karate		Ladies Basketball Club				
	Dance Studio					Gymnastics					Badminton						
	Main Pool				Learn To Swim	Aerobic	20-20-20	Step	Public Swimming		Dance Classes		Parties	Women's Only Session			
	Activity Pool				Learn To Swim				Public Swimming				Parties	Women's Only Session			
					Yoga												
Sunday	Sports Hall — Court 1–6	CLOSED			Council Sports Development: Mini Football			Aerobics	Parties			Thai Boxing					
	Dance Studio				Pilates	Yoga	Step							Body Pump			
	Main Pool			Swim Club		Public Swimming							Learn To Swim				
	Activity Pool			Swim Club		Public Swimming							Learn To Swim				

APPENDIX 2: E-LEISURE (PRIVATE) PROGRAMME

Friday

Targeted Customer Groups: Adults, Corporates, Mums, 50+, Families

	06:00	07:00	08:00	09:00	10:00	11:00	12:00	13:00	14:00	15:00	16:00	17:00	18:00	19:00	20:00	21:00
Sports Hall – Court 1	Badminton Free Play			Creche			Badminton Free Play				Badminton Free Play		Football group coached session		Badminton Free Play	
Court 2																
Court 3																
Court 4				Badminton Free Play		Netball						Kids activity sessions				
Court 5																
Court 6																
Dance Studio		Express		Toning	Fitness	M&B	Express				Strength	Toning	Fitness	Circuits	M&B	
Main Pool					Aqua		Lane Swimming at least two lanes at all times				Swim Lessons					
Activity Pool													Diving Lesson			

Saturday

Targeted Customer Groups: Adults, Corporates, Mums, 50+, Families

	06:00	07:00	08:00	09:00	10:00	11:00	12:00	13:00	14:00	15:00	16:00	17:00	18:00	19:00	20:00	21:00
Sports Hall – Court 1	Closed	Badminton Free Play		Kids Activity Sessions			Football group coached session		Netball		Badminton Free Play		Circuit Training		Badminton Free Play	
Court 2																
Court 3										Toning						
Court 4				Creche		Badminton Free Play	Circuits	M&B								
Court 5																
Court 6																
Dance Studio				Toning	Strength	Fitness										
Main Pool					Aqua		Splash		Lane Swimming at least two lanes at all times							
Activity Pool						Swim Lessons										

APPENDIX 3

Typical time-targeted customer groups for E-Leisure (private sector)

Corporate

These are busy workers with limited time and so short intense workouts are programmed into early mornings and lunchtime. For example, each week day has an express workout at 7 am. This is a high-intensity class (spin, body pump, boxercise) which lasts for 45 minutes (15 minutes less than a traditional class).

Adults

These are for those who may wish to attend and workout individually. There are a wide range of individual activities available all day such as classes, lane swimming and badminton. The IHRSA (2004) research that suggests that adults will stay longer at a facility if they are included in group activities means that team games such as football, netball and basketball should also be provided at peak times.

Mums with pre-school children

For this group a crèche has been included as part of the facility between 9 am and 12 noon during week days to support their attendance. In the E-Leisure example a number of activities are programmed in between these hours (two fitness and toning classes, aqua aerobics, group sports session [indoor hockey, netball] and swimming).

50+

This group has moderate-impact activities provided at off peak times during the day. These activities can last slightly longer than other activities to meet the needs of this group of members. Sessions which fit into this profile are badminton, indoor bowls, mind and body classes, aqua aerobics.

Families

To encourage family use after school activities and gym availability for older children is important. There are after-school activities on from 4 pm to 6 pm each week day; junior gym sessions take place between 5 pm and 6.30 pm each evening also.

CHAPTER 28

SELF-EMPLOYMENT – PROGRAMMING TO MANAGE TIME AND ENERGY

Simon Rea

INTRODUCTION

In the sport and fitness sector there are a range of self-employed people who work in roles such as coaches, personal trainers, sports nutritionists or sports masseurs. These people will either be based at a facility or be itinerant and visit their customers rather than have their customers come to them. Self-employed people have particular issues to face in scheduling their work to achieve maximum efficiency. Their most important resources are the finite qualities of time and energy and these need to be carefully managed.

The chapter will draw on the author's own self-employed background and, in addition, the experiences of three self-employed people investigated by in-depth semi-structured interviews: a cricket coach who coaches a university team (coach 1), an exercise coach who works from a studio within a health and fitness club (coach 2), and a personal trainer who visits customers in their homes (coach 3). For the purpose of this chapter I will refer to all three of the professionals in the case studies as 'coaches' without discussing the complex features of this term. The coaches' focus will be on meeting the needs of each of their customers and fitting these customers into a time schedule which will ensure the effective use of the coach's time.

INFLUENCES ON PLANNING THE PROGRAMME

When planning the programme it is important to look at four main factors: the values of the coach; the profile of the customers; the financial viability of activities; the resources required and their availability. The values of the coach will influence the amount of time they make available and when this time is allocated. The first value evident from the coaches interviewed was ensuring that they were giving 100% of their effort and attention to the customers they work with, particularly as the customer was paying for their time and they wanted to give value for money. Coach 2 (exercise coach) expressed the importance of looking after her own welfare, in terms of eating, sleeping and training, so she could look after her customers. The importance of maintaining a work/life balance and having boundaries as to when you will work was highlighted by coach 3 (personal trainer) who ensured his weekends were protected to spend with his partner.

In terms of the second factor, customer profile, it is vital to identify the characteristic of the target group, for example, where they live and the likely working hours that the group maintains. Coach 1 (cricket coach) faced issues with his target group of students as each had a specific schedule of lectures and commitments which means that he had to maintain flexibility. During his programming he had to consider that some of his coaching was on an individual basis and some was with the team. The itinerant coach 3 (personal trainer) found that his clients were in occupations or positions where they could dictate their working hours to a greater extent and this provided flexibility. He also set a guideline limit of 20 minutes of travel from his home when targeting customers.

The third factor, the financial implications of delivering the service to a customer, heavily influences coaches working hours. Coach 2 (exercise coach) reported that they needed to work a certain number of hours to pay the rent on her studio and this was always at the back of her mind. Coach 3 (personal trainer) had no such overheads but had to consider the cost of his time, the cost of petrol and depreciation on his vehicle when deciding whether to take on a customer.

The final influencing factor is resources. Coaches 1 and 2 had to consider the competition for the facilities they needed and fitted in with the demands of other user groups. Coach 3 (personal trainer) had to consider his resources, such as weights, benches and stability balls, as he 'brings the gym' to the customer, in terms of the equipment, rather than the customer coming to the gym in the traditional manner. As well as tangible resources there is also the personal resource of time and energy which the coaches have to consider. In particular, managing energy is vital as each coaching session will have a physical and mental 'cost' on the coach and this can affect their performance. Loehr and Schwartz agree with this belief as they said 'managing energy, not time, is the fundamental currency of high performance' (Loehr and Schwarz, 2005: p. 17).

315

CUSTOMER EXPECTATIONS

Due to the nature of the product that is being delivered each customer will have different expectations based on their own knowledge and experiences of training. Coach 2 (exercise coach) explains that customers would come to her with set goals and expect to achieve these goals. However, these goals might have been unrealistic or the process for achieving these goals may have been flawed. First, it is important to help the customer be sure of what the goals of their training are and whether they are the best goals for them. There may need to be some negotiation, particularly in relation to the amount of time they need to dedicate to their training. Some customers also need to be educated that rest is as important as training. Customers will want results and they will expect the coach to deliver excellence whether their session is at 7 am or 9 pm.

PROGRAMME DESIGN

When designing the weekly programme of appointments, customers' needs must be met but also the requirements of the coach. Coach 2 (exercise coach) explains her experiences of working in a studio:

> The studio is divided into set allotted hours. The pattern is the same every day and every week. Thus we are able to give customers a regular training time. For example, one customer has 5 pm on Monday and Thursday. I get people to fit their time to the time I have in the studio and what I can do. It is my interest that they do that time but it is also in their interest as it gets them into a routine for when they train and they make it a habit.

Working a programme to meet both parties' needs is important for coach 2. She can programme her customers so that they follow immediately after each other and she maximises her time. Effective use of time such as this also ensures she has time to write training programmes, complete administration and keep studying for more qualifications. Her view is that studying for further qualifications will benefit the customers as her knowledge grows, so it is important to build in that time.

Coach 3 (personal trainer) has to consider the following factors when scheduling his time. First, there is the travel time, time for loading and unloading his vehicle, the proximity of the customers, customer availability and his time for eating and recovery. The big issue is the time between appointments as this is wasted time and can minimise efficiency. He explains how he deals with this issue of scheduling time:

> When I started my business I would go wherever there was a customer and do whatever was needed. However, over the months I have become more in demand and have more control in selecting customers. I like to get up early and start work as far away as possible and work towards home. I have customers who always have the same times and I have a few who are flexible and I can use their flexibility to my advantage by fitting them into my schedule to make it manageable.

Time needs to be scheduled into their weekly session to allow for planning sessions, updating records and general administration of the business. Coach 2 (exercise coach), finds this a challenge, as well as managing her life, and has a solution for buying some time from the customer:

> I keep detailed notes on their session on their repetitions, weights and what has being going well and what has been going badly. Because I go from one session to the next I get them to start stretching themselves and I get their notes out and have a read through. This buys me a bit of time to get myself up to date and then into the right frame of mind for the session.

In summary, both these coaches say it is important to get the customers into a regular routine where they train on the same days at the same times; if it is important to customers they will fit in with a coach's schedule. If the coach cannot fit the customer into their schedule they need to offer an alternative, such as finding another coach, as it can affect the quality of the training they deliver to their other customers.

MANAGING THE PROGRAMME

One of the practicalities of time management involves consideration of the methods used to communicate with customers. Coach 1 (cricket coach) has the most difficult job as he is communicating with around 20 players on a group and

317

individual basis. He has addressed this problem by appointing a communications manager within the group. This is one of his senior players, who coordinates the communication through a social networking site which is used by all the players. This appeals to his players who are in their late teens and early twenties who are comfortable with this method.

Communication through social networking will also generate emails when a message is posted and these can be accessed through a mobile phone. This method fits the profile of the group of players he is coaching. He will also use text messages and emails for the immediacy of contact that they provide.

Coach 2 (exercise coach) and her colleagues use mainly electronic diaries to schedule all appointments and she blocks out training times, time for writing programmes and time for study. Her daily work, in terms of additional tasks, is scheduled as a 'to do list' which is paper based. Coach 3 (personal trainer) has used an electronic diary but found it did not always suit the itinerant demands of his work. He relies on a paper diary as it is easily portable and easily accessible. Coach 2 summarises the methods of scheduling their programme very well:

> Try different things to find out what suits you and what works for your brain because everyone is different. What works for one person is useless for another.

EVALUATION AND MEASUREMENT

Knowing whether the coach is successful or not in programming their time is a matter of reflection and talking with other coaches often helps. Coach 2 (exercise coach) says she is able to deal with delivering 30–35 training sessions a week; one of her colleagues can manage up to 40 while the other colleague can only deal with 15–20 training sessions. Coach 3 (personal trainer) finds that the nature of his work, which involves a lot of travel and setting up of equipment, can cope with up to 20 sessions a week. Through experience he has found that this number of sessions is his absolute maximum. Coach 2 gives some sound advice on planning the weekly schedule:

> Work out what is a manageable amount of time which enables you to sustain your energy levels and deal with all your clients and their needs. You also need to keep paperwork up to date and be

able to fit your life in as well as your own training and household chores.

Coach 3 (personal trainer) says he does not always realise when he gets his programming right but he always knows when he has got it wrong. He realises that if he is late for appointments or continually rushing then something has gone wrong. Both coaches use customer retainment as a crucial measure of their success and will examine the reasons that lie behind losing a customer and this helps to inform them of any issues in their programming.

Another reported intuitive method of evaluating success is to examine your own mood and its resulting behaviour. Coach 3 (personal trainer) says that if his schedule is wrong he will become tired and stressed, resulting in a bad mood which may be picked up on by customers. Both coaches 2 and 3 mentioned that not working enough can be as stressful as working too much. Both have had previous careers where working for 10 to 12 hours a day was normal and they felt guilty and under motivated if they aren't working enough. Coach 3 summed up his own intuitive reflection on the success or failure of his programming:

> If I'm too busy I moan and if I'm not busy enough I moan. So if I'm not moaning then I know I am getting it right!

Therefore, it is vital for coaches to be sensitive to customer satisfaction and also self-aware of whether they are appropriately prepared for sessions, their own mood and energy level.

CONCLUSION

In summary there is no set way to develop a programme or schedule. However, coaches need to be conscious of the needs of their customers as well as personal needs. Customers will expect delivery of a quality product at a time which is mutually agreed. Self-employed workers have to decide whether this can be done and if it is financially viable. Crossley (2006) says you always need to be aware how many sessions you need to perform to become financially viable. While this is important, if the customer cannot be fitted into the schedule it is often the best solution to decide not to engage them as a customer. Most of all it is vital to be realistic about what can be done, when it can be done it and be true to your own values because the success of self-employment depends upon how well the schedule of appointments is operated and managed.

REFERENCES

Crossley, J. (2006) *Personal Training: Theory and Practice*. Abingdon: Hodder Arnold.

Loehr, S. and Schwartz, T. (2005) *The Power of Full Engagement*. New York: The Free Press.

CHAPTER 29

THE SPORT MARKETING COMMUNICATIONS MIX[1]

Maria Hopwood

INTRODUCTION

This chapter introduces the reader to one of the 4 P's of the traditional marketing mix: promotion.

No matter what organisations do, whether they are large or small, profit or non-profit making, commercial or government, educational or sporting, they all have one thing in common: in order to be successful and to survive they have to engage in communication. Communication can take place within and between organisations and a whole range of other 'publics' or 'audiences' with whom the organisation would like to have a relationship. In today's hugely competitive and 'noisy' marketing environment, those marketing communications messages that get noticed and listened to are those that are precisely targeted and of relevance to the person or persons on the receiving end and that have some degree of originality and memorability about them. For a whole range of reasons, audiences nowadays are proving increasingly difficult to reach, so it is a constant challenge for organisations to try to make and maintain contact. The primary way that organisations make contact is through marketing communications, a process that, at the beginning of the twenty-first century, is moving towards greater integration in order to attempt to achieve coherence and consistency of the message.

Traditionally, the marketing communications mix consists of five main tools: advertising, sales promotion, public relations, personal selling, and direct marketing. This combination of tools is also sometimes more narrowly referred to as the promotions mix and also includes the range of different media via which

[1] Adapted version of Hopwood, M. 'Sports public relations' in Beech, J. and Chadwick, S. (2007) *The Marketing of Sport*, pp. 213–235, Harlow: FT Prentice Hall/Pearson Education.

messages are delivered to targeted audiences. To attempt to understand what marketing communications does, it is useful to have a definition of the process as a starting point. Perhaps as a reflection of the intangible qualities of the process, there is no single universal definition, and there is a wide range of interpretations of the discipline. Perhaps this definition of marketing communications will aid understanding:

> Marketing communications is a management process through which an organisation enters into a dialogue with its various audiences. Based upon an understanding of the audience's communications environment, an organisation develops and presents messages for its identified stakeholder groups, and evaluates and acts upon the responses received. The objective of the process is to (re)position the organisation and/or its products and services, in the minds of the members of the target market, by influencing their perception and understanding. The goal is to generate attitudinal and behavioural responses.
>
> (Fill, 2002: p. 12)

This definition emphasises two-way communication and the aim of influencing attitudes and behaviour.

Increasing numbers of sport and fitness organisations recognise that the creation and maintenance of long-term relationships is a critical success factor and that engaging target audiences in dialogue is crucial. The Bradford Bulls Rugby League team is an example of a club intent on using proactive relationship-building strategies in its sport marketing communications armoury. Stuart Duffy, the club's media and public relations manager, is adamant that the customer should form the focus of the Bull's marketing communications strategies. He describes how the general approach used to be very inward looking, neglecting the fact that if the paying customer was not satisfied, then this could have serious negative consequences for the well-being of the club. Using customer relationship marketing strategies, the Bradford Bulls now actively engages with research to find out what its customers want and communicates with them regularly on all manner of issues. This is an example of two-way communication in which a direct dialogue exists between the sender of the message and the receiver. Two-way communication is generally considered to be the 'richest' form of communication because the main objective of both parties in the exchange process is mutually beneficial: long-term relationship building upon which future communications transactions will be founded.

Research amongst contemporary sport organisations shows that 'new media' communications tools (the internet and email) play a significant role in their communications armoury and that successful two-way communication can be achieved just as well by using these methods. During the first County Championship match of the 2005 England and Wales cricket season, Durham County Cricket Club capitalised on its email database contacts by sending out a number of emails informing readers of the tremendous start new Captain Mike Hussey was making with a match-winning innings of more than 200 runs. The fixture was an away one, so this communications technique allowed those supporters who could not get there in person to feel part of the occasion.

If long-term mutually beneficial exchange relationships are established and nurtured, then the potential for repeat and more frequent buying behaviour becomes a reality.

COMPONENTS OF THE SPORT MARKETING COMMUNICATIONS MIX

A variety of sport marketing communications, or promotions, mixes can be found in recent sport marketing theory. They each have their strengths and weaknesses.

The sport marketing communications mix presented here is an amalgamation of Kotler's (1982) non-profit promotion mix and Irwin *et al.*'s (2002) sport promotion mix. However, in addition, it is thought that to fully represent current thinking in sport communications the additional dimension of relationship building and management should be incorporated. The mix is broken down into its eight constituent parts below.

RELATIONSHIP BUILDING AND MANAGEMENT

A fundamental shift in marketing thinking has been developing during recent years, the outcome of which has seen the emergence of new marketing concepts, such as customer relationship marketing (CRM), which are very different in essence to that of traditional transactional marketing.

CRM is defined as '... the values and strategies of relationship marketing – with particular emphasis on customer relationships – turned into practical application'. These basic principles are integral to relationship building and management. Gummesson (2002) states that 'relationships are at the core of human behaviour' and relationships are vital to successful sport business.

However, it is suggested that to confine relationships to marketing is too limiting. In an article written for *Public Relations Quarterly* (Fall, 2000), Ledingham states that a relationship approach to public relations is vital for any organisation 'seeking to initiate, nurture and maintain positive, mutually beneficial relationships between their organisation and its key publics'. Sport organisations are intent on getting and keeping their customers because their livelihood depends on it just like any other business. However, loyalty, tradition and emotion are characteristics of the sport product that are rarely manifested in other consumer products. Consider the number of loyal football supporters, often in family groups, who, from one season to the next, doggedly follow their team through the good times and the bad.

Just as with any relationship, it has to be nurtured and worked at over the years. An excellent example of how sporting relationships can be managed and improved is Twenty20 Cricket. In recent years, the England and Wales Cricket Board (ECB) came to realise that the traditional 4-day County Championship was losing its appeal and beginning to create a negative image for professional cricket. Pictures of almost empty grounds, apart from the stereo-typical 'one man and his dog' and comments from players, who were increasingly disappointed by not having an audience to whom they could display their hard-earned skills, were beginning to have an impact. Consequently, the ECB launched a comprehensive market research campaign, the direct outcome of which was the Twenty20 Cup. The research findings told the ECB that their core audience was on the wane and that for cricket to become more meaningful and to attract the players of the future, it would have to make some fundamental changes. Intended to appeal to a different demographic, the matches generally started at 5.30 pm and lasted around three hours. The success that Twenty20 has now become throughout the world is testament to the understanding that if you talk to your customers, listen to what they say and give them what they want in a format that suits them, then they will respond favourably. Relationship management in the twenty-first-century UK cricket is alive and well and proving its value within the sport context.

ADVERTISING

It used to be the case that advertising was the predominant and most popular marketing communications tool; however, in recent years, the reliance on advertising has diminished in favour of the application of other techniques. There are a number of reasons for this, but the most obvious is to do with cost. Advertising is still widely used because of what it can achieve – it has the potential to reach global audiences with attention of grabbing and persuasive messages. But in certain situations, advertising has become prohibitively expensive and audiences have become resistant to its appeals.

In sport marketing communications, each available technique should be used for the things it is good at doing, and advertising's strength in sport is that it is highly visible and therefore widely used by sport marketers. Advertising achieves a wide range of sport marketing communications objectives: it can create and maintain brand awareness and brand loyalty and it can create a strong identity for sport products and services. Although there is much academic debate surrounding the issue of how advertising works, there is no doubt that advertising can directly affect how consumers behave.

But what exactly is advertising? The meaning of advertising is often confused, and the term is frequently used as a 'catch-all' phrase to describe a whole range of different promotional activities such as sales promotions and direct marketing, which are well beyond the scope of advertising. There are many definitions of advertising, but one of the most helpful is this one by Duncan:

> Advertising is nonpersonal, paid announcements by an identified sponsor. It is used to reach large audiences, create brand awareness, help differentiate a brand from its competitors, and build an image of the brand.
>
> (2005: p. 9)

From this, we can see that advertising is always paid for; we know who has generated the advertisement; and we are exposed to it through the press or broadcast media and are then persuaded or influenced by it.

For contemporary sport marketers, the internet is taking a significant role in sports-related advertising strategies. The internet is another example of how the traditional definitions of advertising have become too narrow and how the predominance of mass media usage in advertising is being challenged. Internet advertising is a product extension to traditional advertising in that it has allowed this usually non-personal communications technique to become interactive and much more personalised. There are a number of advantages in using the internet such as flexibility, currency and cost effectiveness. The Football Association (FA) in 2007 employed four full-time staff members to work constantly on keeping the FA's website (www.thefa.com) up to date because it has become such an important advertising and communications medium. Sports organisations work hard at making their websites attractive because they provide the distinct possibility of attracting a worldwide audience. Advertising has many distinct advantages that, when used in combination with the other elements of the mix, create a powerful mechanism for encouraging customer loyalty.

PUBLICITY

Like advertising, the true meaning of publicity is frequently misunderstood, and the word tends to be used in all manner of incorrect ways. According to Marconi:

> Publicity is a process of managing information and bringing it to the attention of the public … the task of generating publicity does not have to be loud and excessive to be effective
>
> (2004: p. 137)

Managing information and bringing it to the attention of the public in a way that is appealing to them is a distinct skill because it is something that has to be done properly if it is to be prevented from thinking that all publicity is hype and all publicists are liars. Media decision-makers and influencers such as editors, journalists and commentators have to be persuaded to take an interest, so publicity has to be shaped to suit their requirements, and relationships built on trust, openness and honesty are critical success factors. Publicity is a great way of generating goodwill and understanding at no financial cost to the organisation, so it is not surprising to learn that it is a tool widely used in public relations practice. The limited financial resources of many sport organisations mean that there is a considerable reliance on publicity. News stories are examples of the type of publicity that is widely used in sport. The back pages of almost all the national and local newspapers are where we turn to for our daily update on what is going on in the work of sport. In our contemporary time-poor lifestyles, many sport consumers are increasingly turning to the internet for the same news stories that can be found in the online versions of the daily newspapers, designated internet news sites and the proliferation of dedicated sports websites. An example was given earlier of how Durham County Cricket Club trialled 'e-publicity' at the start of the 2005 season and the fact that, if you want to pay for them, you can get sports updates via SMS text messaging on your mobile phone is a further indication of how such forms of publicity are developing.

Because many sport organisations have limited financial resources, publicity is a tool upon which they have come to rely. Publicity undoubtedly has many distinct advantages, but it is disingenuous to think that it is an entirely free form of communication. Much time and energy has to be expended on developing excellent media relations (i.e. relationships with journalists) by designated personnel in sport organisations in order to ensure constant adequate and accurate media and press overage. Stuart Duffy, media and public relations manager at Bradford Bulls rugby league club, says that much of his job is concentrated on developing excellent media relationships, particularly with journalists from the local press and broadcasting organisations. Local media are crucially important to sport organisations because they are the ones to whom the vast majority of the local target population turns for information. Stuart Duffy cites the example of competitions for free tickets to Bulls matches on a local radio breakfast show as a highly successful technique for reaching people who have never previously attended a game. The potential for converting first-time visitors into regular customers should be a key objective for sports publicity.

PERSONAL CONTACT

In a very well-known study into international business organisations, Peters and Waterman (1982) identify a range of organisational activities that set excellent organisations apart from the rest. One of these activities is what they describe as staying close to the customer (p. 156), which is another way of describing personal contact. Personal selling is one of the five major components in the traditional integrated marketing communications mix, but this, in its commercial sense, does not work particularly well for sport organisations because a sale is not always the intended or desired outcome. For sport organisations, the words *personal contact* are much more applicable.

According to Irwin *et al.*:

> Personal contact is critical to the success of an effective promotional campaign. Whereas advertising is very public, indiscriminate and impersonal, personal contact can be tailored to the target customer's interests and needs
>
> (2002: p. 8)

As with relationship building and management, the concept of personal contact is rooted firmly in the practice of public relations. Personal contact adds the human element to the relationships that are developed between the sport organisation and the customer which, in turn, are the foundation for the creation of dialogue and that all-important two-way communication.

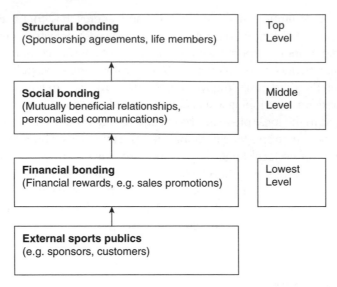

Figure 29.1 Levels of loyalty

The principles of relationship marketing are integral to sports personal contact because long-term contact is characteristic of some sport organisations whose ultimate goal is to engender loyalty. In sports relationship marketing, there are three distinct levels of loyalty (shown in Figure 29.1) that need some explanation and clarification.

The lowest level is financial bonding, which is 'bought' through a range of financial rewards or sales promotion initiatives such as reduced price gym memberships for a limited period after Christmas, or buy one ticket for a game, get another half price. Although such techniques are attractive and designed to appeal to customer requirements, they do not focus on long-term loyalty building; after the offer has passed or expired, the customer may go elsewhere.

The middle level of the sports loyalty scheme is social bonding, which is aimed at developing a mutually beneficial relationship between the sport organisation and the customer. At this level, contact needs to be much more personalised because there is the very good chance that when customers are happy with this level of their relationship with the sport organisation, they will move up to the desired final loyalty level. Communications at the social bonding level should be personalised. For example, when you buy your first season ticket from your favourite football club, you might expect to receive preferential treatment or special offers that are particularly targeted at you and your interests. Many sporting organisations use their database information to send out personalised

maria hopwood

birthday cards or Christmas cards, which make the customer feel that the organisation has a genuine interest in them and that they are not just another anonymous number. If such a relationship is achieved, then the step up to the final level of loyalty, known as structural bonding, is a small one. At this level, each party has an equal role in the relationship, which is particularly evident in relationships that exist between sports clubs and sponsors. Long-term membership of a sports club is another example of structural bonding. Because this involves considerable financial outlay on behalf of the member during the lifetime of the relationship, it is only right that the member should be consulted on club business and development.

To move people up through the three stages of the sports loyalty scene, it is essential that the sport organisation makes a commitment to value the public more as equals in a long-term relationship and less as transactional figures. Regular, high-quality personal interaction, communication and contact are required to maintain the relationship, which should be quite naturally and, if properly nurtured, increase purchase and the likelihood of repurchase. For the sports organisation, this requires a heavy investment in terms of time and resources, but the return on that investment is high.

Many sport organisations, such as cricket, rugby and football clubs, have a distinct advantage as far as personal contact is concerned, and that is the players. One of the most powerful ways of getting youngsters interested in a sport is by making the players, many of whom will also be role models, accessible and approachable. Durham County Cricket Club has an annual pre-season 'meet the players' night to which all members are invited. Players are also encouraged to work towards acquiring coaching qualifications, which means they get the opportunity to encourage keen youngsters in the sport. Examples such as these show how personal contact in sport can create distinct stakeholder impressions of both the sporting organisation and the sport itself, which in turn can be translated into long-term, structural bonding, which can then provide a measurable representation of relationship management.

INCENTIVES

Just as personal contact has been described as an extension of personal selling, incentives in sport can be thought of as an extension to the sales promotion component of the traditional integrated marketing communications mix. Incentives, to Kotler (1982), incorporate all the emotional, social, psychological, functional, or financial conditions that serve to encourage some overt behavioural response.

However, within the mix presented here it must be realised that not all sporting consumption experiences are of a transactional nature, meaning that incentives are not only used in order to generate sales, but also image and reputation. Understanding how to best use incentives also requires an understanding of what motivates sports publics and how they behave, which in this short overview there is not scope to explore (see Irwin et al., 2002).

The final three components of the sport marketing communications mix presented here mainly apply to professional spectator sports. As a result they may not apply to general sport and fitness contexts as clearly as earlier components.

ATMOSPHERICS

This component of the mix consists of everything that is done to ensure that the place of purchase or consumption of the sport product is designed to create specific behavioural or emotional effects in the consumer. This includes everything that appears at the point of sale, such as posters, displays, signs and other promotional material, such as athlete endorsements, that is intended to persuade people at the point of purchase. Atmospherics also includes features that are intended to influence choice or outlet in which the sport product is to be consumed. So, for example, the actual place where a sporting event occurs becomes an integral element of the overall promotional strategy.

LICENSING

According to Irwin et al. (2002: p. 14), licensing has emerged as the fastest growing component of the contemporary sport promotion mix. Just as with a corporate brand or logo, a recognisable symbol for a team or event increases consumer awareness and creates an identity in the marketplace. Such globally recognised logos as the Nike Swoosh and the Adidas Stripes are emblazoned on a whole range of consumer products, not all of which are immediately sports related. Many of these logos and brands have achieved iconic status. For example, an advertisement for Nike is immediately recognisable by the Swoosh; there is no need for the company to include the name as well.

In buying and wearing a favourite team's shirts, supporters are not only demonstrating their allegiance but are also extending the promotional opportunities for any sponsor or corporate logo that might be emblazoned on the replica shirt.

Royalty fees are paid by second parties in return for the right to use a logo, name, symbol, or mark associated with an event or an athlete.

SPONSORSHIP

Sponsorship within contemporary sports is probably the most financially lucrative way that contemporary sport organisations make their presence felt. Anyone you speak to in the world of sport will have a different interpretation of what sponsorship means. To the professional cricket team chief executive, sponsorship can mean the long-awaited building of the new stand. In fact, any sport organisation (and player) will tell you that sponsorship is critical to their success.

Lagae (2005) describes sponsorship as a business agreement between two parties, based on reciprocity. This means that both parties get something from the exchange, which is usually demonstrated by the sponsor providing funds, resources or equipment to the organisation in return for some form of association or user rights, which can be then used to the sponsor's commercial advantage. In other words, through the benevolent and high-profile association with sport, businesses are able to reach out to a range of potential audiences and markets that they may not be able to reach through other marketing communications techniques.

CONCLUSIONS

Getting your message across to your targeted audiences sounds easy, but it is clear that the reality for people involved within promoting sport organisations is rather more challenging. It is evident that for any sport organisation intent on maximising its full potential in the contemporary sports environment, a business focus is essential. A thorough understanding of the benefits of a well-planned, strategic communication mix has to be fundamental to successful long-term planning. In today's increasingly competitive environment, in which competition might be in the form of an afternoon spent at the local out-of-town shopping centre rather than attendance at the local club, sport organisations cannot afford to neglect the power of communications. As identified in the chapter, there are examples of sport organisations adopting excellent strategic marketing communications thinking that is making measurable differences to their existence.

Having an understanding of some of the theory that underpins the marketing communications is also extremely useful for those charged with the job of communicating on behalf of sport organisations. Basing communication strategies on these principles can be much more cost effective than relying on the ad hoc, shoestring approach that has been characteristic of sport organisations in the past.

Some knowledge of the characteristics, advantages and disadvantages of the components of the communication mix means that those engaged in developing effective sport communications strategies can have a much better understanding and insight into how each of the distinct techniques can be used synergistically to greatest effect. It also allows individual sport organisations to stamp their own unique personality on the generic sport product.

REFERENCES

Duncan, T. (2005) *Principles of Advertising and IMC*, 2nd international edn. New York: McGraw-Hill/Irwin.

Fill, C. (2002) *Marketing Communications Contexts, Strategies and Applications*, 3rd edn. Harlow: Pearson Education Limited.

Gummesson, E. (2002) *Total Relationship Marketing*, 2nd edn. Oxford: Butterworth-heinemann.

Irwin, R. Sutton, W.A. and McCarthy, L.M. (2002) *Sport Promotion and Sales Management*. Champaign, IL: Human Kinetics.

Kotler, P. (1982) *Marketing for Non Profit Organisations*. Englewood Cliffs, NJ: Prentice Hall.

Lagae, W. (2005) *Sport Sponsorship and Marketing Communications: A European Perspective*. Harlow: Pearson Education Limited.

Ledingham, J.A. (2000) *Guidelines to Building and Maintaining Strong Organization-Public Relationships*. *Public Relations Quarterly*, 45(3): 44–7.

Marconi, J. (2004) *Public Relations: The Complete Guide*. Mason, OH: Thomson Learning.

Peters, T. and Waterman Jr, R.H. (1982) *In Search of Excellence: Lessons from America's Best Run Companies*. London: Harper-Collins.

INDEX